KESAHARU IMAI

ROLEX

3,621 WRISTWATCHES

4880 Lower Valley Road, Atglen, Pennsylvania 19310

Note: The various dial indications, such as precision, chronometer, indications of watertightness, etc., will not always be noted in the descriptions, since these details are visible in the pictures.

The original data appeared in 1997 as Vol. 2 of the periodical *ROLEX Fan* and 2003 as No. 435 in the periodical *World Mook*, published by World Photo Press in Tokyo.

Translated from the German by Dr. Edward Force
Edited by Douglas Congdon-Martin

Copyright © 2009 by Schiffer Publishing Ltd.
Library of Congress Control Number: 2009932060

All rights reserved. No part of this work may be reproduced or used in any form or by any means—graphic, electronic, or mechanical, including photocopying or information storage and retrieval systems—without written permission from the publisher.
The scanning, uploading and distribution of this book or any part thereof via the Internet or via any other means without the permission of the publisher is illegal and punishable by law. Please purchase only authorized editions and do not participate in or encourage the electronic piracy of copyrighted materials.
"Schiffer," "Schiffer Publishing Ltd. & Design," and the "Design of pen and ink well" are registered trademarks of Schiffer Publishing Ltd.

Designed by Mark David Bowyer
Type set in Zurich Lt BT / Zurich BT

ISBN: 978-0-7643-3380-4
Printed in China

Schiffer Books are available at special discounts for bulk purchases for sales promotions or premiums. Special editions, including personalized covers, corporate imprints, and excerpts can be created in large quantities for special needs. For more information contact the publisher:

Published by Schiffer Publishing Ltd.
4880 Lower Valley Road
Atglen, PA 19310
Phone: (610) 593-1777; Fax: (610) 593-2002
E-mail: Info@schifferbooks.com

For the largest selection of fine reference books on this and related subjects, please visit our web site at
www.schifferbooks.com
We are always looking for people to write books on new and related subjects. If you have an idea for a book please contact us at the above address.

This book may be purchased from the publisher.
Include $5.00 for shipping.
Please try your bookstore first.
You may write for a free catalog.

In Europe, Schiffer books are distributed by
Bushwood Books
6 Marksbury Ave.
Kew Gardens
Surrey TW9 4JF England
Phone: 44 (0) 20 8392 8585; Fax: 44 (0) 20 8392 9876
E-mail: info@bushwoodbooks.co.uk
Website: www.bushwoodbooks.co.uk

CONTENTS

- 4 THE HISTORY OF THE ROLEX FIRM
- 5 INTRODUCTION
- 6 NON-OYSTER
- 16 AIR-KING
- 22 PRINCE
- 25 QUARTER CENTURY
- 27 BUBBLE BACK
- 52 CHRONOGRAPH
- 64 WATERPROOF WATCHES
- 77 OYSTER
- 114 OYSTER PERPETUAL
- 156 SUBMARINER
- 168 SEA-DWELLER
- 172 YACHT-MASTER
- 174 EXPLORER
- 187 GMT-MASTER
- 198 LADIES' WATCHES
- 222 POCKET WATCHES

THE HISTORY OF THE ROLEX FIRM

When the 19-year-old Hans Wilsdorf left his home town of Kulmbach in 1900 to move to La Chaux-de-Fonds, Switzerland, and enter a watch dealer's firm, no one could have suspected that his firm of Rolex would rise to such heights. A few years later he moved to London and, with a friend, founded the firm of Wilsdorf and Davis there, buying watches in Switzerland and selling them in Britain. In 1908 he registered his first brand name: "ROLEX," an abbreviation for "Horlogerie Exquise."

The connection with Aegeler of Biel, a movement manufacturer who was already building very high-quality products then and continues it to this day, delivered the first watches with the "ROLEX" name on the dial. In 1914 there came the first Kew A certificate for a wristwatch from the Kew Observatory. In the 1920s Hans Wilsdorf returned to Switzerland, first to Biel, then to Geneva. There he devoted himself solely to mastering the hardest problem, then as now: designing a dust- and watertight case. In 1926 the "Oyster," the world's first watertight watch, saw the light of day. It was praised in a full-page in the *Daily Mail* after a London secretary, Mercedes Gleitze, swam the English Channel with an Oyster on her arm. A little later, in 1931, this watch gained an automatic movement, and so the Kulmbach merchant's son had taken a giant step forward toward solving the two most important problems of the everyday, practical wristwatch. For the firm's 40th anniversary the "Datejust" (with date) was introduced, a watch that, with minor changes, is still built today.

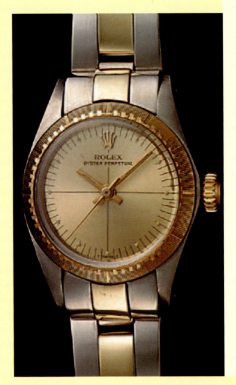

But building only functional watches did not satisfy Hans Wilsdorf; he also wanted something "for the eye." From this desire arose the "Prince" series, a big family of rectangular watches with hand-wound movements in very beautiful cases. They still fetch very good prices today, after fifty years.

INTRODUCTION

The vast and varied array of Rolex wristwatches may not have been fully appreciated until now. In a way not unlike a catalogue raisonné, this book presents a very large number of Rolex wristwatches, along with a few pocket watches. They are organized by the general type—"Non-Oyster," "Oyster," "Bubble Back," "Submariner," "Chronograph" and more—and then further organized by reference number, when known, date of manufacture, or shape. This will be of great assistance to collectors as they seek to determine the catalog number or year of manufacture of their own watches. The often overlooked Rolex "Ladies' Watches" are included, as are the rare "1/4 Century Club," the "Milgauss" with its turning glass and the second hand in the shape of a lightning bolt, and the "Oyster Perpetual" with moon phase and full calendar, the legendary catalog number 6062. The "Zerograph/Centregraph" from the late thirties, a hybrid chronograph with just one push button, is also shown.

The more than 3,620 pictures are accompanied by brief descriptions, including material, movement, date, and size. They will astonish the reader with the almost unlimited designs. As Christian Pfeiffer-Belli noted in the introduction to the German version of this book, "there is scarcely anything that Rolex has not made, from the most varied metal bands to the most remarkable dials. Among the 'Non-Oyster' watches one finds everything that other firms have also made: military watches with grids over the dial, rectangular watches, the red 12 on the enameled dial, elaborate hinged gold cases, colorful enamel dials."

There is much to be learned about the history and production of Rolex, and most will not be discovered until the company chooses to share it. In the meantime, this imposing work offers many important insights.

NON-OYSTER

The designation "Oyster" has become almost a synonym for Rolex. But the claim that there were no outstanding non-Oyster models is not true.

In the time between the patent application for the screwed Oyster case bottom in 1926—most non-Oyster watches were not yet fitted with a snap-in bottom—many interesting models were produced. Numerous variations of non-Oyster models like the Tonneau, Prince, rectangular and pillow shapes offer interesting things to the watch fan.

NON-OYSTER

NON-OYSTER 1910s

NON-OYSTER / faultless enamel dial, 1910, silver case, hand-wound, 20.5 x 30 mm,

NON-OYSTER / original enamel dial in very good condition, 1910s, silver case, hand-wound, 14 x 35.5 mm

NON-OYSTER / 1913-14, very rare model, enamel dial, dealer's signature "Dunklings", 11.5 x 34 mm

NON-OYSTER / enamel dial, pressed Arabic numerals, 1915-20s, hand-wound, silver, 11.5 x 34 mm

NON-OYSTER / very rare model with hinged lid, 1915, 10 x 35 mm

NON-OYSTER / 1916, silver hinged lid, enamel dial, blue steel hands, London hallmarks, 11 x 35 mm

NON-OYSTER / case with hinged lid, silver, original enamel dial, signed "D & W" inside lid, 10.5 x 35 mm

NON-OYSTER / hinged lid with glass inset, case opens by pushing, enamel dial, 11 x 34 mm, good condition

NON-OYSTER / 1917, hinged lid with inset glass, case opens by pushing, black enamel dial, 11 x 35.5 mm

NON-OYSTER / silver case, hinged lid with inset glass, numerals visible through glass, 12 x 35 mm

NON-OYSTER 1920s

PARKS / British dealer's name on enamel dial with crystal guard, hand-wound, 1910-20s, 12 x 32 mm

NON-OYSTER /oval silver case, still with button for hand-setting, 9.5 x 33.5 mm

NON-OYSTER / black enamel dial, silver case, 1920s, hand-wound, 12.2 x 29.9 mm

BIRKS / rebuilt pocket-watch movement, 1920-30s, original dial, silver case, 10 x 34.5 mm

NON-OYSTER / early model, original enamel dial, silver case, hand-wound, 1920s, 11.5 x 30 mm

NON-OYSTER / early model with largest crown, original enamel dial, silver case, hand-wound, 1920s, 9.5 x 30 mm, crown 6.5 mm

NON-OYSTER / silver case, wrong crown, enamel dial, 1920s, 12 x 29 mm

NON-OYSTER / dial signature "Marconi" and "James Walker," 1920-30s, hand-wound, silver case, 10.5 x 25 mm

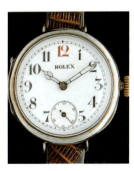

NON-OYSTER / 1920s, original silver case, skeletal hands, enamel dial, all original, Ref. 514, 12.5 x 34 mm

NON-OYSTER "OCTAGON FIRST," stainless steel case, late 1920s, hand-wound, 11 x 28 mm

NON-OYSTER

OCTAGON / dealer's signature "Dunklings" (Austrian dealer), 14 karat gilded case, 1920s, hand-wound, 10 x 25.5 mm

NON-OYSTER / double signature Levinson and Rolex, 1920s, 9 karat plaque, 9.5 x 26 mm

NON-OYSTER / 1920s, tonneau case, 11 x 33.5 mm

NON-OYSTER / good condition, 1920s, rare black enamel dial, silver case, 12 x 33 mm

NON-OYSTER / double case of 9 karat yellow gold, hand-wound, 1920, 12 x 31 mm

NON-OYSTER / rare early screwed watertight gold case, 1924-25, Glasgow hallmarks, 11.5 x 33 mm

NON-OYSTER / early screwed watertight case, hidden crown, hand-wound, 9 karat gold case, 1920s, 12 x 31.5 mm

NON-OYSTER / early screwed watertight case of silver, unusual hand shape, 11 x 33 mm

NON-OYSTER / 9 karat plaque tonneau case, late 1920s, hand-wound, 9 x 30 x 25 mm

NON-OYSTER / silver tonneau case, late 1920s, hand-wound, 9.5 x 30 x 26 mm

NON-OYSTER 1930s

NON-OYSTER / original two-tone dial with signature "Marconi", 1925, silver case, hand-wound, 11 x 33 mm

NON-OYSTER / silver case in good condition, 1930s, enamel dial, 12 x 34mm

NON-OYSTER / 1930s, typical model with red no. 12, enamel dial, 13 x 36 mm

NON-OYSTER / enamel dial, three-piece silver case, hand-wound, 1930s, 10 x 30 mm

NON-OYSTER / flexible band attachments, original dial, 1930s, steel case, 10 x 29 mm

NON-OYSTER / small second, stainless steel case, hand-wound, 1930, 9 x 28 mm

NON-OYSTER / 9 karat plaque case, original enamel dial, 1930s, 9 x 31.5 mm

SKYROCKET / 1930s, red 24 hour indication, gilded, 10.5 x 27 mm

NON-OYSTER / classic model with steel hands, indices and Arabic numerals, 1930s, 10 karat gold-filled, hand-wound, 11 x 30.5 mm

NON-OYSTER / 1930s, double second ring, one with fifth-of-second division, easily read, 10 x 30 mm

NON-OYSTER

NON-OYSTER / Roman numerals with red 12, 1930s, hand-wound, 10 x 27 mm

OCTAGON / gilded case, hand-wound, 1930s, 10 x 32 mm

NON-OYSTER / decorative dial (freshened up) and gold case, 1930s, hand-wound, 8 x 33.5 mm

NON-OYSTER / pillow-shaped case, 9 karat gold, freshened-up dial, 1930s, hand-wound, 8.5 x 28.5 x 28.5 mm

PRECISION / earlier model of dial, nickel case, 1930s, hand-wound, 9 x 28.5 mm,

NON-OYSTER / original dial, pillow-shaped 14 karat gold case, hand-wound, 1930s, 9 x 29 x 29 mm

NON-OYSTER / original dial with very fine engraving, silver case, 1930s, hand-wound, hour hand later, 9.5 x 28 mm, stem 6 mm

NON-OYSTER / original dial with small second, 1930s, nickel case, hand-wound, 10 x 27.5 mm

NON-OYSTER / 1930s, 9 karat rose gold case, lady's size, 10 x 27 mm

NON-OYSTER / 9 karat red gold tonneau case, 1930s, 10 x 30 mm

NON-OYSTER / double signature Rolex Watch & Company & Marconi, steel case, hand-wound, 1930s, 8 x 26.5 mm

NON-OYSTER / yellow gold tonneau case, hand-wound, 1930s, 9 x 30 mm

NON-OYSTER / ca. 1935, very rare formed movement, 9 karat gold, 8 x 30 x 21.5 mm

NON-OYSTER / 1930s, rare tonneau model, double signature Rolex and Marconi, original dial, chromed case, 9.5 x 28.5 mm

NON-OYSTER / rectangular stainless steel case, small second, original dial, 1930s, hand-wound, 9.5 x 30.5 x 20.5 mm

NON-OYSTER 1940s

NON-OYSTER / rectangular case with integrated glass, 1930s, 8.5 x 32 x 22.5 mm

NON-OYSTER / rectangular gold case, "just fit" model, 1930s, two-tone dial, elegant design, hand-wound, 9 x 33.5 x 22 mm

PRECISION / wedge-shaped numerals, 9 karat gold case, 1930s, hand-wound, 9 x 30.5 x 20.5 mm

DENNISON / small second, Dennison case of red gold, 1940s, 9 x 36 mm

DENNISON / freshened-up dial, case of 9 karat plaque, 1940s, 9 x 30.5 mm

NON-OYSTER

DENNISON / Dennison case of stainless steel, original guilloched dial, 1940s, 10 x 29.5 mm

DENNISON / small second, stainless steel Dennison case, hand-wound, 1940, 10 x 30 mm

DENNISON / small second, original dial, 9 karat gold case, 1940s, hand-wound, 10 x 31.5 mm

DENNISON / "shock resisting", hand-wound, 1940s, raised numerals on original dial, 10.5 x 30 mm, 6 mm stem

DENNISON / elegant 9 karat gold Dennison case, 1940s, hand-wound, signed "Chronometre", 12 x 31 mm

NON-OYSTER / small second, stainless steel case, hand-wound, 1940, 9 x 32 mm

NON-OYSTER / simple design with round 9 karat plaque, hand-wound, 9 x 35.5 mm

NON-OYSTER / later stem, original dial, 1940s, hand-wound, steel case, 9.5 x 30.5 mm

NON-OYSTER / pressed-on gold Arabic numerals and indices, "Chronometer" lettering in red, 9 karat, 1940s, 9 x 32 mm

PRECISION / 1947, original dial, 10 x 33.5 mm

PRECISION / raised Arabic numerals, gold hands, bicolor plaque-steel case, 1940s, 11.5 x 35 mm

VICTORY / original dial, medium size, 1940s, stainless steel case, 11.5 x 29.5 mm

NON-OYSTER / 1940s, gold case, fine hands, 8.5 x 35.5 mm

SKY ROCKET / red 24-hour markings on rim of dial, luminous hands, hand-wound, 1940s, 10 x 29 mm

NON-OYSTER / dealer's signature "Northern Goldsmiths Newcastle", freshened-up dial, hand-wound, 1940s, silver case, 10 x 28 mm

NON-OYSTER / blue steel hands, pillow-shaped 9 karat gold case, 1940s, hand-wound, 9 x 27 x 27 mm, 5 mm stem

AIR-LION / inside second markings, original dial, 1948, pillow-shaped case, 11.5 x 30 mm

PRECISION / rare square 14 karat gold case, 1940s, 9 x 29 mm

PRECISION / original rose dial, stainless steel case, 1940s, hand-wound, 9 x 25.5 x 25.5 mm

NON-OYSTER 1950s

NON-OYSTER / 1950s, 9 karat gold case, hand-wound, freshened-up dial, 10.5 x 34 mm

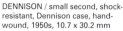

PRECISION / 9 karat yellow gold coin-shape case, hand-wound, 1950s, 12.3 x 33.6 mm

PRECISION / 9 karat yellow gold case, hand-wound, 1950, 9 x 33 mm

PRECISION / 18 karat gold case, 1950s, stamped dial, 10 x 36 mm

DENNISON / raised numerals, 9 karat gold Dennison case, 1950s, hand-wound, 10 x 31.5 mm

DENNISON / small second, shock-resistant, Dennison case, hand-wound, 1950s, 10.7 x 30.2 mm

DENNISON / 1950s, Dennison case, leaf hands, raised numerals, 10 x 35 mm

DENNISON / stainless steel case, raised Arabic numerals and indices, 1950s, 9.5 x 35 mm

DENNISON. Original dial, "shock resisting", 9 karat gold case, hand-wound, 1950s, 10 x 36 mm

DENNISON / hand-wound, raised numerals, original dial, 9 karat gold Dennison case, 1950s, Cal. 1210, 10 x 32 mm

PRECISION / staff numerals, 1950s, 18 karat gold case, hand-wound, 10 x 34 mm

NON-OYSTER / overhauled, 14 karat gold case, hands and numerals, 1950s, Cal. 16539, 9.5 x 34 mm

PRECISION / 9 karat yellow gold case, hand-wound, 1950, 9 x 32 mm

NON-OYSTER / central second, hand-wound, 1950, 10 x 31 mm

NON-OYSTER / stamped pattern on dial, stainless steel case, 1950s, hand-wound, 11 x 32.5 mm

NON-OYSTER / heart-shaped numerals, freshened-up dial, 1950s, 18 karat gold case, 9 x 34.5 mm, crown 5.5 mm

PRECISION / 1950s, British model, dial with raised Arabic numerals and indices, plaque case, 9 x 32 mm

NON-OYSTER / fine line pattern on dial, hand-wound, signed "Chronometer", 1950s, 9 karat gold case, 9.5 x 30 mm

PRECISION / 1950s, 9 karat gold case, gold numerals and hands, hand-wound, 9 x 34 mm

NON-OYSTER / yellow gold case, hand-wound, 1950s, 10 x 34 mm

NON-OYSTER / square 14 karat yellow gold case, hand-wound, 1950s, 8 x 26 mm

NON-OYSTER

NON-OYSTER 1960s

NON-OYSTER / square 9 karat plaque case, dial in very good condition, 1950s, 9 x 27 mm

PRECISION / 9 karat yellow gold case, hand-wound, 1960s, 10.3 x 33 mm

PRECISION / raised rod-shaped indices and hands of gold, 1960s, 9 karat gold case, hand-wound, 9.5 x 33 mm

PRECISION / three-piece case, side channels, 1960s, hand-wound, 9 karat gold case, 10 x 34 mm

DENNISON / Dennison case, 1960s, British design, 8.5 x 31.5 mm

DENNISON / Dennison case, stainless steel, hand-wound, 1960s, 10 x 34 mm

PRECISION / 1960s, freshened-up dial, hand-wound, stainless steel case, 10 x 33.5 mm

PRECISION / simple design, freshened-up dial, stainless steel case, 1960s, hand-wound, 9.5 x 35 mm

NON-OYSTER / short band attachments, chronometer, 1960s, hand-wound, 18 karat plaque case, 9 x 32 mm

PRECISION / raised numerals on original dial, 1960s, hand-wound, 9 karat gold case, 10 x 33 mm

Ref. 136
Ref. 859

NON-OYSTER / raised Rolex crown on freshened-up dial, 1960s, 14 karat gold case, hand-wound, Cal. 1210, 10 x 33.5 mm

PRECISION / 1960s, 18 karat gold case, 8.5 x 36.5 mm

PRECISION DATE / 9 karat yellow gold case, hand-wound, 1960, 12 x 34 mm

NON-OYSTER / original dial with red 24.hour indication, 9 karat gold case, hand-wound, 1930s, Ref. 136, 11.5 x 32.5 mm

NON-OYSTER / classic tonneau case, gilded, 1930s, hand-wound, Ref. 859, 29.5 x 29.5 mm,

Ref. 1917
Ref. 2008
Ref. 2568
Ref. 2732

UNICORN / tonneau case, signature "ROLEX" later, 9 karat gold case, Ref. 1917, 9 x 32 x 27 mm

NON-OYSTER / curved-rectangular case of 9 karat gold, original dial, dealer's signature "Marconi Maxim", Ref. 2008, 9 x 23.5 mm

NON-OYSTER / round stainless steel case, hand-wound, 1930, Ref. 2568, 10 x 27 mm

NON-OYSTER / medium size, covered band attachments, stainless steel case, 1930s, Ref. 2568, 10 x 26.5 mm

NON-OYSTER / rectangular 9 karat yellow gold case, hand-wound, 1920s, Ref. 2732, 8 x 30 mm

NON-OYSTER

Ref. 2877

NON-OYSTER / rectangular chrome case, hand-wound, Ref. 2877, 10 x 31 x 22 mm, 5.5 mm stem

Ref. 2942

NON-OYSTER / signed "Scientific", enamel dial in good condition, 9 karat gold case, Ref. 2942, 10 x 30 mm

Ref. 2985

NON-OYSTER / pillow-shaped 9 karat gold case, Ref. 2985, 9.5 x 29 mm

Ref. 3066

DENNISON / medium size, Dennison case of stainless steel, hand-wound, 1950s, Ref. 3066, 9.8 x 30.2 mm

Ref. 3103

NON-OYSTER / double second ring, one with fifths of seconds, 1930s, hand-wound, 9 karat gold case, Ref. 3103, 12 x 29 mm

Ref. 3255

PRECISION / 1934, rectangular case with hidden band attachments, Ref. 3255, 9 x 31.5 mm

Ref. 3428

NON-OYSTER / small pillow-shaped case, original dial in good condition, 1920s, Ref. 3428, 8.5 x 29 mm

Ref. 3892

NON-OYSTER / pillow-shaped metal case, hand-wound, Ref. 3892, 9.5 x 29 x 29 mm

Ref. 4029

PRECISION / square case, round movement, bicolor steel, hand-wound, Ref. 4029, 11.5 x 29.s x 27.5 mm

Ref. 4107

DENNISON / Dennison case of 18 karat gold, hand-wound, 1940s, Ref. 4107, 9.5 x 36 mm

Ref. 4270

ROYAL / stamped numerals and indices, 1940s, stainless steel case, hand-wound, Ref. 4270, 11.5 x 27.5 mm

Ref. 4325

DENNISON / 18 karat yellow gold case, hand-wound, 1950s, Ref. 4325, 9.3 x 33.9 mm

Ref. 4363

PRECISION / 1950s, Ref. 4363, stainless steel case, hand-wound, 10 x 35 mm

Ref. 4383

PRECISION / pillow-shaped case, hand-wound, stamped numerals and indices, stainless steel case, Ref. 4383, Cal. 12102, 9 x 29 mm

Ref. 4516

PRECISION / nice band attachments, elegant model, 9 karat gold case, Ref. 4516, 11 x 33 mm

Ref. 4643

NON-OYSTER / square 18 karat gold case, 12.5 x 26.5 mm, Ref. 4643

Ref. 4658

NON-OYSTER / raised numerals, signed "Officially Certified Chronometer", hand-wound, stainless steel case, Ref. 4658, 11 x 32.5 mm

Ref. 6411

NON-OYSTER / small second, square 18 karat gold case, hand-wound, 1950, Ref. 6411, 7 x 27 x 25 mm

Ref. 6466

PRECISION / medium-sized, two-tone dial, hand-wound, 1960s, stainless steel case, Ref. 6466, Cal. 1220, 9.5 x 29 mm

Ref. 6908

PRECISION / 9 karat yellow gold case, hand-wound, 1950, Ref. 6908, 9 x 32 mm

NON-OYSTER

Ref. 9714

CUSHION

NON-OYSTER / 1940s, pillow-shaped case, larger movement installed, Ref. 9714, 9 x 32 x 32 mm

ROLCO / freshened-up dial, case of 9 karat plaque, hand-wound, 9.5 x 30 mm

NON-OYSTER / pillow-shaped 9 karat gold case, hand-wound, 9.5 x 27.5 mm

NON-OYSTER / complete signature "Rolex Watch Co. Ltd.," original dial, 10 x 25.5 mm

NON-OYSTER / lightly bowed pillow-shaped 9 karat gold case, attached numerals, blue steel hands, 10 x 27 mm

RECTANGULAR

NON-OYSTER / square gold case with interesting dial design, 9.5 x 28 mm

NON-OYSTER / rectangular bicolor case of steel and 18 karat gold, two-tone dial, 9,5 x 24.5 mm

NON-OYSTER / so-called "driving watch", arched case, hand-wound, 9 x 18.5 mm

NON-OYSTER / rectangular model with small second, hand-wound, 18 karat gold case, 4.5 x 31.5 mm

NON-OYSTER / freshened-up dial with small second, hand-wound, rectangular 18 karat gold case, 10.5 x 36 mm

ROUND

NON-OYSTER / patterned dial, case with gold inlays and side relief, wrong hour hand, 9 x 31 mm

NON-OYSTER / movable band attachments, railway minutery, 9.5 x 26.5 mm

NON-OYSTER / luminous hands, medium size, hand-wound, 11 x 28 mm

DENNISON / Dennison 10 karat plaque case, hand-wound, 9.5 x 34 mm

DENNISON / signed "Chronometre", original dial, Dennison 18 karat gold case, hand-wound, 8.5 x 34.5 mm

DENNISON / rare combination of Dennison case and black dial, 9.5 x 35 mm

DENNISON / Dennison case, serial number and Dennison name engraved on bottom, 9 karat gold case, hand-wound, 9 x 32 mm, stem 4 mm

DENNISON / "Precision" model, 9 karat gold case, hand-wound, original dial, 9.5 x 30 mm

PRECISION / 1960s, hand-wound, original dial with bar indices, 9 karat gold case, 9 x 33 mm

NON-OYSTER / rod-shaped indices on original dial, hand-wound, 18 karat gold case, 10 x 36 mm

NON-OYSTER

NON-OYSTER / original dial with red 24 hour indication, 10 x 29 mm

NON-OYSTER / medium size, Arabic numerals, 9.5 x 27 mm

PRECISION / Non-Oyster model, 14 karat gold case, freshened-up dial, hand-wound, 9 x 37.5 mm

NON-OYSTER / medium size, luminous hands, Roman numerals and indices, hand-wound, 9.5 x 27.5 mm

NON-OYSTER / medium size, stainless steel case, original dial, 8.5 x 30.5 mm

PRECISION / bar odd numerals, leaf hands, 10 x 33.5 mm

NON-OYSTER / slightly arched glass, gold-filled case, hand-wound, 12 x 35 mm

NON-OYSTER / stepped lunette, 9 karat gold case, original silver dial, 9 x 26 mm

PRECISION / stainless steel, lunette with raised 18 karat gold indices, 9 x 35 mm

NON-OYSTER / original dial with stamped indices, "Aqua" model, gilded steel case, 10.5 x 32 mm

NON-OYSTER / small second, hand-wound, long band attachments, stainless steel case, 10.5 x 32 mm, 6 mm crown

NON-OYSTER / simple modern design, 10 karat plaque, 10.5 x 30.5 mm

SUPER PRECISION / 1960s, sighed "Perpetual", 9 karat gold case, Cal. 1530, 11.5 x 34 mm

PRECISION / 1940s, 9 karat gold case, black dial with white numerals, 9 x 30 mm

NON-OYSTER / screwed case bottom, 10 x 28.5 mm

TONNEAU/PILLOW   SQUARE

PRECISION / 9 karat gold case, gold Arabic numerals and hands, hand-wound, 10 x 32 mm

NON-OYSTER / medium-size pillow-shaped model, stainless steel case, hand-wound, 10 x 28.5 mm

NON-OYSTER / flower relief on the dial, hands in cathedral form, gold case, special model, 9.5 x 27 x 26 mm

NON-OYSTER / typical 1950s model, freshened-up black dial, 18 karat gold case, hand-wound, 9 x 26 mm

NON-OYSTER / square case with guilloched lunette of 18 karat gold, dial with gold indices, 7.5 x 26 mm

AIR-KING

The "AIR-KING" is one of the oldest Rolex models, and the only model that has been produced essentially unchanged to this day. It is the typical Rolex watch. If one views the whole array from a present-day standpoint, the "AIR-KING" model, because it is a "NON-CHRONOMETER" watch, is the most reasonable model. The Caliber 1520 used in the 1860s to 1980s, was very robust and reliable, and the Submariner was also equipped with it. Most models have an engine-turned lunette and no date indication.

Old catalog from 1966. The AIR-KING is the oldest and longest-sold Rolex model.

AIR-KING

AIR-KING 1940s

AIR-KING / early model, stainless steel case, original dial with raised Arabic numerals, hand-wound, 1940s, 10.5 x 32.5 mm

AIR-KING 1960s

AIR-KING / stainless steel case, freshened-up white dial, hand-wound, 1960s, 11 x 33 mm

AIR-KING / lunette with raised indices, stainless steel case, automatic movement, 1960s, 11.5 x 34 mm

AIR-KING / simple dial, automatic movement, 1960s, 11.5 x 32.5 mm

AIR-KING / black dial with raised bar indices, 1967, 12.5 x 33 mm

AIR-KING 1970s

AIR-KING / stainless steel case and band, white dial with Roman numerals, automatic movement, 1970s, 11.5 x 33.5 mm

AIR-KING / timeless simple design, black dial, 1973, 12 x 33 mm

Ref. 1002

AIR-KING / stainless steel case and arm, original silver dial, automatic movement, Ref. 1002, 12 x 32.5 mm

Ref. 4365

OYSTER AIR-KING / first "AIR-KING" model, hand-wound, Cal. 10 ½ Hunter, 1946, Ref. 4365, 10.5 x 31.5 mm

Ref. 4925

AIR-KING / early model, original dial with Arabic numerals, hand-wound, 1940s, Ref. 4925, 10 x 32 mm

Ref. 5500

AIR-KING / automatic, stainless steel case, 1970, Ref. 5500, 12 x 33 mm

AIR-KING / automatic, stainless steel case, 1966, Ref. 5500, 12 x 33 mm

AIR-KING / automatic, stainless steel case, 1984, Ref. 5500, 12.2 x 32.6 mm

AIR-KING / automatic, stainless steel case, 1987, Ref. 5500, 12.2 x 32.9 mm

AIR-KING / automatic, stainless steel case, 1990, Ref. 5500, Near East military emblem, 12.2 x 32.9 mm

AIR-KING / automatic, stainless steel case, 1970s, Ref. 5500, 12.9 x 34.8 mm

AIR-KING / automatic, stainless steel case, 1970s, Ref. 5500, 12 x 33 mm

AIR-KING / automatic, stainless steel case, 1979, Ref. 5500, 11 x 33 mm

AIR-KING / automatic, stainless steel case, 1970, Ref. 5500, 12 x 33 mm

AIR-KING / automatic, stainless steel case, 1980, Ref. 5500, 12 x 33 mm

AIR-KING

AIR-KING / automatic, stainless steel case, 1988, Ref. 5500, 12 x 33 mm

AIR-KING / stainless steel case and band, black dial with raised numerals and indices, 1960s, Ref. 5500, 12.5 x 33 mm

AIR-KING / signature "DOMINO'S PIZZA", stainless steel case, automatic movement, 12 x 33 mm, Ref. 5500, 12 x 33 mm

AIR-KING / original condition with certificate (Rolex, New York), stainless steel case, automatic movement, 1973, Ref. 5500, 12 x 33 mm

AIR-KING / red signature "AIR-KING" on presumably freshened-up dial, Cal. 1520 movement, 1970s, Ref. 5500, 11 x 33 mm

AIR-KING / stainless steel case, automatic movement, Cal. 1520, Ref. 5500, 12.5 x 33 mm

AIR-KING / freshened-up piece, 14 karat gold case and channeled lunette, black dial, automatic movement, 1970s, Ref. 5500, 12 x 33 mm

AIR-KING / very simple model, stainless steel case, 1970s, Ref. 5500, 12,5 x 33 mm

AIR-KING / freshened-up black dial, automatic movement, Cal. 1520, 1970s, Ref. 5500, 12 x 33 mm

AIR-KING / dial with Chicago petroleum firm's logo, 1970s, Ref. 5500, 11 x 33 mm

AIR-KING / dial with firm's signature, stainless steel case and band, automatic movement, 1970s, Ref. 5500, 12 x 33 mm

AIR-KING / 1980s, Ref. 5500, 10 x 33 mm

AIR-KING / signature "DOMINO'S PIZZA", stainless steel case, 1970s, Ref. 5500, 12.5 x 32.5 mm

AIR-KING / stainless steel case, freshened-up dial, raised gold indices, gold hands, 1978, Ref. 5500, 11.5 x 33 mm

AIR-KING / original fine matte silver dial, automatic movement, Cal. 1520, Ref. 5500, 11.5 x 33 mm

AIR-KING / timeless simple design, stainless steel case and band, Cal. 1520 Ref. 5500, 12 x 33 mm

AIR-KING / dial with dealer's signature "Tiffany & Co" (added later), original band, Cal. 1520, 1960s, Ref. 5500, 12 x 33 mm

AIR-KING / silver dial, raised gold bar indices, Cal. 1520, Ref. 5500, 11.5 x 33 mm

AIR-KING / silver dial, stainless steel case, 1980s, Ref. 5500, 12.5 x 33.5 mm

AIR-KING / stainless steel case and band, original black dial, automatic movement, 1970s, Ref. 5500, 11.5 x 33 mm

AIR-KING

AIR-KING 1970s, Ref. 5500, 12 x 33 mm

AIR-KING / very simple model, stainless steel case, automatic movement, 1971, Ref. 5500 12 x 33 mm

AIR-KING signature "DOMINO'S PIZZA", certificate, original dial, 1988, Ref. 5500, 12 x 33 mm

AIR-KING / original model, leather band, matte silver dial, Cal. 1520, 1970s, Ref. 5500, 11 x 33 mm

Ref. 5501

AIR-KING / automatic, 14 karat yellow gold and stainless steel bicolor case, 1970, Ref. 5501, 12 x 32 mm

AIR-KING / original box, certificate and receipt, channeled lunette, 14 karat gold and stainless steel bicolor case, Cal. 1520, 1967, Ref. 5501, 12 x 33 mm

AIR-KING / channeled lunette, 14 karat gold and stainless steel bicolor case, original dial, Cal. 1530, 1960s, Ref. 5501, 11 x 33 mm

Ref. 5504

AIR-KING / automatic, stainless steel case, 1958, Ref. 5504, 12.1 x 34.1 mm

Ref. 5506

AIR-KING / original certificate, 18 karat gold-coated case, original dial with raised indices, Ref. 5506, 12 x 33 mm

Ref. 5520

AIR-KING / 14 karat gold-filled case, 1978, Ref. 5520, 11 x 33 mm

AIR-KING / 14 karat gold case, hand-wound, 1970, Ref. 5520, 12 x 33 mm

AIR-KING / original tag, case and gold hood, raised gold bar indices, automatic movement, Ref. 5520, 11.5 x 33 mm

Ref. 5700

AIR-KING DATE / automatic, stainless steel case, 1963, Ref. 5700, 12 x 33 mm

AIR-KING / automatic, stainless steel case, 1970s, Ref. 5700, 12.9 x 36.1 mm

AIR-KING / automatic, stainless steel case, 1970s, Ref. 5700, 12 x 33 mm

AIR-KING DATE / automatic, stainless steel case, 1983, Ref. 5700, 12 x 33 mm

AIR-KING / automatic, stainless steel case, 1971, Ref. 5700, 12 x 33 mm

AIR-KING DATE / flexible band, finely shaped original indices, Cal. 1530, Ref. 5700, 1960s, 12.5 x 33.5 mm

AIR-KING DATE / 14 karat yellow gold and stainless steel case and flexible band, automatic movement, Cal. 1535, 1960s, Ref. 5700, 12 x 33 mm

AIR-KING DATE / second stop, Cal. 1520, Ref. 5700, 12 x 33.5 mm

AIR-KING

Ref. 5701

Ref. 6500

Ref. 6552

Ref. 7784

AIR-KING DATE / simple model, champagne-colored dial, raised bar indices, 1970s, Ref. 5700, 12 x 33 mm

AIR-KING DATE / date loupe, channeled yellow gold lunette, stainless steel case, nice gold dial, Ref. 5701, 13 x 33.5 mm

AIR-KING / white dial with Arabic numerals, 1960s, Ref. 6500, 12 x 32.5 mm

AIR-KING / leather band, lunette with raised indices, leaf hands, automatic movement, 1950s, Ref. 6552, 12 x 32 mm

AIR-KING / 9 karat yellow gold case, leather band, elegant blue dial, 1970s, Ref. 7784, 11.5 x 32.5 mm

Ref. 14000

AIR-KING / automatic, stainless steel case, 1994, Ref. 14000, 12 x 33 mm

AIR-KING / automatic, stainless steel case, 1970s, Ref. 14000, 12 x 34 mm

AIR-KING / automatic, stainless steel case, 1999, Ref. 14000, 11 x 34 mm

AIR-KING / automatic, stainless steel case, 1989, Ref. 14000, 12 x 33 mm

AIR-KING / automatic, stainless steel case, 1998, Ref. 14000, 12 x 33 mm

AIR-KING / automatic, stainless steel case, 2000, Ref. 14000, 12 x 33 mm

AIR-KING / automatic, stainless steel case, 1970s, Ref. 14000, 12 x 34 mm

AIR-KING / automatic, stainless steel case, 1970s, Ref. 14000, 12 x 34 mm

AIR-KING / automatic, stainless steel case, 1998, Ref. 14000, 11 x 34 mm

AIR-KING / automatic, stainless steel case, 1990s, Ref. 14000, 12 x 33 mm

AIR-KING / automatic, stainless steel case, 2000, Ref. 14000, 12 x 33 mm

AIR-KING / automatic, stainless steel case, 1995, Ref. 14000, 12 x 35 mm

AIR-KING / automatic, stainless steel case, Ref. 14000, 12 x 33 mm

AIR-KING / automatic, stainless steel case, 1996, Ref. 14000, 12 x 33 mm

AIR-KING / automatic, stainless steel case, 1998, Ref. 14000, 11.7 x 33.4 mm

AIR-KING

Ref. 14000M

AIR-KING / automatic, stainless steel case, 2003, Ref. 14000M, 11 x 33 mm

AIR-KING / automatic, stainless steel case, 2003, Ref. 14000M, 12 x 34 mm

AIR-KING / good condition, automatic, stainless steel case, 2003, Ref. 14000M, 12 x 34 mm

AIR-KING / good condition, automatic, stainless steel case, 2003, Ref. 14000M, 12 x 34 mm

AIR-KING / good condition, automatic, stainless steel case, 2003, Ref. 14000M, 12 x 34 mm

AIR-KING / automatic, stainless steel case, 2003, Ref. 14000M, 12 x 33 mm

Ref. 14010

AIR-KING / automatic, stainless steel case, 1997, Ref. 14010, 12 x 33 mm

AIR-KING / automatic, stainless steel case, 1994, Ref. 14010, 11.6 x 34 mm

AIR-KING / automatic, stainless steel case, Ref. 14010, 11 x 34 mm

AIR-KING / automatic, stainless steel case, 1999, Ref. 14010, 11 x 34 mm

Ref. 14010M

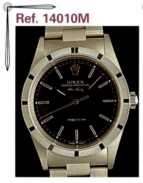

AIR-KING / automatic, stainless steel case, 2001, Ref. 14010M, 12 x 34 mm

Ref. 114000

AIR-KING / automatic, stainless steel case, 1999, Ref. 114000, 11 x 33 mm

PRINCE

The "PRINCE" is a model from the 1930s. Because of the second hand's position below the dial, it was used gladly by doctors. Thus it was known as the "Doctor's Watch". Its classic rectangular shape is just as modern now as it was 80 years ago. It is one of the loveliest watches that Rolex ever made.

PRINCE

PRINCE 1920s

PRINCE / original box, platinum case, two-tone dial, hand-wound, 1920s, 9 x 35 x 25 mm

BRANCARD / silver case, freshened-up dial, hand-wound, 1929, 9 x 36 x 23.5 mm

PRINCE 1930s

PRINCE / red-gold case, 1930s, hand-wound, 10 x 33 mm

BRANCARD / 9 karat white gold and yellow gold bicolor case, freshened-up dial, Arabic numerals, hand-wound, 1930s, 9 x 36.5 mm

BRANCARD / stainless steel case, hand-wound, 1930s, 9.5 x 35.5 x 23.5 mm

PRINCE / 9 karat yellow gold case, original dial with Arabic numerals and dot indices, hand-wound, 1930s, 9 x 35 x 25 mm

BRANCARD / 9 karat yellow gold case, hand-wound, signed "Chronometer", 1930s, 9 x 35.5 x 25.5 mm

PRINCE / 9 karat rose gold case, 1937, 9 x 36 x 20 mm

BRANCARD / dealer's signature "Bucherer", white and yellow gold bicolor case, 1935, 9 x 36 x 25 mm

PRINCE 1950s

RAILWAY / matte silver dial, printed Arabic numerals, 9 karat gold and stainless steel bicolor case, hand-wound, 1950s, 8 x 35.5 mm

PRINCE / 9 karat gold case, freshened-up dial, raised Arabic numerals, hand-wound, 1950s, 9 x 36 mm

JUMPING HOUR / digital hour indication, second indication with Arabic numerals, hand-wound, 1950s, 8.5 x 35.5 mm

Ref. 971

BRANCARD / striped white and yellow gold case, hand-wound, 1935, Ref. 971, 9 x 35.5 x 23.5 mm

BRANCARD / link band, 14 karat white gold case, unusual hand shape, Ref. 971, 8.5 x 36 x 25 mm

BRANCARD / dial with printed numerals, silver case, hand-wound, 1930s, 10 x 35 , 25 mm

Ref. 1490

BRANCARD / with box and certificate, silver case, early 1930s, Ref. 971, 9 x 35 x 24 mm

BRANCARD / dealer's signature "Bucherer", 9 karat gold case, original dial, hand-wound, Ref. 1490, 9.5 x 35.5 x 25 mm

BRANCARD / white and yellow gold bicolor case, luminous hands, dial with Arabic numerals, 6 mm crown, Ref. 1490, 8.5 x 36.5 x 23 mm

BRANCARD / 14 karat yellow gold case, black numerals and hands, hand-wound, 1948, Ref. 1490, 9 x 36 x 21.5 mm

Ref. 1491

JUMPING HOUR / digital hour indication, silver case, hand-wound, Ref. 1491, 1920s, 13.5 x 35 x 23 mm

PRINCE

Ref. 1527

RAILWAY / dealer's signature "SERPICO", gold and white gold bicolor case, Ref. 1527, 9 x 35.5 mm

Ref. 1862

PRINCE / very rare classic model, black dial, 1930s, Ref. 1862, 8.5 x 35.5 x 23 mm

Ref. 1862

PRINCE / 9 karat gold and stainless steel bicolor case, Ref. 1862, 8.5 x 35.5 x 20.5 mm

Ref. 2246

JUMPING HOUR / digital hour indication, 18 karat white gold and yellow gold bicolor case, hand-wound, Ref. 2246, 8.5 x 36 x 23 mm

Ref. 4376
JUMPING HOUR / 18 karat gold and white gold bicolor case in railway form, hand-wound, Ref. 4376, 9 x 36.5 x 20.5 mm

OTHER PRINCES
PRINCE / very elegant model, 10 karat gold-coated case, small second with indices, hand-wound, 9 x 35 x 21 mm

QUARTER CENTURY

QUARTER CENTURY

QUARTER CENTURY 1940s

LADY'S WATCH / rare "Quarter Century" model, 14 karat gold, 1948, 8.5 x 36.5 mm

PRINCE / firm signature "Eaton" (Canada), 25th anniversary gift, 14 karat gold case, 1946, 9 x 35.5 mm

PRINCE / scarcely used, very nice piece, 14 karat gold case, 1948, 8.5 x 35.5 x 25 mm

PRINCE / rolled attachments, 1944, 10 x 35 x 25 mm

QUARTER CENTURY 1950s

ANNIVERSARY WATCH / firm signature "Eaton", very nice model, smooth 14-karat gold lunette and case, hand-wound, 1955, 10.5 x 32.5 mm

BOMBAY / use time "1936-1961" engraved, 14 karat gold, 1950s, 11.5 x 32.5 mm

BOMBAY / original dial, 14 karat gold case, 18 karat gold band, 1953, 12 x 32.5 mm

ROUND / firm signature "Eaton", good condition, 14 karat gold, 1953, 12 x 32 mm

ANNIVERSARY WATCH / for Mr.. Gordon B. Daglus 1939-1954, 12 x 33 mm

Ref. 3937

PRINCE / case, dial and movement in mint condition, 14 karat gold case, Ref. 3937, 10 x 35.5 x 25 mm

PRINCE / for Mr.. Cambel for 1924-1949 anniversary, Ref. 3937, 9.5 x 35.5 x 25 mm

Ref. 4622

BOMBAY / 14 karat gold, Ref. 4622, 10 x 33 mm

Ref. 6422

ANNIVERSARY WATCH / firm signature "Eaton", 14 karat gold case, 1950s, Cal. 1210, Ref. 6422, 9.5 x 33 mm

OTHER QUARTER CENTURY

PRINCE / rare model, 14 karat gold case, 9 x 35.5 mm

PRINCE / Cal. 300 formed movement, 9.5 x 35.5 x 23 mm

BOMBAY / 14 karat gold, 11 x 33 mm

BOMBAY / 11 x 32.5 mm

BOMBAY / discolored dial, flexible gilded band, 11 x 32 mm

BOMBAY / case and movement in good condition, 11 x 33 mm

PRINCE / 9 x 36 x 25 mm

BUBBLE BACK

The Bubble Back is the first absolutely watertight automatic wristwatch, which Rolex itself developed, and whose real name is "Oyster Perpetual." In this model the hand winding used in other models was replaced by a rotor. This first self-winding mechanism, working only in one direction, was very thick. To house the automatic winding system, a special rounded case bottom was used instead of the former Oyster case bottom, hence the "Bubble Back" name. In the 22 years of production, from the beginning in 1933 to the end of production in 1955, Rolex put the most varied variants of the Bubble Back on the market.

BUBBLE BACK

BUBBLE BACK 1930s

BUBBLE BACK / 18 karat gold Empire case, original black dial, 1930s, 14 x 32

BUBBLE BACK / 18 karat gold Empire case, rare dial with Rolex crown, 1934, 13.5 x 32

BUBBLE BACK / early model, three-piece case, gold lunette, early 1930s, 12.5 x 29 mm

BUBBLE BACK / early model, Cal. 8 3/4 Hunter movement, 1934, 13 x 29 mm

BUBBLE BACK / early model with central second, 1930s, 12 x 29 mm

BUBBLE BACK / early model, two-tone dial, stainless steel lunette, 1930s, 13 x 30 mm

BUBBLE BACK / early model with dealer's signature "Asprey's", Breguet numerals, 1930s, 12 x 28 mm

BUBBLE BACK / early model, 1933-39, original dial, "flat rotor" Cal. 8 3/4 Hunter movement, 12 x 29 mm

BUBBLE BACK / early model, classic design, two-tone dial, rod hands, stainless steel case, 1933-35, 12 x 29 mm

BUBBLE BACK / rare "scientific" dial with red central second, covered steel band attachments, original dial, 1930s, 13 x 30 mm

BUBBLE BACK / Roman numerals and indices, small second, 1930s, 12 x 29 mm

BUBBLE BACK / three-piece case is original Rolex Perpetual case, gold lunette, 1934, 13 x 30 mm

BUBBLE BACK / three-piece gold and steel case, small second, 1935, 12 x 28.5 mm

BUBBLE BACK / three-piece 18 karat gold case, Cal. 8 ¾ Hunter rotor movement, 1930s, 12.5 x 29 mm

BUBBLE BACK / three-piece 18 karat gold case, late 1930s, 12.5 x 30 mm

BUBBLE BACK / three-piece steel case, original dial, 1930s, 12.5 x 29.5 mm

BUBBLE BACK / 18 karat three-piece case, railway minutery on dial, 1930s, 13 x 30.5 mm

BUBBLE BACK / original dial, only 3 Arabic numerals, 1930s, 13 x 29 mm

BUBBLE BACK / matte silver dial, small second, stainless steel case, 1930s, 13 x 29 mm

BUBBLE BACK / made between 1935 and 1938, yellow dial with raised Roman numerals, 13 x 29 mm

BUBBLE BACK

BUBBLE BACK 1940s

BUBBLE BACK / bicolor model, stainless steel case, 14 karat gold lunette and covered band attachments, in this form since 1939, 13 x 29 mm

BUBBLE BACK / medium size, 18 karat gold case, original dial, late 1930s, 14 x 28 mm

NON-OYSTER / 1930s, steel case (Bubble Back), original dial, automatic, 12 x 31 mm

BUBBLE BACK / 18 karat gold "Empire" case, unique dial, Mercedes hands, 1944, 13.5 x 31.5 mm

BUBBLE BACK / rare model, steel pillow-shaped case, 1940s, 13.5 x 31.5 mm

BUBBLE BACK / stainless steel case, Arabic numerals and indices, luminous hands, original dial, 1940s, 14 x 29 mm

BUBBLE BACK / 14 karat gold case, raised gold Arabic numerals and hands, original dial, small second, 1940s, 13 x 30 mm

BUBBLE BACK / original dial with Roman numerals and indices, stainless steel case, 1944, 13 x 29 mm

BUBBLE BACK / Arabic numerals, Mercedes hands, good condition, 1940s, 13.5 x 29 mm

BUBBLE BACK / two-piece case, black dial, 1940s, 13 x 29 mm

BUBBLE BACK / Roman and Arabic numerals and indices, original black dial, stainless steel case, 1940s, 13 x 29.5 mm

BUBBLE BACK / 18 karat gold case, two-tone dial, 24-hour markings, faultless condition, 1940s, 13 x 30 mm

BUBBLE MACK / simple steel model, almost new condition, original dial, 1946, 15.5 x 30.5 mm

BUBBLE BACK / 14 karat gold case, two-tone dial, 24-hour markings, 1946, b 14 x 30 mm

BUBBLE BACK / dealer's signature "Mappin", original dial, 1940s, 15 x 29.5 mm

BUBBLE BACK / two-tone dial and Mercedes hands, 1943, 16 x 30 mm

BUBBLE BACK / bicolor 14 karat gold and steel case, wedge indices, Mercedes hands, 1940s, 14 x 29 mm

BUBBLE BACK / 18 karat gold case and crown, numerals 3 and 9 lying, 1940s, 13 x 30 mm

BUBBLE BACK / Arabic numerals, red 24-hour markings, 1944, 15 x 29.5 mm

BUBBLE BACK / steel case, gold lunette, late 1940s, 14 x 30 mm

BUBBLE BACK

BUBBLE BACK / 14 karat gold case, railway minutery, Roman and Arabic numerals and indices, original dial, 1940s, 13 x 30 mm

BUBBLE BACK / red central second, 1940s, 14.5 x 30 mm

BUBBLE BACK / 14 karat gold case, original white dial, 1947, 14 x 30 mm

BUBBLE BACK / gold raised Arabic numerals and indices on original white dial, stainless steel case, 1940s, 13.5 x 30 mm

BUBBLE BACK / 9 karat gold case, gold Arabic numerals and indices, original dial, 1940s, 12.5 x 30 mm

BUBBLE BACK / automatic, stainless steel case, 1940, 12 x 30 mm

BUBBLE BACK / gilded stamped Arabic numerals, modern leaf hands, original dial, 1940s, 13 x 29 mm

BUBBLE BACK / original white dial, stainless steel case, 1940s, 13.5 x 29.5 mm

BUBBLE BACK / rare printed bar indices, matching hands, original dial, 1940s, 13 x 30 mm

BUBBLE BACK / bicolor model, gold lunette, stainless steel case, good condition, 1940s, 13.5 x 29.5 mm

BUBBLE BACK / Arabic numerals and wedge-shaped indices, red central second, 1940s, 14 x 29.5 mm

BUBBLE BACK / 14 karat rose gold case, same dial color, freshened-up dial, 1947, 14 x 30.5 mm

BUBBLE BACK / original two-tone dial, NA movement, late 1940s, 13 x 29 mm

BUBBLE BACK / black dial, Mercedes hands, 1940s, 13.5 x 29 mm

BUBBLE BACK / discolored dial, red 24-hour markings, 1940s, 14 x 29 mm

BUBBLE BACK / small second, stainless steel case, hand-wound, 1940s, 13 x 30 mm

BUBBLE BACK / 18 karat gold three-piece case, matte yellow dial, Roman numerals and indices, small second, 1940s, 14 x 30 mm

BUBBLE BACK / 14-karat gold and steel three-piece case, freshened-up dial, 1945, 14.5 x 30 mm

BUBBLE BACK / three-piece 14 karat gold case, freshened-up dial, 1947-48, 12.5 x 29 mm

BUBBLE BACK / three-piece bicolor case, gold lunette and stainless steel, original rose dial, 1940s, 13.5 x 30 mm

BUBBLE BACK

BUBBLE BACK two-piece case, central second, 1946, 13 x 29 mm

BUBBLE BACK / Arabic numerals and indices, white dial, original flexible band, 1946, 13 x 29 mm

BUBBLE BACK / unique dial, 14 karat gold and steel bicolor case, 1940s, 14 x 29 mm

BUBBLE BACK / small deeply grooved crown, 1940s, 14 x 30.5 mm

BUBBLE BACK / unique dial, Roman and Arabic numerals and indices, Mercedes hands, 1942, 14.5 x 29 mm

BUBBLE BACK / rare dial design, 1940s, 15.5 x 29.5 mm

BUBBLE BACK / 14 karat gold, Cal. NA 9 ¾ Hunter movement, 1944, 13 x 34 mm

BUBBLE BACK / flat case bottom, Arabic numerals (3 and 9 lying), rose gold lunette, 1940s, 14.5 x 30 mm

BUBBLE BACK / red gold case, original black dial, 1940s, 13.5 x 30 mm

BUBBLE BACK / raised Arabic numerals and wedge indices, 1940s, 13 x 28.5 mm

BUBBLE BACK / 14 karat gold case, gold raised indices, nice original dial, 1940s, 13 x 30 mm

BUBBLE BACK / large Arabic numerals and indices, bar hands, original dial, 1943, 13 x 29 mm

BUBBLE BACK / 14 karat gold case, raised Roman numerals and indices, original dial, 1940s, 13.5 x 30.5 mm

BUBBLE BACK / simple design, baton hands, Roman numerals and indices, stainless steel case, original dial, late 1940s, 14 x 29 mm

BUBBLE BACK / black dial, luminous hands, stainless steel case, 1940s, 13 x 31 mm

BUBBLE BACK / discolored dial, Arabic numerals and indices (this dial variant was made 1939-1942), 14.5 x 29 mm

BUBBLE BACK / signed "CERTIFIED PRECISION", raised gold Roman numerals and indices, late 1940s, 13.5 x 29 mm

BUBBLE BACK / 18 karat gold case, gold hands on original black dial, 1940s, 14 x 30 mm

BUBBLE BACK / gold and steel bicolor model, original dial, 1943-46, 13 x 30 mm

BUBBLE BACK / three-piece 14 karat gold and steel case, raised crown, numerals and indices, original dial, 1945, 14 x 29.5 mm

BUBBLE BACK

BUBBLE BACK / original red central second and luminous hands, stainless steel case, Cal. NA, late 1940s, 14 x 29.5 mm

BUBBLE BACK / 14 karat gold case, freshened-up dial, Arabic numerals, 1949, 15 x 31 mm

BUBBLE BACK / early model, 14 karat gold case, discolored dial, 1940s, 13 x 30 mm

BUBBLE BACK / movable band attachments, steel and gold bicolor case, 1940s, 12.5 x 31.5 mm

BUBBLE BACK / 14 karat gold and steel bicolor case, flat lunette, covered band attachments, 1943, 13 x 30 mm

BUBBLE BACK / bicolor model with covered band attachments, gold and steel band, 1940s, 14 x 30 mm

BUBBLE BACK / automatic, 18 karat red gold and stainless steel bicolor case, covered band attachments, 1940, 13 x 30 mm

BUBBLE BACK / 18 karat gold model, hidden band attachments, original band, 1940s, 13.5 x 30 mm

BUBBLE BACK / bicolor model, gold lunette, covered band attachments, matte rose dial, small second, 1940s, 14 x 30 mm

BUBBLE BACK / automatic, original dial, 14 karat red gold case, covered band attachments, 1940, 13 x 30 mm

BUBBLE BACK / automatic, original dial, 14 karat yellow gold case, covered band attachments, 1940, 13 x 30 mm

BUBBLE BACK / bicolor model, 14 karat gold lunette, covered band attachments, original dial with Arabic numerals, 1940s, 13.5 x 30 mm

BUBBLE BACK / steel case, gold lunette, covered band attachments, black dial, Bicolor band, 1940s, 13.5 x 30 mm

BUBBLE BACK automatic, 18 karat yellow gold, 1947, 13 x 30 mm

BUBBLE BACK / automatic, stainless steel case, so-called "lifesaver" model, 1940, 13 x 30 mm

BUBBLE BACK / bicolor case and band, rose dial, gold hands, 1945, 14.5 x 30 mm,

BUBBLE BACK / covered band attachments, Arabic numerals, gold band not original, 13 x 30 mm

BUBBLE BACK / 18 karat gold case, covered band attachments, gold Arabic numerals and hands, 1940s, 13.5 x 30 mm

BUBBLE BACK / discolored 24-hour markings and dial with small second, flexible band, 14 karat gold case, 1940s, 14 x 30 mm

BUBBLE BACK / original dial and flexible bicolor band, bicolor steel and 14 karat gold case, Cal. 9 ¾ Hunter movement, 1940s, 13 x 30.5 mm

BUBBLE BACK

BUBBLE BACK / smooth lunette, shell-shaped covered band attachments, 14 karat gold and steel bicolor case, original dial, 1940s, 13.5 x 27 mm,000

BUBBLE BACK / small model, stainless steel case, covered shell-shaped band attachments, rose dial, 1940s, 11 x 27 mm

BUBBLE BACK / medium size, covered shell-shaped band attachments, Cal. AR, 1940s, 13 x 27.5 mm

BUBBLE BACK / covered shell-shaped band attachments, Cal. AR (520), 1842, 13 x 27 mm

BUBBLE BACK / covered shell-shaped band attachments, 1940s, 12.5 x 27.5

BUBBLE BACK / medium size, Cal. AR or 520 movement, nice covered shell-shaped gold band attachments, 1940s, 14 x 27.5 mm

BUBBLE BACK / automatic, 18 karat red gold and stainless steel bicolor case, 1940, 13 x 28 mm

BUBBLE BACK / discolored dial, lying numerals, stainless steel case, 1940s, 13 x 30 mm

BUBBLE BACK / 18 karat gold case, early model, raised Roman numerals and indices, 1940s, 13 x 30 mm

BUBBLE BACK / bicolor model, gold lunette, stainless steel case, gold leaf hands, late 1940s, 12.5 x 30 mm

BUBBLE BACK / so-called "life saver" model, discolored dial, small second, wide lunette, medium size with AR movement, 1940s, 12 x 27.5 mm

BUBBLE BACK / bicolor model, raised numerals and indices, original white dial, 1940s, 13.5 x 30 mm

BUBBLE BACK / model with AR movement, striking lunette and crown, bicolor case, original dial, 1940s, 13 x 28 mm

BUBBLE BACK / 14 karat gold and steel bicolor case, raised numerals, 1940s, 13.5 x 30 mm

BUBBLE BACK / 18 karat gold case, original matte silver dial, 1940s, 13 x 30 mm

BUBBLE BACK / dial design made 1939-1942, leaf hands since 1944, 13.5 x 30 mm

BUBBLE BACK / 18 karat gold case, original dial, Arabic and Roman numerals, gold band, 1944, 13 x 30 mm,

BUBBLE BACK / raised Arabic numerals and indices, sloping 18 karat gold lunette, 1940s, 14 x 29.5 mm

BUBBLE BACK / luminous white Arabic numerals on black dial, 1940s, 15 x 29 mm

BUBBLE BACK / original crown, lunette and hands, raised Arabic numerals, indices and Rolex crown, 1940s, 13 x 30 mm

BUBBLE BACK

BUBBLE BACK / automatic, stainless steel case, so-called "life-saver" model, 1940, 12 x 28 mm

BUBBLE BACK / original white dial wedge-shaped numerals, 1940s, 14.5 x 30 mm

BUBBLE BACK / stainless steel case, original dial, 1942, 15 x 30 mm

BUBBLE BACK / second division on freshened-up two-tone dial, stainless steel case, 1940s, 14 x 29 mm

BUBBLE BACK / flat steel lunette, projecting crown, late 1940s, 14 x 30 mm

BUBBLE BACK / dealer's signature "Bucherer", three-piece 18 karat gold case, 1940s, 13.5 x 30 mm

BUBBLE BACK / then-modern wedge indices, freshened-up dial, stainless steel case, 1940s, 13 x 30 mm

BUBBLE BACK / rose dial, rod hands, gold central second, 1940s, 12.5 x 30 mm

BUBBLE BACK / Arabic numerals, 10 karat gold-filled case, 1940s, 13.5 x 29.5 mm

BUBBLE BACK unusual dial, bi-color gold and steel case, flexible band, 1940s, 13.5 x 30 mm

BUBBLE BACK / automatic, 18 karat red gold case, 1945, 12 x 29 mm

BUBBLE BACK / medium size, freshened-up dial, Cal. AR 8 ¾ Hunter, 1947, 15 x 29 mm

BUBBLE BACK / medium size, original dial, small second, Cal. AR, 1940s, 13 x 28 mm

BIG BUBBLE / unusual big (original?) hands, Arabic numerals and indices, late 1940s, 14 x 34.5 mm

BUBBLE BACK / elegant design, 18 karat gold case, freshened-up white dial, 1940s, 13 x 29,5 mm

BUBBLE BACK 1950s

BUBBLE BACK / slim lunette, small second, original dial, 1940s, 13.5 x 29 mm

BUBBLE BACK / original two-tone dial, dealer's signature "Serpico", steel case with narrow gold lunette, 1950s, 13 x 29 mm

BUBBLE BACK / rare model with engraved lunette from 1950 Holy Year, 15 x 30 mm

BUBBLE BACK / common model since the 1950s, modern leaf hands, raised indices, original dial, 13 x 29.5 mm

BUBBLE BACK / late model, medium size, stainless steel case, two-tone dial, 1950s, 14 x 29 mm

BUBBLE BACK / gold-plated case, gold hands and indices, freshened-up dial, 1950s, 13 x 29.5 mm

BIG BUBBLE / lightly bowed case bottom, 1951, 14 x 34 mm

BIG BUBBLE / 14 karat gold and steel bicolor case, "Oysterdate" added to dial in freshening-up, 1950s, 13.5 x 32.5 mm

BUBBLE BACK / medium size, 18 karat gold case, Cal. AR (520)m Cal. 8 ¾ Hunter movement

BIG BUBBLE / 18 karat gold case, Cal. 10 ½ Hunter movement, 1950s, 12.5 x 32 mm

BUBBLE BACK / stainless steel case, 1950s, 13 x 32 mm

SEMI-BUBBLE / automatic, stainless steel case, 1950s, 14 x 32 mm

BUBBLE BACK / automatic, stainless steel case, 1950s, 13 x 31 mm

BIG BUBBLE / Bubble Back model with Super-Oyster crown, original dial, 1953, 13 x 33 mm

Ref. 1595

BUBBLE BACK / medium size, so-called "life saver" model, wide gold lunette, dealer's signature "CASA MASSON", 12 x 27 mm, Ref. 1595,

Ref. 1858

BUBBLE BACK / early model, 18 karat gold case, "flat rotor" 8 3/4 Hunter Cal., 13 x 30 mm, Ref. 1858

Ref. 2490

BUBBLE BACK / cream dial, Arabic numerals, case in good condition, 1947, 13 x 29 mm, Ref. 2490

Ref. 2704

BUBBLE BACK / white dial and hands, freshened up, stainless steel case, 14 x 29 mm, Ref. 2704

Ref. 2760

BUBBLE BACK / Cal. NA (620), freshened-up dial, 13 x 30 mm, Ref. 2760

Ref. 2763

OYSTER BUBBLE BACK / classic "Chronometer" model, bar hands, red central second, 1940s, stainless steel case, Ref. 2763, 11.5 x 29 mm

Ref. 2764

BUBBLE BACK / gold hands, indices, dial and hands, striking central second, 1940s, 12.5 x 29 mm, Ref. 2764

BUBBLE BACK / two-tone dial, blue steel central second, Cal. NA, 1940s, 13 x 29 mm, Ref. 2764

BUBBLE BACK / normal model, signed "Centregraph", 1940s, 13 x 29.5 mm, Ref. 2764

BUBBLE BACK / silver case and dial, red central second, 1940s, 13 x 29 mm, Ref. 2764

BUBBLE BACK / 14 karat gold lunette, original white dial, case with pressed-on steel bottom, Cal. NA, 14 x 29.5 mm, Ref. 2764

BUBBLE BACK

BUBBLE BACK / discolored dial, luminous indices, 13.5 x 29 mm, Ref. 2764

BUBBLE BACK / bicolor case and band, freshened up, 1941, 13 x 30 mm, Ref. 2764

BUBBLE BACK / stainless steel case, red central second, original dial, 12 x 29 mm, Ref. 2764

BUBBLE BACK / dealer's signature "Gerv y Sobrinos", original dial, 1940s, 12 x 29 mm, Ref. 2764

BUBBLE BACK / gold Arabic numerals and railway minutery, black dial, formerly freshened up, 13.5 x 29.5 mm, Ref. 2764

BUBBLE BACK / simple design, Arabic numerals and indices, original dial, Cal. 320, 1940s, 14 x 29 mm, Ref. 2764

BUBBLE BACK / original dial with early 1935-37 design, NZ movement, 13 x 29 mm, Ref. 2764

BUBBLE BACK / early model, small second, 1940s, 13 x 29.5 mm, Ref. 2764

BUBBLE BACK / rare model, original white dial, small second, 1948, 12.5 x 29.5 mm, Ref. 2764

BUBBLE BACK / interesting design, larger numerals and indices, luminous hands, small second, freshened up, 13.5 x 29 mm, Ref. 2764

BUBBLE BACK / Arabic numerals and indices, gold dial, small second, stainless steel case, 1936, 13 x 29 mm, Ref. 2764

BUBBLE BACK / model with small second, original two-tone matte-rose dial, railway minutery, 1940s, 12.5 x 29 mm, Ref. 2764

BUBBLE BACK / rare model, small second, 1940s, Cal. NA, 12.5 x 29 mm, Ref. 2764

BUBBLE BACK / automatic, stainless steel case, 1940s, Ref. 2764, 13.5 x 29.2 mm

BUBBLE BACK / stainless steel case, 1940s, Ref. 2764, 13.4 x 28.8 mm

Ref. 2765

Ref. 2768

BUBBLE BACK / small second, automatic, stainless steel case, 1930s, Ref. 2764, 13.3 x 32 mm

BUBBLE BACK OYSTER / elegant original dial, engraving on small second, 1939, stainless steel case, Ref. 2765, 12 x 20 mm

BUBBLE BACK OYSTER / original dial with raised numerals, signed "Chronometre" and "Observatory", stainless steel case, Ref. 2765, 12 x 29 mm

BUBBLE OYSTER / white dial signed "Chronometre" and "Observatory", hand-wound, stainless steel case, Ref. 2765, 10.5 x 29 mm

BUBBLE BACK / original dial, Roman numerals and indices, small second, 1940s, 13 x 29.5 mm, Ref. 2768

BUBBLE BACK

Ref. 2784

BUBBLE SPEEDKING / elaborate dial, red central second, 1940s, Ref. 2784, 11 x 30 mm

BUBBLE OYSTER / Centregraph (printed later), 24-hour markings, 1940s, Ref. 2784, 12 x 30 mm

BUBBLE JUNIOR SPORT / two-tone dial, 1940s, stainless steel case, Ref. 2784, 12 x 29.5 mm

Ref. 2940

BUBBLE BACK / dealer's signature on original rose dial, 1940s, 13 x 29 mm, Ref. 2940

BUBBLE BACK / unique dial and Mercedes hands, original box and guarantee, Cal. NA, 1940s, 13.5 x 29.5 mm, Ref. 2940

BUBBLE BACK / central second, Mercedes hands, striking Roman numerals, 1940s, 13.5 x 29 mm, Ref. 2940

BUBBLE BACK / black dial with Roman and Arabic numerals and indices, 1940s, 12.5 x 29 mm, Ref. 2940

BUBBLE BACK / black dial, Mercedes hands, original movement and case, flexible band, 1940s, 15 x 29 mm, Ref. 2940

BUBBLE BACK / sporting, semi-unique dial, Mercedes hands, 15.5 x 30 mm, 1941, Ref. 2940

BUBBLE BACK / discolored original dial, stainless steel case, 1942, 12.5 x 29 mm, Ref. 2940

BUBBLE BACK / original matte rose dial, case in good condition, Cal. NA, 15.5 x 29.5 mm, Ref. 2940

BUBBLE BACK / rare jewel hands, 1940s, 15 x 29 mm, Ref. 2940

BUBBLE BACK / automatic, stainless steel case, 1940s, Ref. 2940, 13.4 x 28.8 mm

BUBBLE BACK / two-tone dial, red 24-hour markings, Cal. NA, 1940s, 14 x 29.5 mm, Ref. 2940

BUBBLE BACK / Arabic numerals and indices, red 24-hour markings, stainless steel case, 1940s, 13.5 x 29.5 mm, Ref. 2940

BUBBLE BACK / automatic, stainless steel case, 1940s, Ref. 2940, 13 x 29 mm

BUBBLE BACK / automatic, stainless steel case, 1940s, Ref. 2940, 14.1 x 29.4 mm

BUBBLE BACK / automatic, stainless steel case, 1940s, Ref. 2940, 13.7 x 29 mm

BUBBLE BACK / automatic, black dial, 1940s, Ref. 2940, 13 x 29 mm

BUBBLE BACK / automatic, stainless steel case, 1940s, Ref. 2940, 13.7 x 28.8 mm

BUBBLE BACK

BUBBLE BACK / timeless model, steel bicolor case with gold lunette, simple dial, Cal. NA, 1940s, Ref. 2940, 13 x 30 mm

BUBBLE BACK / striking silver markings and Arabic numerals, three-piece steel case, 1940s, 13.5 x 30 mm, Ref. 2940

BUBBLE BACK / automatic, stainless steel case. 1942, Ref. 2940, 13 x 30 mm

BUBBLE BACK / original dial, raised gold Roman numerals and indices, 13.5 x 29 mm, Ref. 2940

BUBBLE BACK / dial freshened up after the original, original crown not worn, 1950s, 14 x 30 mm, Ref. 2940

BUBBLE BACK / discolored original dial, fifth Bubble Back movement from 1945-46, 15 x 31 mm, Ref. 2940

BUBBLE BACK / original Arabic numerals and hands, 14 x 31 mm, Ref. 2940

BUBBLE BACK / original dial, stainless steel case, late 1940s, 14 x 30 mm, Ref. 2940

BUBBLE BACK / wedge-shaped indices and dots, freshened-up dial, 1940s, 13 x 29 mm, Ref. 2940

BUBBLE BACK / freshened-up early dial, Arabic numerals, Cal. NA, 1940s, 15 x 29 mm, Ref. 2940

BUBBLE BACK / Breguet numerals, freshened-up white dial, 1940s, 13 x 29 mm, Ref. 2940

BUBBLE BACK / stainless steel case, freshened-up white dial, Arabic numerals and indices, 1947, 13 x 29 mm, Ref. 2940

BUBBLE BACK / Arabic numerals and indices combined, 1940s, 13.5 x 29 mm, Ref. 2940

BUBBLE BACK / wide Roman numerals and indices, rod hands, red central second, 1940s, 13 x 29 mm, Ref. 2940

BUBBLE BACK / stainless steel case, 1940s, 15 x 29.5 mm, Ref. 2940

BUBBLE BACK / white dial, raised Arabic numerals and indices, blue steel hands, 13.5 x 28.5 mm, Ref. 2940

BUBBLE BACK / black dial with 24-hour markings, original dial and band, 13.5 x 39 mm, Ref. 2940

BUBBLE BACK / gold raised Roman numerals and indices, leaf hands, stainless steel case, freshened-up dial, 1945, 14 x 29 mm, Ref. 2940

BUBBLE BACK / two-tone dial, stainless steel case, 1945, 14 x 29 mm, Ref. 2940

BUBBLE BACK / two-tone dial, stainless steel case, 13 x 29.5 mm, Ref. 2940

BUBBLE BACK

BUBBLE BACK / bicolor model with gold lunette and stainless steel case, raised Arabic numerals, 1940s, 14.5 x 30.5 mm, Ref. 2940

BUBBLE BACK / 24-hour markings on original rose dial, stainless steel case, Cal. NA, 1940s, 14 x 29 mm, Ref. 2940

BUBBLE BACK / raised Arabic numerals and indices, original flexible band, 1950s, 14 x 29 mm, Ref. 2940

BUBBLE BACK / small raised numerals and indices, stainless steel case, 1945, 14.5 x 29.5 mm, Ref. 2940

BUBBLE BACK / stainless steel case, raised Arabic numerals, leaf hands, 1945, 14 x 29 mm, Ref. 2940

BUBBLE BACK / Roman numerals and indices, gold and steel bicolor case, 1940s, 13 x 30 mm, Ref. 2940

BUBBLE BACK / stainless steel case, gold lunette, 15 x 30 mm, Ref. 2940

BUBBLE BACK / gold lunette, original dial with 24-hour markings, Cal. NA, 1940s, 11.5 x 30 mm, Ref. 2940

BUBBLE BACK / stainless steel case, original dial, Arabic numerals, Cal. 9 3.4 Hunter Cal., 1940s, Ref. 2940, 14 x 30 mm

BUBBLE BACK / stainless steel case, original dial, red central second, Cal. NA, 1940s, 13 x 29 mm, Ref. 2940

BUBBLE BACK / stainless steel case, silver dial, red central second, Cal. NA, 1940s, 14 x 30 mm, Ref. 2940

BUBBLE BACK / unique dial, red central second, Mercedes hands, Cal. NA, 1940s, 14 x 30 mm, Ref. 2940

BUBBLE BACK / airplane on dial at buyer's request, original, 1940s, 13 x 30 mm, Ref. 2940

BUBBLE BACK / flat lunette, three-piece case, signed "Chronometre", stainless steel case, 1940s, 13.5 x 29 mm, Ref. 2940

BUBBLE BACK / Arabic numerals with shadowing, 1940s, 14.5 x 29 mm, Ref. 2940

BUBBLE BACK / dealer's signature "RANDLES DURHAM", original dial, 1940s, 13.5 x 29 mm, Ref. 2940

BUBBLE BACK / dealer's signature "Mappin", early model, three-piece 14 karat gold and steel case, small second, 1940s, 14 x 30 mm, Ref. 2940

BUBBLE BACK / dealer's signature "Gammeter", original dial, Cal NA, 1940s, 13.5 x 29.5 mm, Ref. 2940

BUBBLE BACK / Arabic numerals and indices on rose dial, luminous hands, stainless steel case and band, 1940s, 12 x 29 mm, Ref. 2940

BUBBLE BACK / automatic, small second, stainless steel case, 1940s, Ref. 2940, 13.9 x 32 mm

BUBBLE BACK

BUBBLE BACK / stainless steel case, original rose dial, small Roman numerals, Cal. NA, 1940s, 15 x 29 mm, Ref. 2940

BUBBLE BACK / rare model, silver dial, case and band, small second, late 1940s, 13.5 x 29 mm, Ref. 2940

BUBBLE BACK / rare model with flexible band, original dial, 1939, 13.5 x 30 mm, Ref. 2940

BUBBLE BACK / "Chronometer", original dial, 15 x 29 mm, Ref. 2940

BUBBLE BACK / gold wedge indices, stainless steel case, freshened-up dial, 13 x 28.5 mm, Ref. 2940

Ref. 3009 Ref. 3042 Ref. 3064 Ref. 3065

OYSTER BUBBLE BACK / original dial, hand-wound, "Chronometre". 14 karat gold case and hands, Ref. 3009, 11.5 x 28 mm

BUBBLE BACK / glass missing, so-called "life saver" model, original dial, early 1940s, 13 x 27.5 mm, Ref. 3042

BUBBLE BACK / first model with covered band attachments, 14 karat gold and steel bicolor case, bamboo band, 1930s, 13 x 30 mm, Ref. 3064

BUBBLE BACK / bicolor model, gold covered band attachments and lunette, silver case, 13.5 x 30 mm, Ref. 3065

BUBBLE BACK / 24-hour markings, 18 karat gold and steel bicolor case, Jubilee band, 1940s, 14 x 30 mm, Ref. 3065

BUBBLE BACK / gold and steel bicolor model, Arabic numerals, Mercedes hands, 14 x 30 mm, Ref. 3065

BUBBLE BACK / bicolor model, covered gold band attachments, stainless steel case, discolored original dial, Cal. NA, 14 x 30 mm, Ref. 3065

BUBBLE BACK / covered band attachments (later?), original dial, good condition, 1940s, 14 x 29 mm, Ref. 3065

BUBBLE BACK / 14 karat gold case, covered band attachments, original dial, 1939, 13.5 x 30 mm, Ref. 3065

BUBBLE BACK / original flexible bicolor band, rose/ gold lunette, 13.5 x 30 mm, Ref. 3065

BUBBLE BACK / gold and steel bicolor case, covered band attachments, flexible band, Ref. 3065, 1945, 13.5 x 30 mm

BUBBLE BACK / bicolor model, gold lunette, stainless steel case, discolored dial, all original, 1940s, 14 x 29.5 mm, Ref. 3065

BUBBLE BACK / automatic, 14 karat yellow gold and stainless steel bicolor case, 1940s, Ref. 3065, 15 x 30 mm

BUBBLE BACK / automatic, bicolor case of gold and stainless steel, covered band attachments, 1940s, Ref. 3065, 13 x 30 mm

BUBBLE BACK / gold lunette and covered band attachments, bicolor steel and gold case, original dial with 24-hour markings, 1940s, 15 x 30 mm, Ref. 3065

BUBBLE BACK

BUBBLE BACK / gold lunette and covered band attachments, bicolor case, leather band, 14.5 x 30 mm, Ref. 3065

BUBBLE MACK / automatic, 14 karat yellow gold and stainless steel bicolor case with covered band attachments, 1945, Ref. 3065, 13 x 30 mm

BUBBLE BACK / dealer's signature "Cartier", 14 karat gold case with serial number, 13.5 x 29 mm, Ref. 3065

BUBBLE BACK / gold indices and hands, 14 karat gold case, hidden band attachments, 1950s, 14 x 29.5 mm, Ref. 3065

BUBBLE BACK / small Roman numerals and indices, slim blue steel hands, bicolor 18 karat gold case, 1940s, Ref. 3065

Ref. 3130

BUBBLE BACK / bicolor model with gold lunette, covered band attachments, 14.5 x 30 mm, Ref. 3065

BUBBLE BACK / covered band attachments, small second, 14 karat gold case, original dial, 1940s, 14 x 30 mm, Ref. 3065

BUBBLE BACK / covered band attachments, small 18 karat gold second, original dial with raised numerals, 1940s, 13 x 30 mm, Ref. 3065

BUBBLE BACK / 14 karat gold case, Cal. NA, 1940s, 12.5 x 31 mm, Ref. 3130

BUBBLE BACK / Mercedes hands, semi-unique dial, 14 karat gold case, 1945, 13 x 30 mm, Ref. 3130

Ref. 3131

BUBBLE BACK / original dial, gold case, 12 x 30.5 mm, Ref. 3130

BUBBLE BACK / 14 karat gold case, small second, Cal. NA, 1940s, 12.5 x 31.5 mm, Ref. 3130

BUBBLE BACK / semi-unique dial with small second, double 12-hour markings, 14 karat gold case, freshened-up dial, 13 x 30 mm, Ref. 3130

BUBBLE BACK / automatic, 14 karat yellow gold case, 1940s, Ref. 3131, 13.5 x 30 mm

BUBBLE BACK / Roman numerals, Mercedes hands, black dial, original in good condition, 14 karat gold case, 13.5 x 30 mm, Ref. 3131

BUBBLE BACK / 14 karat gold case, Roman and Arabic numerals and indices, Mercedes hands, Cal. NA, 1940s, 13 x 30 mm, Ref. 3131

BUBBLE BACK / automatic, semi-unique dial, 14 karat yellow gold case, 1940s, Ref. 3131, 13.9 x 29.7 mm

BUBBLE BACK / automatic, 14 karat red gold case, 12940s, Ref. 3131, 14.1 x 30 mm

BUBBLE BACK / 14 karat gold case, unique original dial, good condition, 1940s, 14 x 30 mm, Ref. 3131

BUBBLE BACK / original rose dial, 14 karat gold case, Cal. NA, early 1940s, 14 x 30 mm, Ref. 3131

BUBBLE BACK

BUBBLE BACK / 18 karat gold case, original rose dial, 1940s, 13 x 30 mm, Ref. 3131

BUBBLE BACK / 14 karat gold case, added "Self Winding" printed on dial, 1947, 13.5 x 30 mm, Ref. 3131

BUBBLE BACK / automatic, stainless steel case, 1940s, Ref. 3131, 12 x 29 mm

BUBBLE BACK / gold case, two-tone dial, small second, 14.5 x 30 mm, Ref. 3131

BUBBLE BACK / freshened-up white dial, 14 karat gold case, movement in good condition, 1940s, 13.5 x 30 mm, Ref. 3131

BUBBLE BACK / 18 karat gold case, Arabic numerals, 1940s, 12 x 30 mm, Ref. 3131

BUBBLE BACK / 14 karat gold case, black dial, flexible band, 1940s, 14.5 x 30 mm, Ref. 3131

BUBBLE BACK / original black dial, Arabic numerals, 14 karat gold case, 14.5 x 30 mm, Ref. 3131

BUBBLE BACK / 14 karat gold case, original two-tone dial, Cal. NA, 1940s, 13 x 30 mm, Ref. 3131

BUBBLE BACK / 14 karat gold case, railway minutery, raised numerals, 1947, 13 x 30 mm, Ref. 3131

BUBBLE BACK / simple design, raised Roman numerals and indices, 18 karat gold case, original dial, 1940s, 13 x 30 mm, Ref. 3131

BUBBLE BACK / printed gold bar hands, 14 karat gold case, original dial, 13.5 x 30 mm, Ref. 3131

BUBBLE BACK / automatic, 18 karat red gold, 1940s, Ref. 3131, 13 x 30 mm

BUBBLE BACK / numerals and hands go well with 14 karat gold case, original dial with small second, 13.5 x 29.5 mm, Ref. 3131

BUBBLE BACK / automatic, 18 karat red gold case, 1940s, Ref. 3131, 14 x 29.8 mm

BUBBLE BACK / white dial with raised numerals and indices, 14 karat gold case, 1940s, 13.5 x 30 mm, Ref. 3131

BUBBLE BACK / 14 karat gold case, raised Arabic numerals and indices, 1940s, 13.5 x 30 mm, Ref. 3131

BUBBLE BACK / 14 karat gold case, gold Arabic numerals and indices, modern leaf hands, 1943, 12.5 x 30 mm, Ref. 3131

BUBBLE BACK / three-piece 14 karat gold case, gold leaf hands, blue central second, Cal. 9 ¾, 13.5 x 30 mm, Ref. 3131

BUBBLE BACK / 14 karat gold case, original dial, Arabic numerals and indices, 1940s, 13 x 32 mm, Ref. 3131

BUBBLE BACK

Ref. 3133

BUBBLE BACK / bicolor gold and steel case, original dial, Mercedes hands, 1946, 13 x 31 mm, Ref. 3133

BUBBLE BACK / gold lunette, stamped gold numerals and indices, Mercedes hands, 1944, 14 x 30 mm, Ref. 3133

BUBBLE BACK / semi-unique dial, 13x 30 mm, Ref. 3133

BUBBLE BACK / luminous hands and numerals, bicolor gold and stainless steel case, original dial, 13.5 x 30 mm, Ref. 3133

BUBBLE BACK / original white dial, Arabic numerals and wedge indices, 14.5 x 30 mm, Ref. 3133

BUBBLE BACK / three-piece stainless steel case, gold dial, 1945, 13.5 x 29 mm, Ref. 3133

BUBBLE BACK / three-piece gold and steel bicolor case, original dial, Cal. NA, 13 x 30 mm, Ref. 3133

BUBBLE BACK / rounded case bottom, 1940s, 14 x 30 mm, Ref. 3133

Ref. 3134

BUBBLE BACK / stainless steel case, wedge indices, 13.5 x 30 mm, Ref. 3134

Ref. 3135

BUBBLE BACK / printed Arabic numerals and indices, small second, Cal. NA, 1940s, 12.5 x 29 mm, Ref. 3135

BUBBLE BACK / normal model, red central second, late 1940s, 14 x 30 mm, Ref. 3135

Ref. 3348

BUBBLE BACK / so-called "boys bubble", dealer's signature, Cal. AR, 1940s, 12.5 x 27.5 mm, Ref. 3348

Ref. 3353

BUBBLE BACK / covered shell-shaped band attachments, original dial with Roman numerals, 1939, 12.5 x 27 mm, Ref. 3353

Ref. 3358

VICEROY / lunette with raised indices, original dial, 1940s, stainless steel case, Ref. 3358, 10.x 27.5 mm

Ref. 3372

BUBBLE BACK / stainless steel case, flexible band, original dial, late 1940s, 13 x 29 mm, Ref. 3372

BUBBLE BACK / three-piece 14 karat gold case, freshened-up rose dial, 1946, 13.5 x 30 mm, Ref. 3372

BUBBLE BACK / 18 karat gold case, dial in good condition, 1940s, 12.5 x 30 mm, Ref. 3372

BUBBLE BACK / leaf hands, Arabic numerals, small second, stainless steel case, freshened-up dial, 13 x 30 mm, Ref. 3372

BUBBLE BACK / 14 karat gold and steel bicolor case, rose dial, flexible gold band, 1940s, 12.5 x 30 mm, Ref. 3372

BUBBLE BACK / black dial, Mercedes hands, 14 karat gold case, 1940s, 14.5 x 29 mm, Ref. 3372

BUBBLE BACK

BUBBLE BACK / stainless steel case, 13 x 30 mm, Ref. 3372

BUBBLE BACK / luxury model, 14 karat gold lunette, 12.5 x 29.5 mm, Ref. 3372

BUBBLE BACK / Arabic numerals, rod hands, rose dial, original, Cal. NA, 1940s, 13.5 x 30 mm, Ref. 3372

BUBBLE BACK / automatic, stainless steel case, red 24-hour markings, 1940s, Ref. 3372, 13.2 x 30.5 mm

BUBBLE BACK / /gold two-tone dial, 9 karat gold lunette, bicolor band, 12.5 x 30 mm, Ref. 3372

BUBBLE BACK / bicolor steel case/gold lunette, Roman numerals and indices, 1945, 13 x 30 mm, Ref. 3372

BUBBLE BACK / luxury model, 18 karat gold case and lunette, 9 karat gold flexible band, original dial, Roman numerals and indices, 13 x 30 mm, Ref. 3372

BUBBLE BACK / bar hands, gold lunette and crown, 1940s, 14 x 30 mm, Ref. 3372

BUBBLE BACK / gold and steel three-piece case, 13 x 30 mm, Ref. 3372

BUBBLE BACK / case and dial in good condition, 1942, 13 x 28.5 mm, Ref. 3372

BUBBLE BACK / semi-unique dial, small second, flat steel lunette, 1940s, 13.5 x 30.5 mm, Ref. 3372

BUBBLE BACK / 14 karat gold case, original dial, 12.5 x 30 mm, Ref. 3372

Ref. 3458

BUBBLE BACK / railway minutery on original dial, stainless steel case, Cal. NA, 1940s, 13.5 x 29 mm, Ref. 3458

BUBBLE BACK / stainless steel case, original dial, lying Arabic numerals 3 and 9, 13 x 29 mm, Ref. 3458

Ref. 3548

BUBBLE BACK / stainless steel Empire case, Ref. 3548, 13 x 32 mm

BUBBLE BACK / 18 karat gold Empire case, small second, Cal. NA, 1930s, 14.5 x 32 mm, Ref. 3548

BUBBLE BACK / 18 karat gold "Empire" case, freshened-up white dial with small second, 1940s, 13 x 38 mm, Ref. 3548

Ref. 3595

BUBBLE BACK / smooth gold lunette and hidden rippled band attachments, 12.5 x 30 mm, Ref. 3595

BUBBLE BACK / covered band attachments with five-line engraving, model for USA, 1941, 13 x 30 mm, Ref. 3595

Ref. 3599

BUBBLE BACK / model with wide lunette and covered band attachments, on the market since 1943, few produced, Cal. NA, 1940s, 14 x 31 mm, Ref. 3599

BUBBLE BACK

Ref. 3696

Ref. 3716

BUBBLE BACK / rare model, Scientific dial, covered steel band attachments, all original, 1930s, 13 x 30 mm, Ref. 3599

BUBBLE BACK / interesting dial, original, stainless steel case, 1939, 14 x 30 mm, Ref. 3599

BUBBLE BACK / damaged minute hand, 9 karat gold case, original dial, 1944, 13 x 30 mm, Ref. 3696

BUBBLE BACK / Dauphin hands, raised bar indices, 14 karat gold case, 1940s, 13 x 30 mm, Ref. 3696

BUBBLE BACK / freshened-up dial, Arabic numerals and indices, gold modern leaf hands, 1945, 14 x 29 mm, Ref. 3716

Ref. 3725

Ref. 3767

Ref. 3772

Ref. 3794

BUBBLE BACK / 14 karat gold case, stainless steel bottom, original dial, 13 x 30 mm, Ref. 3725

BUBBLE BACK / automatic, stainless steel case, 1940s, Ref. 3767, 13 x 29 mm

BUBBLE BACK / automatic, stainless steel case, 1940s, Ref. 3772, 14 x 29 mm

BUBBLE BACK / medium size, smaller AR movement, bamboo band, 1930s, 13.5 x 27.5 mm, Ref. 3772

BUBBLE BACK / medium size, so-called "life saver" model, automatic, stainless steel case, 1940s, Ref. 3794, 12.3 x 29 mm

Ref. 4362

Ref. 4392

Ref. 4467

BUBBLE BACK / wide lunette, so-called "life saver" model, small second, 1940s, 12 x 27.5 mm, Ref. 3794

BIG BUBBLE / Big Bubble case but Cal. Nader normal Bubble Back movement, 1940s, 15 x 35.5 mm, Ref. 4362

BUBBLE BACK / automatic, stainless steel case, 1940s, Ref. 4392, 14 x 29 mm

BUBBLE BACK / slim lunette, 14 x 31 mm, Ref. 4392

BIG BUBBLE / model with date indication, 9 karat gold case, original dial, 1940s, 14 x 33.5 mm, Ref. 4467

Ref. 4777

Ref. 4961

Ref. 4984

Ref. 5006

BUBBLE BACK / gold case, very rare diamond hand, 1948, 13.5 x 30 mm, Ref. 4777

BUBBLE BACK / pillow-shaped case, NA movement, 1940s, 15 x 31.5 mm, Ref. 4961

BUBBLE BACK / "Army" case type, improved Viceroy case, 14 x 30.5 mm, Ref. 4961

BUBBLE BACK / gold lunette, nice dial, early 1940s, 13.5 x 30 mm, Ref. 4984

BUBBLE BACK / medium size, stamped hands, freshened-up dial, AR movement, 1940s, 14 x 27.5 mm, Ref. 5006

BUBBLE BACK

BUBBLE BACK / stainless steel case, raised Arabic numerals and indices, leaf hands, 1949, 13.5 x 27.5 mm, Ref. 5006

BUBBLE BACK / medium size, presumably made after 1949, 12.5 x 27.5 mm, Ref. 5006

BUBBLE BACK / small Bubble Back model, AR movement, 14 x 29 mm, Ref. 5006

Ref. 5009
BUBBLE BACK / bicolor steel and gold case, gold bar indices and hands, black dial, 1950s, 13.5 x 29.5 mm, Ref. 5009

BUBBLE BACK / bicolor model, gold lunette, steel case, original dial, 1940s, 13.5 x 29.5 mm, Ref. 5009

Ref. 5010

Ref. 5011

BUBBLE BACK / 10 karat yellow gold and stainless steel bicolor case, 1940s, Ref. 5010, 13.3 x 29.3 mm

BUBBLE BACK / bicolor case, rare hand form, freshened-up black dial, larger lettering, 13 x 29.5 mm, Ref. 5010

BUBBLE BACK / gold leaf hands and raised Arabic numerals and indices, 14 karat gold lunette, 1940s, 13 x 29.5 mm, Ref. 5011

BUBBLE BACK / lunette slopes to outside, gold and steel bicolor case, clearly legible dial, 13.5 x 29.5 mm, Ref. 5011

BUBBLE BACK / gold lunette, 14 x 30 mm, Ref. 5011

Ref. 5015

BUBBLE BACK / gold wedge indices on white dial, 12.5 x 29 mm, Ref. 5011

BUBBLE BACK / rare model, stainless steel case, small second, 1949, 13 x 29.5 mm, Ref. 5015

BUBBLE BACK / Arabic numerals, wedge and dot indices, stainless steel case, 1940s, 14 x 29 mm, Ref. 5015

BUBBLE BACK / dealer's signature "Dobbies Ltd Nairobi", bicolor model, 14 karat gold lunette, 1940s, 14 x 29 mm, Ref. 5015

BUBBLE BACK / 18 karat gold case, original dial, raised gold numerals, indices and hands, 13.5 x 29 mm, Ref. 5015

Ref. 5018

Ref. 5026

BUBBLE BACK / original case, dial and leaf hands, 1940s, 14 x 30 mm, Ref. 5015

BUBBLE BACK / indices for 12, 3 6 and 9 set with diamonds, freshened-up dial, steel Bombay case, 1950s, 14.5 x 32 mm, Ref. 5018

BIG BUBBLE / interesting design, original dial, striking Arabic numerals, Bombay case, 1949, 15.5 x 32 mm, Ref. 5018

BIG BUBBLE / steel Bombay case, original dial, Cal. 9 ¾ Hunter movement, 1950s, 15 x 32 mm, Ref. 5018

BUBBLE BACK / Big Bubble size, classic model, Arabic numerals, small second, 1945, 14.5 x 33 mm, Ref. 5026

BUBBLE BACK

Ref. 5028

BUBBLE BACK / automatic, stainless steel case, 1950s, Ref. 5028, 14 x 34 mm

BIG BUBBLE / two-tone dial with attached gold Roman numerals and hands, 1950s, 14 x 33 mm, Ref. 5028

Ref. 5029

BIG BUBBLE / wedge indices stamped on the freshened-up white dial, 1950s, 14 x 33.5 mm, Ref. 5029

Ref. 5031

SEMI-BUBBLE / automatic, yellow gold and stainless steel bicolor case, 1950s, Ref. 5031, 14 x 34 mm

Ref. 5048

BUBBLE BACK / white dial with raised numerals and indices, original dial, 1950s, 14 x 30.5 mm, Ref. 5048

Ref. 5050

BUBBLE BACK / red 24-hour markings, Arabic numerals, 14.5 x 28.5 mm, Ref. 5050

BUBBLE BACK / larger lettering on the dial, interesting numerals, freshened-up, 1940s, 15 x 30 mm, Ref. 5050

BUBBLE BACK / discolored dial, leaf hands, raised Arabic numerals, 1940s, 14.5 x 30 mm, Ref. 5050

BUBBLE BACK / three-piece 9 karat gold case, black dial, 14.5 x 29 mm, Ref. 5050

BUBBLE BACK / white dial with raised Arabic numerals and indices, stainless steel case, overhauled, 1949, 14 x 29 mm, Ref. 5050

BUBBLE BACK / normal size, wedge-shaped indices, 18 karat gold case, 13.5 x 29.5 mm, Ref. 5050

BUBBLE BACK / stainless steel case, flexible band, simple white original dial, 1950s, 13.5 x 30 mm, Ref. 5050

BUBBLE BACK / gold and steel bicolor case and band, covered attachments, original dial, Cal. 3159, 13 x 30 mm, Ref. 5050 mm

Ref. 5052

BUBBLE BACK / small second, automatic, stainless steel case, 1950s, Ref. 5052, 12 x 30 mm

Ref. 5054

BUBBLE BACK / gold lunette and dial, red central second, 1949, 14.5 x 29.5 mm, Ref. 5054

Ref. 5055

BUBBLE BACK / AR model, 14 karat gold lunette, freshened-up dial, 1950s, 14 x 28 mm, Ref. 5055

Ref. 5284

BIG BUBBLE / normal model, original white dial, stainless steel case, 1950s, 13 x 33 mm, Ref. 5284

BIG BUBBLE / dealer's signature "Broeck" on guilloched dial, flexible band, 13 x 32.5 mm, Ref. 5284

Ref. 6011

BUBBLE BACK / 14 karat gold case, 1940s, 13 x 29.5 mm, Ref. 6011

BUBBLE BACK / rippled lunette, 14 karat gold case, original dial, 15 x 30 mm, Ref. 6011

BUBBLE BACK

Ref. 6015

Ref. 6022

BUBBLE BACK / stainless steel case, steel lunette, dial freshened up earlier, 13.5 x 29.5 mm, Ref. 6015

BUBBLE BACK / stainless steel case, Super-Oyster crown, freshened-up dial, 14 x 30 mm, Ref. 6015

BUBBLE BACK / freshened-up black dial, Mercedes hands, 13.5 x 30 mm, Ref. 6015

BUBBLE BACK / stainless steel case, Roman numerals and indices, 13 x 29.5 mm, Ref. 6015

BIG BUBBLE / Dauphin hands, wedge indices, 9 karat gold case, white dial, 12.5 x 31.5 mm, Ref. 6022

Ref. 6029

Ref. 6075

Ref. 6050

BIG BUBBLE / slim lunette, 18 karat gold case, original dial, 1950s, 13.5 x 33 mm, Ref. 6029

BIG BUBBLE / gold case with rippled lunette, date indication, original dial, 1950s, 15 x 33 mm, Ref. 6075

BIG BUBBLE Oyster Perpetual Date model, gold and steel bicolor case, 15.5 x 33.5 mm, Ref. 6075

BUBBLE BACK / freshened-up white dial, Arabic numerals, stainless steel case, Cal. NA, 14.5 x 29 mm, Ref. 6050

BUBBLE BACK / automatic, stainless steel case, 1950s, Ref. 6050, 14 x 30 mm

BUBBLE BACK / last model, two-piece case, raised Rolex crown, 1950s, 13.5 x 30 mm, Ref. 6050

BUBBLE BACK / rare stamped numerals and indices, stainless steel case, early 1950s, 13 x 30 mm, Ref. 6050

BUBBLE BACK / Big Bubble size, case repaired, 1950s, 13.5 x 29.5 mm, Ref. 6050

BUBBLE BACK / like Big Bubble model but late normal model, flexible band, 1950s, 14 x 29.5 mm, Ref. 6050

BUBBLE BACK / very discolored white dial, gold Arabic numerals, indices and hands, 1950s, 13.5 x 29.5 mm, Ref. 6050

Ref. 6084

BUBBLE BACK / stamped, gilded Arabic numbers and indices, freshened-up dial, 1950s, 14 x 29 mm, Ref. 6050

BUBBLE BACK / normal steel model, teardrop indices on white dial, a940s, 13.5 x 29.5 mm, Ref. 6050

BUBBLE BACK / freshened-up dial, 1950s, 13.5 x 30 mm, Ref. 6050

BIG BUBBLE / 14 karat gold case, rippled lunette, wedge indices, 1956, 12.5 x 32 mm, Ref. 6084

BIG BUBBLE / golden leaf hands and wedge indices on white dial, stainless steel case, 15 x 32.5 mm, Ref. 6084

BUBBLE BACK

BIG BUBBLE / different wedge indices, discolored white dial, 14 karat gold case, 1950s, 13 x 32 mm, Ref. 6084

BIG BUBBLE / dial guilloched inside, rare Super-Oyster crown by 12, 1952, 13.5 x 32 mm, Ref. 6084

BIG BUBBLE / stainless steel case, freshened-up white dial, 1950s, 13 x 32 mm, Ref. 6084

Ref. 6085
SEMI BUBBLE / automatic, engine-turned lunette, 18 karat yellow gold case, 1951, Ref. 6085, 13 x 32.4 mm

SEMI-BUBBLE / gold and stainless steel bicolor case, 1950s Ref. 6085, 13 x 32 mm

BIG BUBBLE / Super-Oyster stem, 14 karat gold case, dial in Big Bubble style, 1950s, 13.5 x 33 mm, Ref. 6085

BIG BUBBLE / guilloched dial, rippled lunette, 12.5 x 31.5 mm, Ref. 6085

BUBBLE BACK / silver dial, case with steel lunette, flexible stainless steel band, 1950s, 12.5 x 32.5 mm, Ref. 6085

BIG BUBBLE / 14 karat gold case, black dial, original box, clasp and Rolex tag, overhauled, 1950s, 13 x 32.5 mm, Ref. 6085

BIG BUBBLE / stainless steel case, lunette sloping to outside, original dial, 1950s, 13 x 22.5 mm, Ref. 6085

Ref. 6092
Ref. 6098

Ref. 6106
Ref. 6108

BIG BUBBLE / guilloched dial, Bombay case, typical wedge indices, 1950s, Cal. 8603, Ref. 6092, 13 x 32.5 mm

BIG BUBBLE / original box and guarantee, stainless steel case, 1952, 13.5 x 35 mm, Ref. 6098

BIG BUBBLE / 18 karat gold case, guilloched dial with wedge and star indices, 1953, 13 x 33 mm, Ref. 6098

BIG BUBBLE / freshened-up dial, 13 x 32 mm, Ref. 6106

BIG BUBBLE / luminous indices, so-called "life saver" model, wide gold lunette, dealer's signature "CASA MASSON", 12 x 27 mm, Ref. 6108

Ref. 6206
Ref. 6298
Ref. 6332
Ref. 6102
Ref. 6334

BIG BUBBLE / late model, guilloched black dial, Cal. 9 ¾ Hunter movement, 1950s, 13.5 x 34.5 mm, Ref. 6206

BIG BUBBLE / gold numerals, indices and hands, Cal. 10 ½ Hunter movement, 1950s, 14 x 34.5 mm, Ref. 6298

BIG BUBBLE / simple design, freshened-up dial, Cal. 9 ¾ Hunter movement, 1950s, 13 x 33 mm, Ref. 6332

BIG BUBBLE / Bombay case, Dauphin hands, 1950s, 13.5 x 32 mm, Ref. 6102

BIG BUBBLE / simple model, gold dial, case with gold inlays, bar indices, rod hands, 1950s, 12.5 x 33 mm, Ref. 6334

BUBBLE BACK

Ref. 6352

OTHER BUBBLE BACKS

BIG BUBBLE / stainless steel case and band, freshened-up dial, 1950s, 13 x 34 mm, Ref. 6352

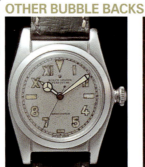
BIG BUBBLE / raised indices and crown, Cal. 10 ½ Hunter movement, 1950s, 14 x 34 mm, Ref. 6352

BUBBLE BACK / stainless steel case, gray dial, white Roman and Arabic numerals and indices, 13 x 29 mm

BUBBLE BACK / black dial with Roman and Arabic numerals, Mercedes hands, stainless steel case, 15 x 29 mm

BUBBLE BACK / original dial, 14 karat gold case, 13.5 x 29.5 mm

BUBBLE BACK / rose dial with blue steel hands, stainless steel case, flexible band, 14 x 29 mm

BUBBLE BACK / original dial with Roman numerals, 15 x 29.5 mm

BUBBLE BACK / printed Roman numerals and indices, original dial, stainless steel case, 14.5 x 29.5 mm

BUBBLE BACK / 9 karat gold case, simple dial, 13 x 30 mm

BUBBLE BACK / Roman numerals, stainless steel case, 13.5 x 29 mm

BUBBLE BACK / stainless steel case, matte rose dial, Roman numerals and indices, 13 x 29 mm

BUBBLE BACK / stainless steel case, raised gold Arabic numerals, 15 x 30 mm

BUBBLE BACK / wedge indices, stainless steel case, discolored original dial, 13.5 x 29 mm

BUBBLE BACK / freshened-up two-tone dial, raised Roman numerals and indices, 14 x 29.5 mm

BUBBLE BACK / rare model, colored enamel dial, 18 karat gold case, 13.5 x 30 mm,

BUBBLE BACK / white dial, small second, Roman numerals and indices, freshened up, 16 x 29 mm

BUBBLE BACK / three-piece steel case, dealer's signature "Mappin", Cal. 8 3/4 Hunter movement, 12 x 29 mm

BUBBLE BACK OYSTER / classic model signed "Observatory", raised railway minutery, bar hands, freshened-up dial, stainless steel case, 11.5 x 29.5 mm

BUBBLE BACK / stainless steel case, white dial, raised indices, 14 x 29.5 mm

BUBBLE BACK / 14 karat gold case, small second, 13 x 31 mm

BUBBLE BACK

BUBBLE BACK / black dial, 14 karat gold lunette and crown, 13 x 30 mm,

BUBBLE BACK / 14 karat gold lunette, dealer's signature "Celpico", 14.5 x 30 mm

BUBBLE BACK / steel and red gold lunette, bicolor band, 14 X 30 mm

BUBBLE BACK / stainless steel case, silver dial, 15.5 x 30 mm

BUBBLE BACK / 14 karat gold case, covered band attachments, Arabic numerals and indices on black dial, new Mercedes hands, 14.5 x 29 mm

BUBBLE BACK / covered band attachments, 14 karat gold case, dial with Mercedes hands, Roman and Arabic numerals, 13 x 29 mm

BUBBLE BACK / bicolor case, 14 karat gold lunette, flexible bicolor band, hidden attachments, original dial, 13.5 x 30 mm

BIG BUBBLE / guilloched dial, gold wedge indices, stainless steel case, 12.5 x 32 mm

BUBBLE BACK / Breguet numerals, freshened up, presumably Cal. AR, 12 x 27 mm

BUBBLE BACK / early model, 14 karat gold lunette, Dauphin hands, bicolor case, 12.5 x 27.5 mm

BUBBLE BACK / medium size, freshened-up dial, smallest movement of its time: Cal. AR (540), 13 x 28 mm

BIG BUBBLE / Arabic numerals and indices, nicely freshened-up white dial, stainless steel case, 12 x 33 mm

BUBBLE BACK / "Bombay" case, "slim-line" lunette, 14 x 31 mm

BUBBLE BACK / so-called "life saver" model, wide lunette, 12.5 x 27 mm

CHRONOGRAPH

Cosmograph Ref. 6239 catalog—still without crown guards in 1970

The "Chronograph" is really the typical sport watch. It is still much desired—not only because of its function of stopping time, but also because of its rarity value.

The Rolex Chronograph of the 1930s and 1940s has a small second and a 30-minute counter. In the 1950s a movement from Valjoux was used with three small accessory dials; since the 1960s the name "OYSTER CHRONOGRAPH" has been on the dial.

In the beginning, "DAYTONA" still appeared on the upper part of the dial, painted in black, but later it appeared in red on the upper part of the 12-hour counter. Until 1987 the Valjoux Caliber 72 with hand-winding was used; as of 1988 the Zenith El Primero movement has been used. At the Basel Fair in 2000 Rolex introduced its own Caliber 4130 movement.

CHRONOGRAPH

CHRONOGRAPH 1940s

CHRONOGRAPH / early hand-wound model, 18 karat gold and stainless steel bicolor case, original dial, 1940s, 12.5 x 30.5 mm

CHRONOGRAPH / rectangular buttons, Valjoux 69 movement, 18 karat rose gold case, 1940s, 11 x 29.5 mm

CHRONOGRAPH / telemeter and tachometer scales, 18 karat yellow gold scale, hand-wound, 1940s, 11 x 32 mm

CHRONOGRAPH / Valjoux 69 movement, one button, stainless steel case, hand-wound, 1930s-1940s, 11.5 x 31.5 mm

CHRONOGRAPH / early model, original gold dial, 9 karat yellow gold case, hand-wound, 1940s, 11.5 x 33 mm

CHRONOGRAPH 1950s

CHRONOGRAPH / telemeter and tachometer scales, stainless steel case, 1940s, 12.5 x 34.5 mm

CHRONOGRAPH / Valjoux 69 movement, stainless steel case and band, 1940, 11.5 x 29 mm

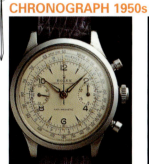
CHRONOGRAPH / blue tachometer scale, 1950s, 14 x 34.5 mm

CHRONOGRAPH / lunette with raised indices, rose gold bicolor case and band, 1950s, 14.5 x 35 mm

COSMOGRAPH / dealer's signature "Tiffany & Co.", tachometer scale on dial, 1950s, 14.5 x 35 mm

CHRONOGRAPH 1960s

CHRONOGRAPH / white dial, hand-wound, 1960s, 14.5 x 33.5 mm

CHRONOGRAPH / blue telemeter and black tachometer scales, 1960s, 14.5 x 34.5 mm

DAYTONA / "Paul Newman" model, "exotic" dial, 14 karat gold case, hand-wound, 1960, 14.5 x 32 mm

CHRONOGRAPH 1970s

CHRONOGRAPH / very rare and valuable 1970s model, original band, 18 karat yellow gold case and band, 13 x 34.5

COSMOGRAPH / "exotic" dial, 1970s, 14 x 36.5 mm

COSMOGRAPH / black plastic lunette, "exotic" dial, screwed buttons, 1970s, hand-wound, 13.5 x 37.5 mm

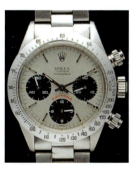
DAYTONA / hand-wound, stainless steel case, silver dial, 1970s, 14 x 37 mm

DAYTONA , 1970s, 13.5 x 37 mm

DAYTONA / dealer's signature "Tiffany & Co.", stainless steel case, 1970s, 13.5 s 37.5 mm

DAYTONA / tachometer scale on stainless steel lunette, stainless steel case, 1970s, 14.5 x 36.5 mm

Paul Newman Model

The well-known actor Paul Newman wore this model, with what is also called the "exotic" dial. It came on the market at the beginning of the 1960s and was produced into the 1970s. The dial can be black or white, the lunette can be stainless steel or plastic.

CHRONOGRAPH

CHRONOGRAPH 1980s

Ref. 2508

COSMOGRAPH / "exotic" dial, screwed buttons, stainless steel case, hand-wound, 1970s, 14 x 37 mm

DAYTONA / probably made to order, lunette and dial set with diamonds, 18 karat yellow gold case, 14 x 36.5 mm

DAYTONA / 1980s, 14 x 37 mm

DAYTONA / early model with black dial and lunette, screwed crown, watertight to 50 meters, 1980s, 13.5 x 37.5 mm

CHRONOGRAPH / 18 karat yellow gold case, hand-wound, 1940s, Ref. 2508, 12/3 x 35.9 mm

Ref. 3055

Ref. 3330

Ref. 3481

CHRONOGRAPH / hand-wound model with tachometer and telemeter scales, leaf hands, stainless steel case, 1950s, Ref. 2508, 13 x 37 mm

CHRONOGRAPH / very early model, hand-wound, stainless steel case, 1937, Ref. 2508, 12 x 37 mm

CHRONOGRAPH "ANTIMAGNETIC" / stainless steel case, hand-wound, 1935, Ref. 3055, 12 x 39 mm

CHRONOGRAPH / rectangular buttons, telemeter and tachometer scales, 18 karat gold case, 1940s, hand-wound, Ref. 3330, 13 x 36 mm

BABY0CHRONO / stainless steel case, hand-wound, 1940s, Ref. 3481, Cal. 69, 12 x 28 mm

Ref. 3525

Ref. 3529

Ref. 3695

Ref. 4500

CHRONOGRAPH / telemeter and tachometer scales, turning lunette, original dial, hand-wound, turning lunette, 1938, Ref. 3481, 11 x 38 mm

CHRONOMETER / Oyster case, original Jubilee band, hand-wound, Ref. 3525, 13.5 x 35 mm

CHRONOGRAPH / very rare model with square case, 1940s, Ref. 3529, 26 x 26 mm

CHRONOGRAPH / rectangular buttons, very rare model, only 48 made, 1941, Ref. 3695, 13 x 36.5 mm

CHRONOGRAPH / blue telemeter scale, hand-wound, gold and stainless steel bicolor case, 1950s, Ref. 4500, 12 x 34 mm

Ref. 4768

Ref. 5512

Ref. 6034

CHRONOGRAPH / pulse-counter scale, 30-minute counter, stainless steel case, hand-wound, calfskin band, 1945, Ref. 4500, 13 x 34 mm

CHRONOGRAPH / rectangular buttons, full calendar, 18 karat yellow gold case, 1951, Ref. 4768, 13 x 38 mm

DAYTONA / automatic, stainless steel case and band, 1970s, Ref. 5512, "Paul Newman" model, 13 x 37 mm

CHRONOGRAPH / red telemeter and blue tachometer scales, 1950s, Ref. 6034, hand-wound, 14.5 x 33.5 mm

CHRONOGRAPH / very well-kept original dial, stainless steel case, hand-wound, 1950s, Ref. 6034, 15 x 34 mm

CHRONOGRAPH

Ref. 6036

Ref. 6234

CHRONOGRAPH / very rare model, dial with tachometer and telemeter scales, 1950s, hand-wound, Ref. 6034, 14 x 34 mm

CHRONOGRAPH / full calendar, hand-wound, 1954, Ref. 6036, 14.5 x 33 mm

CHRONOGRAPH / full calendar, Valjoux 72 movement, 1950s, hand-wound, Ref. 6036, 13 x 32.5 mm

CHRONOGRAPH / round buttons, full calendar, 1940s, Ref. 6036, 13 x 34 mm

CHRONOGRAPH / original black dial, buttons do not screw, 1950s, Ref. 6234, hand-wound, 15 x 34 mm

Ref. 6238

CHRONOGRAPH / simple silver dial with tachometer scale, good condition, Ref. 6234, 14 x 34.5 mm

CHRONOGRAPH / dial with tachometer scale, hand-wound, Ref. 6238, 14 x 35 mm

CHRONOGRAPH / limited model, 3600 made, hand-wound, stainless steel case, 1960, Ref. 6238, 13.5 x 35 mm

COSMOGRAPH / dial with tachometer and telemeter scales, Valjoux 69 movement, 1960s, Ref. 6238, 13.5 x 35.5 mm

CHRONOGRAPH / hand-wound, black dial, stainless steel case, 1957, Ref. 6238, 13.5 x 35 mm

Ref. 6239

DAYTONA / stainless steel case, hand-wound, 1964, Ref. 6239, 14 x 36 mm

DAYTONA / stainless steel case, hand-wound, 1963, Ref. 6239, 14 x 36 mm

DAYTONA / so-called "Paul Newman" model, stainless steel case, hand-wound, 1960s, Ref. 6239, 13 x 37 mm

DAYTONA / automatic, stainless steel case, 1958, Ref. 6239, 13 x 36 mm

DAYTONA / hand-wound, dealer's signature "Tiffany & Co.", Ref. 6239, 14 x 36 mm

CHRONOGRAPH / forerunner of Daytona model, round buttons, 1950s, Ref. 6239, 15 x 34.5 mm

DAYTONA / unusual model with brown auxiliary dials, hand-wound, stainless steel case, 1966, Ref. 6239, 13.5 x 36.5 mm

DAYTONA / white "exotic" dial, 1960S, Ref. 6239, 14 x 36 mm

DAYTONA / Cosmograph, original "exotic" dial, late 1960s, Ref. 6239, 14 x 36.5 mm

DAYTONA / original "exotic" model, hand-wound, perfectly overhauled, 1960s, Ref. 6239, 13.5 x 36.5 mm

CHRONOGRAPH

DAYTONA / Oyster model, plastic lunette, silver dial, screwed buttons, probably 1970s, Ref. 6239, 13.5 x 37.5 mm

DAYTONA / "exotic" dial, hand-wound, stainless steel case, 1966, Ref. 6239, 13.5 x 36.5 mm

COSMOGRAPH / non-Oyster model, screwed buttons, stainless steel case, hand-wound, 1960s, Ref. 6239, 13.5 x 36.5 mm

DAYTONA / "exotic" dial, hand-wound, stainless steel case, 1966, Ref. 6239, 13.5 x 37.5 mm

DAYTONA / "exotic" dial, box and certificate, hand-wound, 1962, Ref. 6239, 13.5 x 37 mm

DAYTONA / stainless steel case and lunette, hand-wound, 1960s, Ref. 6239, 13.5 x 37 mm

DAYTONA / "exotic" matte black dial, non-Oyster, hand-wound, stainless steel case, 1960s, Ref. 6239, 13 x 31 mm

DAYTONA / "Daytona" signature not over small second, hand-wound, 1962, Ref. 6239, 13.5 x 36.5 mm

Ref. 6240

DAYTONA / automatic, stainless steel case, 1963, Ref. 6240, 13 x 37 mm

Ref. 6241

DAYTONA / "Paul Newman" type, hand-wound, plastic lunette with tachometer scale, 14 karat yellow gold case, Ref. 6241, 13 x 38 mm

DAYTONA / "exotic" dial, "Paul Newman" model, Ref. 6241, 13.5 x 37.5 mm

DAYTONA / Cosmograph, original "exotic" dial, hand-wound, late 1960s, Ref. 6241, 13.5 x 37.5 mm

DAYTONA / "exotic" dial, 14-karat massive gold case, hand-wound, 1960s, Ref. 6241, 14 x 33 mm

DAYTONA / "exotic" dial, stainless steel case, Ref. 6241, 14 x 37.5 mm

DAYTONA / original dial with red second markings, stainless steel case, hand-wound, Ref. 6241, 13 x 37.5 mm

Ref. 6262

DAYTONA / stainless steel case, hand-wound, 1968, Ref. 6262, 13.5 x 36.2 mm

DAYTONA / "exotic" model, white inner auxiliary dial, hand-wound, with certificate, late 1960s, Ref. 6262, 13.5 x 37 mm

Ref. 6263

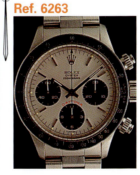

DAYTONA / stainless steel case, hand-wound, 1979, Ref. 6263, 13 x 37 mm

DAYTONA / stainless steel case, hand-wound, year unknown, Ref. 6263, 14 x 37 mm

DAYTONA / stainless steel case, hand-wound, 1969, Ref. 6263, 14 x 37 mm

CHRONOGRAPH

COSMOGRAPH / stainless steel case, hand-wound, 1970s, Ref. 6263, 12 x 37 mm

COSMOGRAPH / stainless steel case, hand-wound, 1970s, Ref. 6263, 11 x 37 mm

DAYTONA / stainless steel case, hand-wound, 1986, Ref. 6263, 13 x 37 mm

DAYTONA / stainless steel case, hand-wound, 1980s, Ref. 6263, 13 x 37 mm

DAYTONA / stainless steel case, hand-wound, 1978, Ref. 6263, 13 x 37 mm

COSMOGRAPH DAYTONA / 18 karat yellow gold case, 1979, Ref. 6263, 13 x 37 mm

DAYTONA / stainless steel case, hand-wound, 1970s, Ref. 6263, 13 x 36 mm

DAYTONA / stainless steel case, hand-wound, 1970s, Ref. 6263, 13 x 36.5 mm

DAYTONA / stainless steel case, hand-wound, 1979, Ref. 6263, 13.5 x 36.5 mm

DAYTONA / black plastic lunette, 1978, Ref. 6263, 13.5 x 37.5 mm

DAYTONA / in best condition with box and certificate from Bucherer, hand-wound, 1985, Ref. 6263, 13.5 x 37.5 mm

DAYTONA / early model with plastic lunette, hand-wound, 1970s, Ref. 6263, 14 x 37 mm

DAYTONA / original black dial and white auxiliary dials, plastic lunette, 1970s, Ref. 6263, 14 x 32,5 mm

DAYTONA plastic lunette, stainless steel case, screwed buttons, hand-wound, 1978, Ref. 6263, 13 x 37.5 mm

DAYTONA / Oyster model, black auxiliary dial, screwed buttons, 1970s, Cal. 727, Ref. 6263, 13.5 x 37.5 mm

DAYTONA / black dial, plastic lunette, tachometer scale, screwed buttons, Ref. 6263, 13 x 37.5 mm

DAYTONA / Oyster Cosmograph, plastic lunette, stainless steel case, original dial, hand-wound, 1978, Ref. 6263, 13.5 x 37.5 mm

DAYTONA / Oyster model, plastic lunette, arched crystal, screwed buttons, certificate, 1974, Ref. 6263, 14 x 38 mm

DAYTONA non-Oyster Chronograph, "exotic" dial, plastic lunette, 18 karat yellow gold case, Ref. 6263, 13 x 37.5 mm

DAYTONA / Oyster model, original silver dial, plastic lunette, 1970s, Cal. 13727, Ref. 6263, 13.5 x 37.5 mm

CHRONOGRAPH

DAYTONA / Oyster model, plastic lunette, hand-wound, screwed buttons, original dial, 1974, Ref. 6263, 13.5 x 37.5 mm

DAYTONA / last Oyster model, screwed buttons, hand-wound, original dial, 1985, Ref. 6263, 13.5 x 37.5 mm

DAYTONA / Chronometer model, 18 karat yellow gold Oyster case, plastic lunette, screwed buttons, 1978, Ref. 6263, 13 x 36 mm

DAYTONA / Oyster model, like-new condition, plastic lunette, hand-wound, 1987, Ref. 6263, 14 x 37.5 mm

COSMOGRAPH / Oyster model, screwed buttons, hand-wound, stainless steel case, 1970s, Ref. 6263, 13.5 x 37.5 mm

Ref. 6264   **Ref. 6265**

DAYTONA / original black dial, hand-wound, stainless steel case, 1977, Ref. 6263, 13.5 x 37.5 mm

DAYTONA / silver dial, plastic lunette, hand-wound, stainless steel case, 1980s, Ref. 6263, Cal. 727, 13.5 x 37.5 mm

DAYTONA / "Paul Newman" model, plastic lunette, black dial, hand-wound, 1960s, Cal. 13722, Ref. 6264, 14 x 37 mm

DAYTONA / stainless steel case, hand-wound, 1979, Ref. 6265, 13 x 36 mm

DAYTONA / 14 karat yellow gold case, hand-wound, 1977, Ref. 6265, 13 x 35 mm

DAYTONA / stainless steel case, hand-wound, 1974, Ref. 6265, 13 x 36 mm

DAYTONA / stainless steel case, hand-wound, 1985, Ref. 6265, 14 x 37 mm

DAYTONA / stainless steel case, hand-wound, 1970s, Ref. 6265, 13 x 36 mm

DAYTONA / 14 karat yellow gold, American gold band, hand-wound, 1977, Ref. 6265, 13 x 36 mm

DAYTONA / stainless steel case, hand-wound, 1986, Ref. 6265, 13 x 37 mm

DAYTONA / stainless steel case, hand-wound, 1978, Ref. 6265, 13 x 37 mm

DAYTONA / stainless steel case, hand-wound, 1974, Ref. 6265, 13 x 27 mm

DAYTONA / stainless steel case, hand-wound, 1970s, Ref. 6265, 13 x 37 mm

DAYTONA / stainless steel case, hand-wound, 1979, Ref. 6265, 13 x 37 mm

DAYTONA / stainless steel case, hand-wound, 1970, Ref. 6265, 13.5 x 36 mm

CHRONOGRAPH

DAYTONA / stainless steel case, hand-wound, 1987, Ref. 6265, 13.5 x 36.5 mm

DAYTONA / stainless steel case, hand-wound, 1978, Ref. 6265, 13 x 36 mm

DAYTONA / stainless steel lunette with tachometer scale, screwed-in buttons, hand-wound, 1979, Ref. 6265, 13.5 x 37 mm

DAYTONA / "Paul Newman" type, stainless steel lunette, screwed buttons, 1974, Ref. 6265, 13.5 x 32 mm

DAYTONA / screwed buttons, silver dial, Oyster case, hand-wound, 1970s, Cal. 727, Ref. 6265, 13.5 x 37 mm

DAYTONA / hand-wound, black dial, overhauled, 1970s, Ref. 6265, 13.5 x 38 mm

COSMOGRAPH / Oyster case of 18 karat yellow gold, hand-wound, screwed buttons, integrated band, 1970s, Ref. 6265, 13 x 37 mm

DAYTONA / Oyster case, screwed buttons, stainless steel case, hand-wound, 1980s, Cal. 727, Ref. 6265, 13.5 x 37 mm

COSMOGRAPH / hand-wound, Oyster case, screwed buttons, original dial, 1973, Ref. 6265, 13.5 x 36.5 mm

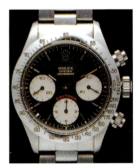

DAYTONA / standard 1970s model, original black dial, hand-wound, Cal. 727, Ref. 6265, 14 x 37 mm

COSMOGRAPH / arched crystal, screwed buttons, hand-wound, 1978, Ref. 6265, 13.5 x 37 mm

DAYTONA / stainless steel lunette, silver dial, screwed buttons, and-wound, Ref. 6265, 1979, 13.5 x 37 mm

DAYTONA / Oyster model, hand-wound, screwed buttons, stainless steel case, 1970s, Ref. 6265, 13 x 37 mm

COSMOGRAPH / chronometer model with 18 karat yellow gold Oyster case, screwed buttons, hand-wound, Ref. 6265, 14 x 37 mm

DAYTONA / Oyster model, black dial, white auxiliary dials, hand-wound, 1969, Ref. 6265, 13.5 x 37.5 mm

DAYTONA /Oyster model, original dial, stainless steel case, hand-wound, 1974, Ref. 6265, 13.5 x 37 mm

DAYTONA / last hand-wound Chronograph, original dial, stainless steel case, 1980s, Cal. 777, Ref. 6265, 13 x 37 mm

DAYTONA / Oyster model, screwed buttons, hand-wound, 1980s, Ref. 6265, 13.5 x 36.5 mm

DAYTONA / Oyster model, stainless steel lunette, tachometer scale, hand-wound, 1960s, Cal. 13727, Ref. 6265, 13.5 x 36.5 mm

DAYTONA / Oyster model, stainless steel lunette, silver dial, screwed buttons, 1984, Ref. 6265, 14.5 x 37 mm

CHRONOGRAPH

   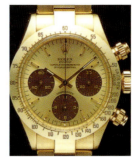 

DAYTONA / Oyster model, chronometer, 14 karat yellow gold case, gold dial and band, Ref. 6265, 13 x 37 mm

DAYTONA / Oyster model, stainless steel case, black dial, screwed buttons, 1970s, Ref. 6265, 13.5 x 36.5 mm

DAYTONA / rare piece, "exotic" dial, Oyster case, plastic lunette, hand-wound, Ref. 6263, 13.5 x 37.5 mm

COSMOGRAPH / Oyster case and band of 18 karat yellow gold, 1973, Ref. 6265, 13 x 37 mm

DAYTONA / stainless steel case, and-wound, certificate, Ref. 6265, 13.5 x 36 mm

Ref. 9239   **Ref. 16518**

DAYTONA /Oyster model with screwed buttons, hand-wound, stainless steel case, 1978, Ref. 6265, 13.5 x 37 mm

DAYTONA / original dial, stainless steel case, hand-wound, Ref. 6265, 13.5 x 37 mm

DAYTONA / "Paul Newman" model, "exotic" dial, original case, hand-wound, 1966, Ref. 9239, 13.5 x 36 mm

DAYTONA / automatic, yellow gold case, 1991, Ref. 16518G, dial with 8 indices set with diamonds, 12 x 39 mm

DAYTONA / automatic, yellow gold case, 2003, Ref. 16518, 13 x 33 mm

Ref. 16519   **Ref. 16520**

DAYTONA / automatic, 18 karat white gold case, 1999, Ref. 16519, dial with 8 indices set with diamonds, 13 x 38 mm

DAYTONA / automatic, stainless steel case, 1989, Ref. 16520, early original dial, 13.7 x 38.5 mm

DAYTONA / automatic, stainless steel case, 1997, Ref. 16520, 12 x 39 mm

DAYTONA / automatic, stainless steel case, 1996, Ref. 16520, 12 x 39 mm

DAYTONA / automatic, stainless steel case, 1999, Ref. 16520, 13 x 38 mm

DAYTONA / automatic, stainless steel case, 1990s, Ref. 16520, 13 x 38 mm

DAYTONA / automatic, stainless steel case, 1991, Ref. 16520, 13 x 38 mm

DAYTONA / automatic, stainless steel case, 1999, Ref. 16520, 13 x 38 mm

DAYTONA / automatic, stainless steel case, 1996, Ref. 16520, 13 x 38 mm

DAYTONA / automatic, stainless steel case, 1990, Ref. 16520, 13 x 38 mm

CHRONOGRAPH

DAYTONA / good condition, automatic, stainless steel case, 2000, Ref. 16520, 13 x 38 mm

DAYTONA / automatic, stainless steel case, 1998, Ref. 16520, 13 x 38 mm

DAYTONA / automatic, stainless steel case, 1999, Ref. 16520, 13 x 38 mm

Ref. 16523

DAYTONA / automatic, yellow gold and stainless steel bicolor case, 1996, Ref. 16523G, 13x 38 mm

DAYTONA / automatic, yellow gold and stainless steel bicolor case, 1990s, Ref. 16523, 13 x 38 mm

DAYTONA / automatic, yellow gold and stainless steel bicolor case, 1994, Ref. 16523, 13 x 39 mm

DAYTONA / automatic, yellow gold and stainless steel bicolor case, 1999, Ref. 16523, 12 x 39 mm

DAYTONA / automatic, yellow gold and stainless steel bicolor case, 1991, Ref. 16523G, dial with 8 indices set with diamonds, 12 x 39 mm

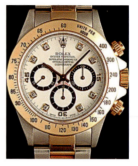

DAYTONA / yellow gold and stainless steel bicolor case, 1991, Ref. 16523G, dial with 8 indices set with diamonds, 12 x 39 mm

DAYTONA / automatic, 18 karat yellow gold and stainless steel bicolor case, 1990, Ref. 16523, 13 x 38 mm

DAYTONA / automatic, 18 karat yellow gold and stainless steel bicolor case, 1998, Ref. 16523G, 13 x 38 mm

DAYTONA / automatic, 18 karat yellow gold and stainless steel bicolor case, 1999, Ref. 16523, 13 x 38 mm

DAYTONA / automatic, 18 karat gold and stainless steel bicolor case, 1996, Ref. 16523, 12 x 39 mm

Ref. 16528

DAYTONA / automatic, 18 karat yellow gold case, 1988, Ref. 16528, 12.7 x 38 mm

DAYTONA / automatic, 18 karat yellow gold case, 1996, Ref. 16528, 12.6 x 38.5 mm

DAYTONA / automatic, 18 karat yellow gold case, 1991, Ref. 16528, 12.4 x 38.3 mm

DAYTONA / automatic, yellow gold case, 1996, Ref. 16528, 12 x 39 mm

DAYTONA / yellow gold case, 1999, Ref. 16528G, dial with 8 indices set with diamonds, 12 x 39 mm

DAYTONA / automatic, 18 karat yellow gold case, 1991, Ref. 16528, 13 x 38 mm

Ref. 116518

DAYTONA / automatic, 18 karat yellow gold and stainless steel bicolor case, 2000, Ref. 116518, mother-of-pearl colored dial, 13 x 38 mm

CHRONOGRAPH

Ref. 116519

Ref. 116520

Ref. 116523

DAYTONA / automatic, 18 karat yellow gold case, 2001, Ref. 116518, 13 x 40 mm

DAYTONA / automatic, 18 karat white gold case, 2001, Ref. 116519, 12 x 38 mm

DAYTONA BEACH / automatic, white gold case, 2002, Ref. 116519NR, 13 x 38 mm

DAYTONA / automatic, stainless steel case, 2003, Ref. 116520, 13 x 38 mm

DAYTONA / automatic, yellow gold and stainless steel bicolor case, 2003, Ref. 116523, 12 x 38 mm

Ref. 116528
OTHER CHRONOGRAPHS

DAYTONA / automatic, 18 karat yellow gold case, 2001, Ref. 116528, 12 x 39 mm

CENTREGRAPH / 1930s, hand-wound, button for resetting second hand, steel case, 11 x 28 mm

CHRONOGRAPH / very rare model with full calendar, 18 karat yellow gold case, hand-wound, 12.5 x 36.5 mm

DAYTONA / hand-wound, screwed buttons, 13.5 x 37 mm

DAYTONA / Oyster case, screwed buttons, hand-wound. 12/5 x 38/5 mm

WATERPROOF WATCHES

WATERPROOF WATCHES

OYSTER PERPETUAL
Ref. 1500, Ref. 14000, Ref. 1601 to 16234

The basic Rolex models are the Oyster Perpetual, DateJust, and Air-King. All the models are made with Oyster cases. The DateJust model was put on the market in 1945. The date switches exactly at midnight. The Air-King model ranks among the oldest Rolex models and is meant for a more reasonably priced category.

DATE

Ref. 1500 Cal. 1520 1970s
Simple silver dial, plastic crystal, bar hands and indices.

DATEJUST

Ref. 1601 Cal. 1520 1970s
Steel and 18-karat yellow gold case, Jubilee band, plastic crystal, gold dial.

Ref. 16233 Cal. 3125 1990s
Champagne-colored dial, yellow gold lunette, Jubilee band,

Ref. 16234 Cal. 3135 1990s
Stainless steel case, 18-karat white gold lunette.

AIR-KING

Ref. 14000 Cal. 3000 1996-1997
The oldest model with the typical blue dial; basic version.

Ref. 14000 Cal. 3000 1996-1997
Beginner's model, silver dial, bar hands and indices.

Ref. 14000 Cal. 3000 1990s
The most-sold version, indices at 3, 6 and 9, looks much like Explorer, thick bar indices with luminous blocks.

WATERPROOF WATCHES

SUBMARINER
Ref. 6204 to Ref. 16610LV

The Submariner is the best-known Rolex diver's watch. Right after sales began in 1953, the Submariner was used not only by divers, but by the most varied other professionals. Its watertightness was developed for depths of 100, 200, and 300 meters. Today almost all Submariner models are made with sapphire crystals. The Submariner is available with the date as a chronometer or without the date as a non-chronometer.

Ref. 6204, Cal. A296, 1954
The first Submariner, turning lunette with 5 minute division, no crown guard, parallel hands, semi-Bubble Back, watertight to 100 meters

Ref. 5510, Cal. 1530, 1958
8 mm Crown diameter, "Brevet" pressed on crown along with a crown, so-called James Bond model

Ref. 5508, Cal. 1530, 1950s
The first model of the 1500 series, 18,000 A/h, modified several times and produced into the 1970s, very reliable

Ref. 6538, Cal. 1030, 1958
The first chronometer in the Submariner series and the only model with a red arrow by the 12 on the lunette to make it easier to read; very large crown

Ref. 5510, Cal. 1530, 1958
James Bond model very rippled lunette

Ref. 5512, Cal. 1570, 1961
The first model with a crown guard. Like the present-day models, it is equipped with a 7 mm diameter crown

Ref. 5513, Cal. 1520, 1973
Long-selling model, opulent crown guard, official Royal Marine diver's watch in the 1970s

WATERPROOF WATCHES

Ref. 6204, Cal. A296, 1954
Reworked model, Mercedes hands, luminous points on second hand, lunette with minute division to 15 minutes

Ref. 6202, Cal. A260, 1954
Turn-O-Graph, which was produced simultaneously with the first model. Watertight to 50 meters, like the other Oyster models. Fitted with a time-recorder lunette.

Ref. 6205, Cal. A260, 1955
The second model. A big difference from the first model is the works with the A260 caliber (600 series). The diameter of the crown is 6 mm; that of the first model was 5 mm.

Ref. 6200, Cal. A296, 1958
Back to Caliber A296 again. The reason was to make it different from the chronometer model Ref. 6538 (Cal. 1030), which had just come onto the market.

Ref. 6536, Cal. 1030, 1950s
Ref. 6536/1 of 1957, Cal. 1030, automatic winding in both directions, 6 mm crown diameter.

Ref. 6205 Cal. A260/1955
Modified 2nd model, equipped with Mercedes hands and lunette with minutes division to 15 minutes

Ref. 1680,
Cal. 1575, 1970s
The first chronometer model with date indication. The so-called "red sub" was produced for only five years (1970-1974)

Ref. 16800, Cal. 3035, 1980s
As early as 1984 Ref. 16800 already had a sapphire crystal, was watertight to 300 meters, and had a calendar with fast switching.

WATERPROOF WATCHES

Ref. 16610 Cal. 3135 1997
31 jewels, Breguet hairspring, 28.800 A/h, chronometer, index with ring

Ref. 14060 Cal. 3000 1998
No date, no chronometer, 27 jewels, 28,800 A/h, the chronometer model with Cal. 3135 has 31 jewels

Sea-Dweller
Ref. 1665 to Ref. 16600

Special diver's watch from 1971, developed especially for the Comex firm, with a valve for helium.

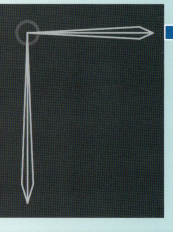

Ref. 1665 Cal. 1570 1972
First model with helium vent, thick bottom and crystal, first presented as the top model of the Submariner series, watertight to 610 meters

Ref. 16600 Cal. 3135 1997
Sea-Dweller 4000, improved legibility

Ref. 16660 Cal. 3035 1980s
Sea-Dweller "Comex" 4000; in the 1980s only 4000 of these special watches were made.

WATERPROOF WATCHES

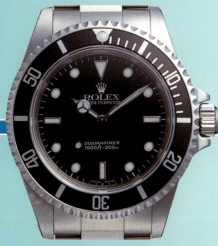

Ref. 14060M Cal. 3130 2001
The alarm is under a bridge. To make it hard to falsify, the sapphire crystal has an etched crown by the 6.

Green lunette, large round index

Called "Red Sea-Dweller," strong base and glass. Overall height 6 mm

Ref. 1665 Cal. 1570 1978
The Sea-Dweller "Comex" is the official Comex watch. There is a Comex logo on the dial; "Rolex" and "Comex" are stamped on the bottom.

Ref. 16660 Cal. 3035 1981
Sea-Dweller 4000, watertight to 1220 meters, total height 15 mm

First Sea-Dweller from the 1980s, without magnifying lens, but with helium valve.

WATERPROOF WATCHES

EXPLORER
Ref. 6350 to Ref. 114270

When the Explorer was placed on the market in 1953, it was not very popular at first and not a great sales success. Thus it was modified several times in the ensuing years.

Ref. 6350 Cal. 10 ½ A296 early 1953
He first model was the official watch for the British Mount Everest expedition.

Ref. 114270 Cal. 3130 2001
Newest model, shock-resistant Cal. 3130, to guard against copying, a crown was etched into the glass at the level of the 6.

Ref. 14270 Cal. 3000 1998
Placed on the market half a year after Ref. 1016 went out of production; indices with metal rim

EXPLORER II
Ref. 1655 to Ref. 16570

With 24-hour hand and lunette, this watch was warn by Reinhold Messner on his climb of Mount Everest and has been available since 1972.

Ref. 1655 Cal. 1570 1970s
Orange 24-hour hand

Ref. 1655 Cal. 1570 1970s
First model with a red 24-hour hand, second hand with luminous points.

WATERPROOF WATCHES

Ref. 6150 Cal. A296 1953
The second model was sold parallel with the first and later replaced it as the main model. Black dial and modified index.

Ref. 6350 end of 1953
The so-called first model was already off the market in 1953.

Ref. 6610 Cal. 1030 1956
Often modified and finally the 3rd model of the Explorer, improved lift function, Cal. 1030

Ref. 1016 Cal. 1570 1980s
The 5th model comes from the late 1980s, Cal. 1570 with second stop, production ended in 1989

Ref. 1016 Cal. 1570 1966
The white outer circle disappears, the bar indices become longer, the first Ref. 1016 had gold indices, which later became white.

Ref. 1016 Cal. 1560 1950s
The 4th model of Ref. 1060 was very popular, is called "Antique Explorer" by collectors, and has a white circle as the outermost ring on the dial. Later models no longer have a white ring.

Ref. 16550 Cal. 3085 1980s
The second model sold out in a short time; ivory dial, metal rim on indices.

Ref. 16570 Cal. 3185 1996-1997
The 3rd model with Cal. 3185 was also used for the GMT-Master II and has higher functionality than its predecessor.

Ref. 16570 Cal. 3185 1999
The newest model with a white dial, independently settable 24-hour hand allows a second time-zone indication.

WATERPROOF WATCHES

GMT-MASTER
Ref. 6542 to Ref. 16700

GMT means Greenwich Mean Time. Besides hour, minute and second hands, there is also a 24-hour hand which can be set to another time. In 1954 the first GMT-Master came onto the market and was often used by pilots. I the 1960s the GMT-Master became the official wristwatch of PanAm Airways.

Ref. 6542 Cal. 1066 1950s
First model without a crown guard, lunette with plastic inlays, later metal.

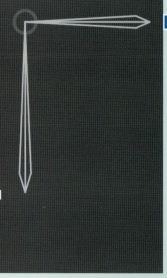

Ref. 16700 Cal. 3175 1990
The newest model, larger indices with metal rim, 31 jewels, Breguet hairspring, 28.800 A/h.

Ref. 16758 Cal. 3075 1986
18-karat yellow gold, developed for pilots on international airlines and business people.

GMT-MASTER II
Ref. 16760 to Ref. 16710

The GMT-Master II came onto the market in 1983. The 24-hour hand can be set individually to a third time zone. At first it was sold parallel to the GMT-Master, but this later caused the GMT-Master to disappear completely from the market.

Ref. 16760 Cal. 3185 1985
First model, sapphire crystal, 3 time zones.

WATERPROOF WATCHES

Ref. 1675 Cal. 1575 early
2nd model, with crown guard and stainless steel lunette. The early model had a 24-hour hand with a smaller arrow, the lunette had a slightly rounded rippling.

Ref. 1675 Cal. 1570
The 2nd model was for export, the whole lunette was black, the 24-hour hand had a larger arrow.

Ref. 16750 Cal. 3075 1980s
It looks like Ref. 1675 but is watertight to 100 meters and has fast date switching.

Ref. 16710 Cal. 3185 1998
2nd model, without tritium, without T symbol by the 6 on the dial.

Ref. 16710 Cal. 3185 2000
Red and blue lunette. With this model the production of the GMT-Master ended.

WATERPROOF WATCHES

COSMOGRAPH DAYTONA
Ref. 6238 to Ref. 116520

A popular collector's item. The boom began in 1988 in Italy. The Cosmograph has existed since 1961. In the 1970s production of the Daytona began. In 1988 the El Primero caliber by Zenith was installed; since 2000 it has had its own movement.

Ref. 6238 Cal. 72 1950s
No lunette and no "Cosmograph" lettering on the dial.

Ref. 6263 Cal. 727 1970
The last hand-wound model, a rare piece with series letter "R", plastic inlays in the lunette, tachometer indication to 200, screwed buttons, watertight to 50 meters.

Ref. 6264 Cal. 727 1968
The last model without screwed buttons, Paul Newman dial, red second indices, lunette on plastic inlay, tachometer indication to 200

Ref. 6263 Cal. 727 1970
Screwed buttons, black dial with small white numerals, plastic lunette inlay.

Ref. 6263 Cal. 727 1987
18 karat yellow gold, last hand-wound model, "Cosmograph" printed over the 12-hour hand, Chronometer

WATERPROOF WATCHES

Ref. 6239 Cal. 72B 1966
With tachometer lunette, Cosmograph Daytona, tachometer indication to 300

Ref. 6239 Cal. 72B 1966
Small second, indication with 15, 30 and 45, Paul Newman model, also called "exotic dial", red "Daytona" signature over the 12-hour indicator, tachometer indication to 200.

Ref. 6239 Cal. 772-1 1960
Standard model with black dial, white second-hand point, tachometer indication to 300

Ref. 6239 Cal. 72B 1966
Standard Daytona, white "Daytona" under Cosmograph, tachometer indication to 200.

Ref. 16520 Cal. 4030 1993
Rare black dial with gray-brown ring with small indications, tachometer indication to 400, chronometer, watertight to 100 meters.

Ref. 116520 Cal. 4130 2001
Newest model, original Rolex movement, alarm under bridge

WATERPROOF WATCHES

YACHT-MASTER
Ref. 68623 to Ref. 16622

The YACHT-MASTER came on the market in 1992 and was at first made only in an 18-karat yellow gold case. The watch is also available in medium size and for ladies. Since about 1997 there is also a steel/gold model which is very luxurious and elegant.

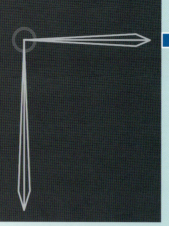

Ref. 68623 Cal. 2135 1996
Medium size, 18-karat yellow gold, gold hands and indices, steel-gold band, lunette diameter is 34 mm,

Ref. 69628 Cal. 2135 1996
Ladies' watch, 18-karat yellow gold, blue dial, lunette diameter 28.5 mm, watertight to 100 meters.

Ref. 68628 Cal. 2135 1995
Medium size, 18-karat yellow gold, blue dial, 18-karat yellow gold band, lunette diameter 34 mm.

Ref. 16622 1999 Yacht-Master
Rolesium, stainless steel case, platinum lunette with 40 mm diameter, red second hand, crown etched in the glass by the 6, watertight to 100 meters.

OYSTER

On October 7, 1927, the London stenographer Mercedes Gleitze was able to swim the English Channel in 15 hours. The watch that she wore on her left wrist became famous—an Oyster.

This is all the more remarkable because in the beginning 20th century the dust- and watertightness of wristwatches was a great problem. In 1926 Rolex received a patent for the watertight Oyster case and developed the screwed-in winding stem. That was the birth of this robust watch that lived up to its name "Oyster." Behind this name lurk many variations of the model. Often they are capable design achievements.

Advertisement from 1936.

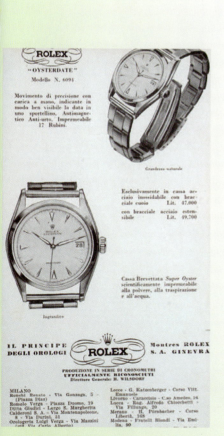
Oyster advertisement; the lower model is called "Super Oyster"

OYSTER

OYSTER 1920s

FLAT BACK / stainless steel case, hand-wound, 1930s, 11 x 28 mm

EXTRA PRECISION / original rose dial, 1927, steel and plaque bicolor case with covered band attachments, 11 x 27.5 mm

CHESTER / octagonal gilded case, matching numerals, 1920s, 10.5 x 30 mm, crown 5 mm

OYSTER / octagonal 18 karat gold case, enamel dial, 1920s, 10.5 x 28 mm

OYSTER / freshened-up dial, replaced crown, massive silver case, 10 x 29 mm

OYSTER / original enamel dial and band attachments, nickel case, 10 x 28.5 mm, crown 6 mm

UNICORN / 1920s, silver case, small second, 10 x 28 mm

OYSTER / enamel dial, pillow-shaped silver case, 1920s, 10 x 28.5 mm

OYSTER / massive silver case, blue steel hands, enamel dial, 1925, Ref. 3281, 9 x 32 mm

OYSTER / original dial, luminous hands, 1920s, pillow-shaped steel case, 9.5 x 28.5 mm

OYSTER 1930s

OYSTER / small second, stainless steel case, hand-wound, 1930, 10 x 28 mm

OYSTER / 1930s, covered stepped band attachments, stainless steel case, 11 x 27.5 mm

OYSTER / covered stepped band attachments, original dial, small second, 1930s, 11 x 28 mm

OYSTER / covered stepped band attachments, 18 karat gold case, 1930s, 11 x 28 mm

OYSTER / steel and gold bicolor case, covered rounded band attachments, 1930s, 11 x 25 mm

OYSTER / classic octagonal stainless steel case, original dial, 1930s, 12 x 27.5 mm

OYSTER / rippled lunette, onion crown, 18 karat gold case, 11 x 28 mm

OYSTER / elegant lunette, octagonal silver case, 1930s, 10 x 27 mm

OYSTER / original dial, Breguet hands, Arabic numerals, 1930s, 9 karat gold case, 10 x 28.5 mm

OCTAGON / 14 karat yellow gold and stainless steel bicolor case, hand-wound, 1930s, 11 x 28 mm

OYSTER

OYSTER / enamel dial, small second, pillow-shaped 9 karat gold case, 1930s, 10 x 27.5 mm, crown 5.5 mm

OYSTER / original dial with Arabic numerals, early model, silver case, 1930s, 10.5 x 28.5 mm

OYSTER / original two-tone dial, bar hands, 1930s, 14 karat gold case, 11.5 x 28.5 mm, crown 6 mm

OYSTER / rippled lunette, early pillow-shaped plaque case, original dial, 10.5 x 28 mm, crown 6 mm

OYSTER / guilloched ray pattern on dial, 1937, stainless steel case, 10.5 x 32 mm

IMPERIAL / "Chronometre", thin blue steel hands, original dial, 1930s, pillow-shaped 9 karat gold case, 9.5 x 28 mm

OYSTER / signed "Pall Mall", pillow-shaped stainless steel case, 1930s, Cal. 10 ½ Hunter movement, 10 x 29.5 mm

OYSTER / clear white markings on black dial, 1930s, stainless steel case, 10 x 26.5 mm, crown 6 mm

OYSTER / freshened-up dial, small second, raised numerals and indices, 1930s, 9 karat gold case, 9.5 x 26.5 mm

OYSTER / dealer's signature "Northern Goldsmiths Newcastle," 1930s, stainless steel case, 10.5 x 28.5 mm

OYSTER / silver dial, 1930s, 10.5 x 28.5 mm, crown 6 mm

ROYAL / stainless steel case like bubble back, hand-wound, 1930s, 11 x 28.5 mm, crown 6 mm

OYSTER / original dial with small second, 1930s, stainless steel case, 11.5 x 28.5 mm, crown 6 mm

OYSTER / original dial with grid muster except crown, 1930s, stainless steel case, 11 x 28.5 mm

FLAT BACK / stainless steel case, hand-wound, 1930, 11 x 28 mm

OYSTER / case like Bubble Back, but case bottom not bowed, hand-wound, 1930s, 14 karat gold case, 10 x 28.5 mm

OYSTER / "ROLEX-OYSTER" signature with hyphen, original bamboo band, 1930s, stainless steel case, 12 x 28 mm

OYSTER / hand-wound, original dial signed "Chronometre", 1930s, 11.5 x 28.5 mm

PRECISION / signed "50 m, 165 ft", 1939, stainless steel case, 10.5 x 33 mm, crown 6.5 mm

TURTLE TIMER / stainless steel case, hand-wound, 1930s, 11.3 x 26.7 mm

OYSTER

OYSTER / small second, stainless steel case, hand-wound, 1930s, 11.4 x 29 mm

OYSTER / black dial, gold numerals, steel case, 1930s, 10 x 27.5 mm

OYSTER / original matte black dial, medium-sized, 1930s, gold-plated case, 11.5 x 28 mm, crown 5 mm

OYSTER / original dial, luminous hands, 1930s, stainless steel case, 11.5 x 29 mm, crown 5.5 mm

LIPTON / 1930s, original dial, rare collector's item, 11.5 x 26.5 mm

OYSTER / original dial, small second, 1930s, 9 karat gold case, 11 x 28.5 mm, crown 5.5 mm

OYSTER / "Chronometre", raised railway minutery, 1930s, hand-wound, 11 x 28 mm

OYSTER / gilded markings on rim of dial, 1930s, hand-wound, "Chronometer", stainless steel case, 10 x 28 mm

OYSTER / raised numerals, medium size, 1938, stainless steel case, 10.5 x 29.5 mm

OYSTER / British dealer's signature over small second, 1930s, stainless steel case, 10 x 27.5 mm, crown 5.5 mm

RALEIGH / original dial, red central second, 1930s, stainless steel case, 12 x 27.5 mm

IMPERIAL / original dial, 1930s, stainless steel case, 11 x 28.5 mm

IMPERIAL / signed "extra precision", original dial, 1930s, 9 karat gold case, 10.5 x 28 mm

IMPERIAL / "Chronometre", original dial with Arabic numerals and dot indices, 1936, stainless steel case, 11 x 27.5 mm

IMPERIAL / medium size, original dial, 1930s, stainless steel case, 10.5 x 27.5 mm

ATHLETE / dealer's signature "Bucherer", stainless steel case, 1937, 11 x 27.5 mm

ROYAL / original black dial, dealer's signature "Bucherer", 1930s, stainless steel case, 11 x 28.5 mm, crown 5.5 mm

ROYAL / dealer's signature "Dochot Berne", two-tone matte white dial, red central second, 1935, stainless steel case, 11 x 28.5 mm, crown 6 mm

ROYAL / classic model, Arabic numerals, bar hands, 1930s, stainless steel case, 10.5 x 29 mm

ROYAL / original dial, small second, 1930s, 10.5 x 29 mm

OYSTER

OYSTER 1940s

ROYALITE / 1930s, raised numerals, red 24-hour markings, 11 x 30 mm

CENTREGRAPH / original dial with dot indices, button for zero setting of second hand, 1938, 12 x 28 mm

OYSTER / dealer's signature "Marconi" on original dial, 1940s, stainless steel case, 12.5 x 28 mm, crown 6 mm

OYSTER / signed "PALL MALL" on original dial, 1940s, steel case, 11.5 x 29.5 mm

EXTRA PRECISION / original dial, 1940s, stainless steel case, 11.5 x 31 mm

VICEROY / red gold and stainless steel case, hand-wound, 1940s, 10 x 28 mm

VICEROY / 9 karat gold case, hand-wound, 1940s, 11 x 26 mm

OYSTER / 1947, bicolor case of steel and plaque, 12 x 27.5 mm

OYSTER / raised numerals, original dial, blue steel hands, 1940s, 9 karat gold case, 10.5 x 26.5 mm

OYSTER / bar indices, white dial, gold and steel bicolor case and band, 1940s, 11 x 27.5 mm

OYSTER / original dial, luminous hands, 1940s, stainless steel case, 12 x 27 mm, crown 5 mm

OYSTER / original dial, leather band, clasp and attachments, like-new condition, 1940s, steel and 14 karat gold bicolor case, 11.5 x 27.5 mm

OYSTER / diamond hands, original dial, 1940s, pillow-shaped steel case, 11 x 31 mm

OYSTER / pillow-shaped stainless steel case, 1944, 11 x 31 mm

ROYAL / gray leather band, pillow-shaped case, original dial, Arabic numerals, leaf hands, 1940s, 10.5 x 31 x 31 mm

ELEGANTE / luminous numerals and bar hands, pillow-shaped 18 karat gold case, 1940s, 12 x 28 mm

OYSTER / medium-sized, 24 hour markings, 1940s, stainless steel case, 13 x 29 mm

OYSTER / stainless steel case, hand-wound, 1940s, 11 x 30 mm

COMMANDER / original dial, 1940s, stainless steel case, 11.5 x 29 mm

OYSTER / Mercedes hands, freshened-up matte rose dial, stainless steel case, 1942, 11 x 30 mm

OYSTER

ELEGANTE / semi-unique matte black dial, gold Mercedes hands, 1940s, gold plated case, 11 x 28.5 mm

ELEGANTE / rose/ dial and 18 karat gold case, 1940s, 11 x 29 mm

ELEGANTE / signed "Precision", flexible band, stainless steel case, 11.5 x 28.5 mm

ELEGANTE / 1940s, stainless steel case, 10.5 x 28 mm, crown 5.5 mm

ELEGANTE / bar hands, original case, 1940s, 14 karat gold case, 11.5 x 29 mm

SPEEDKING / matte rose dial, bar hands, bamboo band, 1940s, stainless steel case, 11 x 29 mm

SPEEDKING / original rose dial, luminous numerals, 1940s, stainless steel case, 11 x 28 mm

SPEEDKING / dealer's signature "ROSCH BERNE", original dial, flexible band, 1940s, 11.5 x 29 mm

SPEEDKING / luminous numerals and hands, matte rose dial, 1940s, 14 karat plaque case, 11.5 x 27.5 mm

SPEEDKING / slim luminous hands, rose dial, 1947, 10.5 x 29 mm

SPEEDKING / Signature 'OYSTER SPEEDKING" in red, freshened-up black dial, 1940s, 11.5 x 29.5 mm

SPEEDKING / raised Arabic numerals and small second, blue steel hands, 1940s, Ref. 4220, 11 x 28.5 mm

SPEEDKING / original white dial, 1940s, stainless steel case, 12 x 29 mm

SPEEDKING / 1940s, nice original cream dial, raised Roman numerals and indices, 12 x 28 mm

SPEEDKING / 1940s, hand-wound, signature "Precision" incomplete, 11.5 x 28.5 mm

OYSTER / original luminous hands, 1940s, 14 karat gold and steel bicolor case, 11.5 x 27.5 mm

LIPTON / original dial with small second, luminous hands, medium size, 1940s, stainless steel case, 12 x 29 mm

OYSTER / black dial, raised gold numerals and indices, 1940s, gold and steel bicolor case, 10.5 x 28.5 mm

ROYALITE / red 24-hour markings and central second, 1940s, 12 x 28 mm

ROYALITE / red 24-hour markings and central second, original dial, stainless steel case, 1940s, 12 x 29 mm

OYSTER

ROYALITE / printed 24-hour markings, two-tone dial, blue steel hands, overhauled, 1930s, 12 x 30 mm

SPEEDKING / matte rose dial, Arabic numerals, hands, all original, stainless steel case, 1946, 11 x 28.5 mm

ROYALITE / red 24-hour markings and central second, original dial, 1942, 12.5 x 29.5 mm

ROYALITE / red 24-hour markings and central second, 1942, 11 x 28.5 mm

ROYAL / original dial, Arabic numerals, red central second, 1940s, stainless steel case, 10.5 x 29 mm, crown 5.5 mm

ROYAL / raised dot indices, original black dial, 1940s, stainless steel case, 12 x 29 mm, crown 5.5 mm

ROYAL / two-tone dial, real Arabic numerals, 1940s, hand-wound, stainless steel case, Cal. 1225, 9.5 x 29.5 mm

OYSTER / original dial, 1940s, stainless steel case, 11 x 27 mm, crown 5 mm

OYSTER / longer minute hand, 1944, stainless steel case, 12 x 29.5 mm, crown 5.5 mm

OYSTER / original dial, 1940s, stainless steel case, 10.5 x 27.5 mm, crown 5.5 mm

OYSTER / Centregraph (printed later), 24-hour markings, gilded stainless steel press-in bottom, 1940s, 12 x 28.5 mm, crown 5.5 mm

OYSTER / dealer's signature "Bucherer", original dial, 1940s, stainless steel dial, 11.5 x 32 mm, crown 5.5 mm

SPORT AQUA / Oyster Company model, printed numerals on original dial, 1940s, stainless steel case, 11 x 29.5 mm

IMPERIAL / "Chronometre", original dial, bar hands. Wider central second, 1940s, stainless steel case, 10 x 25.5 mm

OYSTER / original dial signed "Officially Certified Chronometer", small 18 karat gold case, 1940s, 11 x 29 mm

PRECISION / stainless steel case, hand-wound, 1940, 11 x 33 mm

PRECISION / raised wedge indices, 1940s, 18 karat gold and steel bicolor case, 10 x 25 mm

OYSTER / freshened-up dial, medium-sized, overhauled, 1940s, stainless steel case, 11.5 x 29 mm

OYSTER / block indices on original dial, 1940s, stainless steel case, 10 x 29 mm, crown 5.5 mm

OYSTER / simple model, projecting crown, 1940s, stainless steel case, 10.5 x 30 mm

OYSTER

OYSTER / original dial signed "Chronometre", medium size, 18 karat gold case, 1940s, 11 x 28.5 mm

DATE / 1940s, guilloched dial, red and black date indication, gold plated case, 11 x 29.5 mm

DATE / raised indices, two-tone dial, freshened up, 1940s, stainless steel case, 9 x 33.5 mm. 5.5 mm crown

DATE / date indication in red and black, red central second, 1941, stainless steel case, 10.5 x 33 mm

OYSTER 1950s

OYSTER / medium size, stainless steel case, hand-wound, 1950s, 12 x 30 mm

OYSTER / medium size, bar hands, 1950s, stainless steel case, 11.5 x 30 mm

PRECISION / two-tone dial, raised bar indices, 1953-54, stainless steel case, 10 x 33 mm

OYSTER / "Chronometer", small second, 1957, hand-wound, stainless steel case, 10.5 x 29 mm

OYSTER / "Chronometer", freshened-up dial, hand-wound, 1950s, stainless steel case, 11 x 28.5 mm

SPEEDKING / rose dial with small second, leaf hands, 1950s, 12 x 28.5 mm

OYSTER / white dial with engraving, raised Rolex crown, 1951-52, 11 x 31.5 mm, crown 6 mm

PRECISION / simple model, original dial, 1940s-50s, stainless steel case, 11.5 x 28.5 mm

PRECISION / Super-Oyster crown, 1950s, stainless steel case, 10.5 x 31 mm

OYSTER / raised numerals and indices, medium-sized, freshened-up dial, 1950s, stainless steel case, 9.5 x 28.5 mm

PRECISION / original dial, hand-wound, 1950s, steel and 14 karat gold bicolor case, Cal. 1210, 10 x 33 mm

OYSTER / stainless steel case, hand-wound, 1950s, 10 x 33 mm

PRECISION / turning lunette, crown by 12, 1950s, stainless steel case, Ref. 6233, 11 x 32.5 mm

PRECISION / timeless design, 1950s, stainless steel case, 10 x 33 mm

ROYAL / white dial, leaf hands, Super-Oyster crown, 1950s, stainless steel case, 11 x 33 mm

ROYAL / red "Royal" signature, freshened-up matte gold dial, 1950s, plaque and stainless steel bicolor case, 10 x 33 mm

OYSTER

ROYAL / raised numerals and indices, freshened-up white dial, 1950s, stainless steel case, 10.5 x 30.5 mm

ROYAL / original dial with small second, 1950s, hand-wound, Cal. 10 ½ Hunter, stainless steel case, 12 x 31 mm

ROYAL / two-piece stainless steel Oyster case, freshened-up black dial, 1950s, medium size, 10 x 31 mm

ROYAL / original black dial, Rolex crown by the 12, 1957, stainless steel case, 10.5 x 31 mm

SPEEDKING / two-tone dial, raised gold numerals, 1950s, medium size, stainless steel case, 9 x 29 mm

SPEEDKING / Oyster case, 10 karat gold-filled, original dial, 1950s, 11 x 28.5 mm

SPEEDKING / Oyster model, 1950s, original dial, 10.5 x 28.5 mm

SPEEDKING / leaf hands, Super-Oyster crown, 1951, stainless steel case, 12 x 28.5 mm

DATE / two-tone dial with raised indices, 1951, stainless steel case, 11 x 29.5 mm, 5.5 mm crown

DATE / very striking model, stainless steel case with plaque inlays, 1950s, 11 x 29 mm

DATE / 1950s, guilloched black dial, red and black date indication, 12 x 32.5 mm

DATE / 1950s, Super-Oyster crown, red date indication, orange central second, 12 x 29 mm

DATE / early 1950s, Oysterdate model, red date indication, stainless steel case, 12 x 32 mm, 6 mm crown

DATE / 1950s, wedge indices, red date indication, 13 x 33.5 mm

DATE / 1950s, date indication in red and black, stainless steel case, 10.5 x 33 mm

OYSTER 1960s

DATE / original dial, date indication in red, Super-Oyster crown, 1950s, stainless steel case, 11 x 29 mm

DATE / original white dial, 1950s, stainless steel case, 12 x 32.5 mm, 5.5 mm crown

DATE / raised "Rolex" signature, stainless steel case, 1950s, 11.5 x 33.5 mm

PRECISION / hand-wound, 1960s, stainless steel case, black dial, 10 x 33 mm

PRECISION / finely guilloched dial, 1960s, stainless steel case, 11 x 32.5 mm, crown 6 mm

OYSTER

DATE / 1960s, red "Oyster Date" on white dial, hand-wound, stainless steel case, 10.5 x 33.5 mm

PRECISION / lunette with raised indices, original black dial, stainless steel case, 1960s, 12 x 32.5 mm

ROYAL / matte silver original dial, lunette with raised indices, 1960s, stainless steel case, 10.5 x 32.5 mm

ROYAL / freshened-up matte silver dial, gold plated case, 1960s, 10.5 x 33.5 mm, crown 6 mm

SPEEDKING / rare model, two-tone dial, 1960s, Ref. 6430, 9 x 28 mm

SPEEDKING / original matte silver dial, raised numerals, original, 1960s, stainless steel case, 9.5 x 28.5 mm, crown 5.5 mm

SPEEDKING / freshened-up dial, raised gold numerals, lunette with raised indices, 1960s, stainless steel case, 10 x 29 mm

DATE / 1960s, turning lunette, hand-wound, 11 x 29 mm

DATE / lunette with raised gold indices, date indication in red and black, 1960s, gold and steel bicolor case, 10.5 x 29 mm

DATE / raised indices, medium size, 1960s, stainless steel case, 1.5 x 29 mm

OYSTER 1970s

PRECISION / freshened-up black dial as in Explorer model, 1970s, stainless steel case, 10 x 33 mm

PRECISION / matte silver freshened-up dial, stainless steel case, 1970s, overhauled, 11 x 33 mm

SPEEDKING / freshened-up dial, stainless steel case, 1970s, medium size, 10 x 29 mm

DATE / 1970s, matte silver dial, raised gold bar indices, 11 x 33 mm

DATE / 1970s, gray dial, 11.5 x 33 mm

DATE / 1970s, black dial, gold hands, Oyster band, 11.5 x 33 mm

DATE / 1970s, rare combination of gold hands and gray dial, Oyster band, 11 x 33.5 mm

DATE / freshened-up blue dial with raised silver bar indices, overhauled, 1970s, stainless steel case, 11.5 x 33.5 mm

DATE / freshened-up dial, overhauled, 1970s, stainless steel case, 11.5 x 33.5 mm

DATE / freshened-up black dial, raised bar indices, 1970s, stainless steel case, 11 x 29 mm, 5.5 mm crown

OYSTER

DATE / 1970s, 18 karat yellow gold and steel bicolor case, typical Rolex model, 11.5 x 33.5 mm

DATE / 18 karat gold and steel bicolor case, rare model with hand winding, bicolor Oyster band, 1970s, 10.5 x 33 mm

Ref. 1074

OYSTER / octagonal nickel case, original enamel dial, 1920s, Ref. 1074, 11 x 28 mm

Ref. 1573

OYSTER / original dial, 1930s, steel Viceroy case, Ref. 1573, 10 x 29 mm, crown 5 mm

OYSTER / freshened-up dial, chromed brass case, 1940s, Ref. 1573, 10.5 x 26.5 mm

EXTRA PRECISION / matte gold dial, small second, stainless steel case, Ref. 1573, 9.5 x 27 mm

Ref. 2081

OYSTER / pillow-shaped stainless steel case, hand-wound, 1920s, Ref. 2081, 10 x 32 mm

Ref. 2130

OYSTER / original dial, classic Breguet hands, octagonal steel case, 1930s, Ref. 2130, 11 x 27.5 mm

Ref. 2280

OYSTER / central second, arched crystal, stainless steel case, Ref. 2280, 12 x 28.5 mm

ROYAL / large Mercedes hands, stainless steel case, Ref. 2280, 10.5 x 29 mm

OYSTER / original black dial with luminous hands, stainless steel case, Ref. 2280, 10.5 x 29 mm

OYSTER / three-tone original dial signed "Chronometre", 1940s, stainless steel case, Ref. 2280, 11.5 x 28 mm

OYSTER / medium size, 1936, stainless steel case, Ref. 2280, 10 x 29 mm crown 6 mm

ROYAL / original dial, 1940s, hand-wound, Cal. 10 ½ Hunter, stainless steel case, Ref. 2280, 11 x 29 mm

ROYAL / red central second, 1950s, stainless steel case, Ref. 2280, 11 x 28.5 mm

ROYAL / two-tone dial with small second, 1930-40s, stainless steel case, Ref. 2280, 10 x 28.5 mm, crown 6 mm

ROYAL / dealer's signature "H. G. Bell Salisbury", original dial, large Arabic numerals, 1940s, stainless steel case, Ref. 2280, 11.5 x 29 mm

ROYALITE / rose dial, red 24-hour markings, central second, 1930s, original hands, movement and dial, Ref. 2280, 11.5 x 29.5 mm

ROYAL / large lunette, 1930s, stainless steel case, Ref. 2280, 10.5 x 29 mm

ROYAL / dealer's signature "P. Orr & Sons Ltd", original dial, small second, blue steel hands. 1930s, stainless steel case, Ref. 2280, 10 x 29 mm

OYSTER

ROYALITE / 1937, raised Arabic numerals, original dial and band, Ref. 2280, 11.5 x 28.5 mm

ROYALITE / Oyster model, stainless steel case, 1940s, Ref. 2280, 11 x 29.5 mm

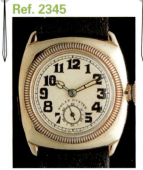

Ref. 2345

OYSTER / skeletal hands, 1940s, pillow-shaped 9 karat plaque case, Ref. 2345, 10 x 27 mm

Ref. 2416

OYSTER / pillow-shaped 9 karat gold case, hand-wound, 1930s, Ref. 2416, 9.5 x 27.9 mm

OYSTER / small second, pillow-shaped 9 karat yellow gold case, hand-wound, 1930s, Ref. 2416, 11.7 x 30.5 mm

PRECISION / raised numerals on original dial, 1940s, stainless steel case, Ref. 2416, 11.5 x 29 mm

OYSTER / hand-wound, signed "Chronometre", 1930s, pillow-shaped 9 karat gold case, Ref. 2416, 11.5 x 28 mm, crown 5.5 mm

Ref. 2574

OYSTER / shock-resistant, 9 karat gold case, hand-wound, 1940s, Ref. 2574, 10.6 x 27.2 mm

IMPERIAL / "Chronometre", original dial with raised railway minutery and Arabic numerals, 1937, stainless steel case, Ref. 2574, 11 x 27.5 mm

Ref. 2595

OYSTER / original dial, "Chronometre", 1940s, hand-wound, stainless steel case, Ref. 2595, 12 x 28 mm

ELEGANTE / original semi-unique dial, Mercedes hands, 1940s, stainless steel case, Ref. 2595, 10 x 29.5 mm

RALEIGH / hand-wound, anti-magnetic, original dial, bar hands, medium size, stainless steel case, Ref. 2595, 12 x 27 mm

IMPERIAL original dial, 1940s, stainless steel, Ref. 2595, 11.5 x 28 mm

PRECISION / early medium-sized model, 18 karat gild case, raised gold indices, 1937, Ref. 2595, 10.5 x 27 mm

Ref. 2781

JUNIOR SPORT / thick lunette, 1930s, 10.5 x 29 mm, crown 6 mm

JUNIOR SPORT / two-tone dial with bar hands, stainless steel case, 1930s, Ref. 2781, 10.5 x 29.5

JUNIOR SPORT / original dial with small second, stainless steel case, engraving on case bottom, 12.5 x 29.5 mm

JUNIOR SPORT / large numerals on original dial, 1930s, stainless steel case, 11 x 29.5 mm, crown 6 mm

JUNIOR SPORT / original dial with small second, 1930s, stainless steel case, 10.5 x 29.5 mm, crown 6 mm

Ref. 3116

VICEROY / original dial, hand-wound, signed "Chronometer", 1948, 18 karat gold, 11.5 x 28.5 mm

OYSTER

VICEROY / polished lunette, stainless steel case, gold central second, Ref. 3116, 10 x 27.5 mm

VICEROY luminous hands, stainless steel case, 10.5 x 27.5 mm

VICEROY / signed "Chronometer", 1940s, stainless steel case, Ref. 3116, 11 x 28 mm

VICEROY / dial signed "Extra Precision", 9 karat gold case, hand-wound, 1930s, 10 x 26 mm

VICEROY / stainless steel case, hand-wound, 1930s, Ref. 3116, 11 x 27 mm

VICEROY / striking Mercedes hands and central second, 1949, 11 x 27 mm, crown 5.5 mm

OYSTER / signed "Chronometer" and "Observatory", 1937, stainless steel case, Ref. 3116, 10 x 29 mm, crown 5 mm

OYSTER / rare original dial with dot and bar indices, 1940s, 14 karat gold case, Ref. 3116, 11.5 x 28 mm

PRECISION / nice Viceroy case, original black dial, 14 karat gold, 1940s, Ref. 3116, 11 x 28 mm, crown 5.5 mm

PRECISION / slightly faded dial, 1946, stainless steel case, Ref. 3116, 10;5 mm

Ref. 3121

SPEEDKING / Viceroy case, large numerals and indices, original dial, 1940s, Ref. 3116, 11 x 27 mm

IMPERIAL / "Chronometre" on original dial, 9 karat gold Viceroy case, 1930s, Ref. 3116, 10 x 27 mm

IMPERIAL / "Chronometre", dial with small second, 1930s, Ref. 3116, 14 karat gold case, Ref. 3116, 10 x 28 mm

IMPERIAL / "Chronometre". Raised railway minutery, original dial, 1940s, 9 karat gold Viceroy case, Ref. 3116, 10.5 x 28 mm

OYSTER / stainless steel case, hand-wound, 1940s, Ref. 3121, 11 x 29 mm

OYSTER / freshened-up dial, small second, stainless steel case, Ref. 3121, 11 x 29 mm

OYSTER / original dial, 1930s, stainless steel case, Ref. 3121, 10.5 x 27.5 mm

PRECISION / 1950s, stainless steel case, Ref. 3121, 11.5 x 27.5

OYSTER / original dial with gold ring, 1930s, stainless steel case, Ref. 3121, 10.5 x 27.5 mm, crown 5 mm

ROYAL / interesting Arabic numerals, 1940s, stainless steel case, Ref. 3121, 10.5 x 27.5 mm, crown 5.5 mm

OYSTER

Ref. 3136

ROYAL / original dial, dealer's signature "Bucherer", medium size, stainless steel case, Ref. 3121, 11.5 x 27.5 mm

ROYAL / very nice original rose dial, Roman numerals, 1930s, stainless steel case, Ref. 3121, 11.5 x 27 mm

LIPTON / original black dial, 1940s, stainless steel case, Ref. 3136, 11 x 29 mm

RALEIGH / numerals printed on original dial, 1940s, stainless steel case, Ref. 3136, 12 x 29 mm

TURTLE RALEIGH / signature "Oyster company" on case, "Zell Bros." (American importer) on dial, 1940s, Ref. 3136, 12.5 x 31 mm

Ref. 3139

ARMY / original dial, gold central second, stainless steel case, 11 x 27 mm, crown 5.5 mm

ARMY / arched crystal, 1941, stainless steel case, Ref. 3139, 11 x 29.5 mm

ARMY / original dial, hand-wound, 10 ½ Hunter movement, stainless steel case, Ref. 3139, 12 x 29.5 mm

ARMY / matte rose dial, fine minute markings on dial rim, overhauled, 1940s, stainless steel case, 12 x 29.5 mm

ARMY / stainless steel case, 1940s, Ref. 4220, 11.5 x 28 mm

ARMY / stainless steel case, hand-wound, 1940s, Ref. 3139, 11 x 31 mm

ARMY / 1940s, Cal. 10 1/2 Hunter movement, Ref. 3139, 12 x 27 mm

ARMY / 9 karat gold case, hand-wound, 1940s, Ref. 3139, 11 x 29 mm

EVEREST / stainless steel "Army" case, original dial, 1943, 10.5 x 31 mm

EVEREST / luminous hands, hand-wound, Cal. 10 1/2 Hunter, Ref. 3139, 12 x 29 mm

EVEREST / 24-hour markings, 1930s, pillow-shaped case, 12.5 x 24.5 mm, crown 5.5 mm

EVEREST / rose dial, raised Arabic numerals, 1940s, stainless steel case, Ref. 3139, 11 x 30 x 30 mm

EVEREST / original two-tone dial, hour hand later, 1930s, stainless steel case, Ref. 3139, 10 x 29.5 mm, crown 5.5 mm

OYSTER / stainless steel case, hand-wound, 1930s, Ref. 3139, 11 x 29 mm

OYSTER / red central second, original white dial, 1940s, pillow-shaped steel case, Ref. 3139, 11.5 x 29.5 mm

OYSTER

Ref. 3156

Ref. 3159

PRECISION / raised numerals on original dial, 1930s, stainless steel case, Ref. 3139, 10 x 29.5 mm

OYSTER / original dial and hands, 1940s, stainless steel case, Ref. 3139, 12.5 x 28 mm

OYSTER / numerals printed on original two-tone dial, 1941, stainless steel "Army" case, Ref. 3139, 10.5 x 29.5 mm

OYSTER / "Scientific" dial, stainless steel case, Ref. 3156, 11.5 x 29 mm

ROYAL / original matte white dial, luminous numerals, 1920-30s, pillow-shaped steel case, 12.5 x 30 mm

Ref. 3242

Ref. 3270

Ref. 3351

ROYAL / arched crystal, 1940s, hand-wound, Cal. 9 3/4 Hunter, pillow-shaped steel case, Ref. 3159, 11.5 x 29 mm

ROYAL / pillow-shaped stainless steel case, 1948, 10.5 x 30.5 mm

OYSTER PROTOTYPE / 14 karat gold and stainless steel bicolor case, hand-wound, Ref. 3242, 11 x 40.8 mm

OYSTER / covered band attachments, original dial, 1930s, 18 karat gold case, Ref. 3270, 11.5 x 27.5 mm

VICEROY / original dial, stainless steel case, Ref. 3351, 9.5 x 27.5 mm, crown 5.5 mm

Ref. 3359

VICEROY CHRONOMETER / 14 karat gold and stainless steel bicolor case, hand-wound, 1940s, Ref. 3359, 11 x 29 mm

VICEROY / older turning lunette, plaque and steel bicolor case, 11.5 x 27.5 mm

VICEROY / Viceroy case, lunette with raised gold indices, 1940s, Ref. 3359, 10.5 x 27.5 mm

VICEROY / original dial, turning plaque lunette, stainless steel case, 1940s, 11.5 x 27.5 mm

PRECISION / guilloched original dial, stainless steel case, 1940s, Ref. 3359, 11 x 27.5 mm

Ref. 3373

Ref. 3386

IMPERIAL / "Chronometre", original two-tone dial, 1943, 14 karat gold and steel bicolor case, Ref. 3359, 13.5 x 30 mm

OYSTER / Centregraph (printed on later), 24-hour markings, 1940s, 9 karat gold-plated case, Ref. 3373, 12 x 30 mm

LINCOLN / Model for USA, original dial, 1940s, Ref. 3386, 12 x 29 mm

LINCOLN / original dial, 1930s, pillow-shaped gold plated case, 11 x 28 mm

OYSTER / 15-jewel hand-wound chronometer, projecting crown, plaque case, Ref. 3386, 10 x 28 mm

OYSTER

Ref. 3478

OYSTER / Centregraph (printed on later), 24-hour markings, stainless steel case, Ref. 3478, 12.5 x 29 mm

COMMANDER / original dial, hand-wound, shock resistance, gold-plated case, Ref. 3478, 12.5 x 26.5mm, crown 5 mm

RALEIGH / original dial, 1940s, stainless steel case, Ref. 3478, 12 x 29 mm

RALEIGH / red central second, stainless steel case, Ref. 3478, 12 x 29 mm, crown 5.5 mm

RALEIGH / blue steel hands, medium size, 1940s, gold plated case, Ref. 3478, 12 x 30 mm

RECORD / original dial, red central second, 1940s, gold plated case, Ref. 3478, 12 x 28.5 mm

LIPTON / nice original dial, medium size, 1940s, stainless steel case, Ref. 3478, 11.5 x 29 mm, crown 5.5 mm

CHESTER / original dial, luminous hands, stainless steel case, Ref. 3478, 12 x 30 mm, crown 5 mm

Ref. 3505

OYSTER / stainless steel case, hand-wound, 1940s, Ref. 3505, 11.4 x 31 mm

Ref. 3980

OYSTER / stainless steel case, hand-wound, 1940s, Ref. 3980, 11.9 x 30 mm

Ref. 4127

ATHLETE / round case, Mercedes hands, 1942, 12.5 x 32.5 mm

ATHLETE / original dial, 1940s, stainless steel case, Ref. 4127, 12 x 32 mm

ATHLETE / stainless steel case, Mercedes hands, 1941, 12 x 31.5 mm

ATHLETE / Mercedes hands, red central second, 1940s, stainless steel case, Ref. 4127, 12 x 32.5 mm, crown 5.5 mm

ATHLETE / Arabic numerals and indices, Mercedes hands, 1940s, round stainless steel case with even rim, 11 x 32 mm, crown 5.5 mm

ATHLETE / long Mercedes hands, luminous numerals, 1940s, stainless steel case, 12.5 x 32 mm

ATHLETE / original matte white dial, Arabic numerals, 1940s, stainless steel case, Ref. 4127, 12.5 x 32 mm

ATHLETE / luminous hands, red central second, 1940s, stainless steel case, Ref. 4127, 11.5 x 32.5 mm

ATHLETE / round stainless steel case with even rim, slim red central second, 1941, 11 x 32 mm, crown 5.5 mm

OYSTER / round stainless steel case with even rim, Ref. 4127, 12.5 x 32 mm

OYSTER

Ref. 4220

OYSTER / freshened-up dial, luminous numerals, 1930s, hand-wound, Cal. 10 1/2 Hunter, Ref. 4127, 12 x 32.5 mm

ROYAL / round stainless steel case, interesting central second, Ref. 4127, 12.5 x 32 mm

SPEEDKING / faded 24-hour markings, original black dial, Ref. 4220, 10.5 x 28.5 mm, crown 6 mm

SPEEDKING / red central second, 1940s, hand-wound, Cal. 10 ½ Hunter, stainless steel case, Ref. 4220, 10.5 x 28 mm

SPEEDKING / original dial, stainless steel case, Ref. 4220, 11.5 x 28.5 mm

SPEEDKING / rose dial with luminous hands and red central second, 1940s, Ref. 4220, 11 x 29 mm

OYSTER / arched crystal, 1940s, hand-wound, "Chronometre", Ref. 4220, 12 x 28.5 mm

ROYALITE / stainless steel case, 1940s, Ref. 4220, 11 x 28.5 mm

SPEEDKING / luminous hands, original dial, stainless steel case, Ref. 4220, 11.5 x 29 mm

ROYAL / faded 24-hour markings, 1940s, stainless steel case, Ref. 4220, 12.5 x 28.5 mm

Ref. 4365

SPEEDKING / raised numerals and indices, central second, 1940s, stainless steel case, Ref. 4220, 11.5 x 28.5 mm

SPEEDKING / printed numerals and indices, matte white dial, stainless steel case, medium size, Ref. 4220, 9.5 x 28.5 mm

SPEEDKING / original dial, gold numerals, 1950s, stainless steel case, Ref. 4220, 10.5 x 28.5 mm

IMPERIAL / original dial, raised numerals, 1940s, stainless steel case, Ref. 4220, 11 x 29 mm

AIR-TIGER / original dial, 1940s, gold plated case, Ref. 4365, 11.5 x 31.5 mm

Ref. 4444

SPEEDKING / signed ELEGANT", 1940s, hand-wound, Cal. 10 ½ Hunter, stainless steel case, Ref. 4365, 11 x 31.5 mm

ROYAL / bar hands, red central second, stainless steel hands, Ref. 4444, 12 x 27.5 mm

ROYAL / original silver dial with raised Arabic numerals, 1940s, stainless steel case, Ref. 4444, 10.5 x 30 mm

OYSTER / small second, shock resistant, stainless steel case, hand-wound, 1940s, Ref. 4444, 10.6 x 32 mm

CHESTER / fine raised numerals and bar hands, 1940s, stainless steel case, Ref. 4444, 12.5 x 30.5 mm, crown 5.5 mm

OYSTER

Ref. 4499

Ref. 4547

PRECISION / elegant model, all original, normal size, 1940s, stainless steel case, Ref. 4499, 11.5 x 32.5 mm

OYSTER / early model, raised Arabic numerals, 1950s, Ref. 4499, 11 x 32 mm

PRECISION / raised numerals, indices and Rolex crown, original dial, 1950s, stainless steel case, Ref. 4499, 12 x 32 mm

PRECISION / original case, dial and crown, 1951, stainless steel case, Ref. 4499, 12 x 32.5

PRECISION / so-called "Army" model, stainless steel, hand-wound, 1940s, Ref. 4547, 11.8 x 33.5 mm

Ref. 5020

Ref. 5056

Ref. 5059

Ref. 6020

SPEEDKING / 14 karat gold and stainless steel bicolor case, two-tone dial with luminous hands, 1940s, Ref. 5020, 11 x 28.5 mm

SPEEDKING / 1950s, stainless steel case, Ref. 5056, 11 x 28 mm

SPEEDKING / freshened-up black dial, Arabic numerals, 1930s, 14 karat gold plated case, Ref. 5056, 11 x 27 mm

OYSTER / elegant leaf hands, 1950s, bicolor plaque and steel case, Ref. 5059, 10.5 x 32 mm

SPEEDKING / raised Arabic numerals, original dial, 10 karat gold case, Ref. 6020, 12.5 x 29 mm

SPEEDKING / raised Arabic numerals and indices, three-piece gold-filled case, original dial, 1950s, Ref. 6020, 10.5 x 29 mm

SPEEDKING / simple model, stainless steel case, Ref. 6020, 11 x 29 mm

SPEEDKING / stamped numerals and indices, leaf hands, 1950s, stainless steel case, Ref. 6020, 11.5 x 29.5 mm

SPEEDKING / Super-Oyster crown, luminous hands, 1950s, stainless steel case, Ref. 6020, 10 x 28 mm

SPEEDKING / 1940s, 9 karat yellow gold case, elegant dial, bar hands, Ref. 6020, 12 x 29 mm

Ref. 6022

PRECISION / Super-Oyster crown, original dial, 1950s, 10 karat gold-filled case, Ref. 6020, 12 x 29 mm

PRECISION / raised indices with luminous paint, 10 karat gold-filled case, Ref. 6022, 11.5 x 32.5 mm

OYSTER / guilloched matte black dial, 1950s, Ref. 6022, 11.5 x 32.5 mm

OYSTER / guilloched black dial, freshened up, star and wedge indices, stainless steel case, 1960s, Ref. 6022, 12 x 32 mm

OYSTER / luminous plaque hands and indices, 1951, stainless steel case, Ref. 6022, 10.5 x 32 mm

OYSTER

Ref. 6034

Ref. 6044

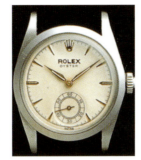

OYSTER / freshened-up dial, raised numerals and indices, 1960s, Ref. 6034, 11.5 x 29 mm, gold or plaque

OYSTER / printed numerals on original dial, good condition, stainless steel case, 1950s, Ref. 6044, 10 x 31.5 mm

OYSTER / raised gold numerals and indices, freshened-up dial, 1960s, stainless steel case, Ref. 6044, Cal. 1200, 11.5 x 29.5 mm

ROYAL / elegant model, raised numerals and indices, leaf hands, Super-Oyster crown, Ref. 6044, 11 x 30 mm

ROYAL / Super-Oyster crown, medium size, original dial, stainless steel case, 1950s, Ref. 6044, 11 x 30 mm

Ref. 6066

Ref. 6082

DATE / gold numerals and indices, medium size, Ref. 6066, stainless steel case, 12 x 29 mm

DATE / stamped-in numerals and indices, Super-Oyster crown, Ref. 6066, stainless steel case, 10.5 x 28.5 mm

OYSTER / 1950, stainless steel case, hand-wound, Ref. 6082, 10 x 33 mm

OYSTER / stainless steel case, hand-wound, 1950, Ref. 6082, 10 x 33 mm

OYSTER / freshened-up black dial, raised numerals and indices, 1950s, Ref. 6082, 11.5 x 32.5 mm, crown 6 mm

Ref. 6083

Ref. 6094

ROYAL / original dial, Super-Oyster crown, 1952, Ref. 6082, 10 x 32 mm

PRECISION / long hands, 1951, stainless steel case, Ref. 6083, 10.5 x 32.5 mm

DATE / freshened-up two-tone dial, raised numerals and indices, red date indication, Ref. 6094, 10.5 x 31.5 mm

DATE / raised numerals and wedge indices with luminous paint, red and black date indication, 1953, Ref. 6094, stainless steel case, 13 x 32.5 mm

DATE / arched crystal, black dial, red central second, 1950s, Ref. 6094, 12 x 31.5 mm

Ref. 6120

Ref. 6144

SPEEDKING / white dial, raised indices, stainless steel case, Ref. 6120, 10 x 29 mm

ROYAL / freshened-up dial, raised pyramidal indices, 1960s, stainless steel case, Ref. 6144, 10 x 30.5 mm

ROYAL / original matte white dial, 1950s, stainless steel case, Ref. 6144, 11.5 x 32 mm, crown 6 mm

ROYAL / Arabic 12 and 6 numerals, original dial, stainless steel case, Ref. 6144, 12 x 30 mm, crown 6 mm

ROYAL / fine mesh pattern on original dial, raised indices, 1950s, stainless steel case, Ref. 6144, 11.5 x 31 mm

OYSTER

Ref. 6145

Ref. 6222

Ref. 6244

ROYAL freshened-up black dial, stainless steel case, Ref. 6145, 12 x 31.5 mm, crown 6 mm

SPEEDKING / luminous numerals, medium size, stainless steel case, Ref. 6145, 11 x 29.5 mm

PRECISION / guilloched dial, 1954, Ref. 6222, 11.5 x 32.5 mm

OYSTER / stainless steel case, hand-wound, 1950s, Ref. 6244, 11 x 31 mm

OYSTER / grid pattern on original dial, 1950s, stainless steel case, Ref. 6244, 11.5 x 31 mm

OYSTER / freshened-up dial, red central second, 1950s, stainless steel case, Ref. 6244, 11.5 x 31 mm

OYSTER / mid-size between large and medium, original dial, 1950s, stainless steel case, Ref. 6244, 11.5 x 31 mm

OYSTER / red central second, original dial, 1960s, stainless steel case, Ref. 6244, 11 x 31 mm

ROYAL / raised numerals and teardrop indices, black dial, stainless steel case, Ref. 6244, 11.5 x 30.5 mm

SPEEDKING / simple model, bar indices, white dial, 1960s, stainless steel case, Ref. 6244, 10 x 28.5 mm

Ref. 6246

Ref. 6266

OYSTER / raised indices and numerals, original dial, 1956, stainless steel case, Ref. 6246, 10 x 31 mm

ROYAL / watertight to 50 meters, rare original dial, hand-wound, Cal. 10 ½ Hunter, stainless steel case, Ref. 6246, 11.5 x 31 mm

ROYAL / elaborate guilloched dial, stamped second markings, 1950s, stainless steel case, Ref. 6246, 10.5 x 31 mm

DATE / 1950s, raised silver numerals and indices, guilloched white dial, red date indication, Ref. 6266, 11 x 28.5 mm

DATE / freshened-up dial, medium size, Ref. 6266, 12 x 29.5 mm

Ref. 6274

Ref. 6282

Ref. 6294

DATE, nice silver dial with raised wedge indices, red date indication, Ref. 6274, stainless steel case, 12.5 x 33 mm

OYSTER / raised gold indices, Dauphin hands, original, Ref. 6282, 1950s, 11.5 x 33 mm

OYSTER / star indices, freshened-up dial, 1960s, stainless steel case, Ref. 6282, 11 x 33 mm

DATE / freshened-up two-tone dial, date indication in red, Ref. 6294, stainless steel case, 11.5 x 33 mm

DATE / 1954, 1/5 second division still easy to read, red date indication, Ref. 6294, 12 x 33 mm

OYSTER

DATE / red and black date indication, 1950s, Ref. 6294, hand-wound, Cal. 10 ½ Hunter, stainless steel case, 12.5 x 33 mm

DATE / guilloched dial, date indication in red, 1950s, Ref. 6294, steel and gold bicolor case, 12.5 x 33 mm

DATE / original dial, date indication in red and black, Ref. 6294, stainless steel case, 12 x 32.5 mm, 5.5 mm crown

DATE // red date indication, gold lunette, raised gold indices, 1953, Ref. 6294, 12 x 33 mm

DATE / small Rolex crown in the center, date indication in red, 1954, Ref. 6294, 12 x 33 mm

DATE / early model, gold leaf hands in good condition, 1950s, Ref. 6294, 13 x 32.5 mm

DATE / stainless steel case, raised plaque indices, 1950s, Ref. 6294, 12 x 32.5 mm

DATE / white dial with raised numerals and indices, Oyster band, 1954, Ref. 6294, 12 x 32.5 mm

DATE / guilloched dial, 1954, Ref. 6294, 12.5 x 32.5 mm

Ref. 6305

DATE / gold dial with raised bar indices, lunette with raised indices, Ref. 6305, 18 karat gold and stainless steel bicolor case, 12 x 34 mm, 6 mm crown

Ref. 6418

SPEEDKING / original black dial, 1960s, gilded case, Ref. 6418, 10 x 29 mm, crown 5.5 mm

Ref. 6420

SPEEDKING / two-tone dial, raised indices, central second, blue steel hands, Ref. 6420, 10 x 28.5 mm

SPEEDKING / freshened-up two-tone dial, stainless steel case, Ref. 6420, 10 x 29 mm

SPEEDKING / matte rose dial, medium size, 1960s, stainless steel case, Ref. 6420, 9 x 29 mm

SPEEDKING / thick leaf hands, slim central second, 1961, stainless steel case, Ref. 6420, 10 x 29 mm

SPEEDKING / medium size, black dial, stainless steel case, Ref. 6420, 11 x 29 mm

SPEEDKING / 1950s, raised bar indices, leaf hands, Ref. 6420, 10.5 x 30 mm

Ref. 6421

OYSTER / original dial, medium-sized, 1950s, 18 karat gold plate and steel bicolor case, Ref. 6421, 10.5 x 29.s mm

SPEEDKING / raised Rolex crown by the 12m freshened-up two-tone dial, stainless steel case, Ref. 6421, 10 x 29 mm

Ref. 6422

OYSTER / stainless steel case, hand-wound, 1960s, Ref. 6422, 11.3 x 33 mm

OYSTER

PRECISION / stainless steel case, hand-wound, 1950s, Ref. 6422, 11.5 x 34 mm

OYSTER / stainless steel case, hand-wound, 1950, Ref. 6422, 11 x 32 mm

PRECISION / guilloched original dial, 1960s, stainless steel case, Ref. 6422, 10 x 33 mm

PRECISION / raised numerals and indices on original dial, hand-wound, 1950s, stainless steel case, Ref. 6422, 10.5 x 33 mm

PRECISION / original pressed two-tone dial, 1950s, stainless steel case, hand-wound, Cal. 1210, Ref. 6422, 10.5 x 33 mm

Ref. 6423

OYSTER / raised gold indices, hand-wound, shock-resistant, stainless steel case, Ref. 6423, 10 x 32.5 mm

Ref. 6424

PRECISION / freshened-up two-tone dial, Ref. 6424, 10 x 34.5 mm, crown 5.5 mm

PRECISION / freshened-up two-tone dial, hand-wound, 1960s, stainless steel case, Cal. 1215, Ref. 6424, 10 x 34.5 mm

PRECISION / hand-wound, 1960s, Ref. 6424, 9.8 x 34.4 mm

PRECISION / hand-wound, rare 20 mm band width, 1960s, stainless steel case, Ref. 6424, 10.5 x 35 mm

PRECISION / matte silver dial, large wedge indices, 1956, stainless steel case, Ref. 6424, 10 x 34.5 mm

PRECISION / 1950s, stainless steel case, Ref. 6424, 10 x 33 mm

Ref. 6426

OYSTER / 9 karat gold case, hand-wound, 1950s, Ref. 6426, 10 x 33 mm

OYSTER / stainless steel case, hand-wound, 1960s, Ref. 6426, 10.1 x 32.8 mm

PRECISION / freshened-up dial as in Explorer model, 1960s, stainless steel case, Ref. 6426, 10 x 32.5 mm

PRECISION / freshened-up dial as in Explorer model, stainless steel case, 1980s, Ref. 6426, 10.5 x 31 mm, crown 6 mm

PRECISION / freshened-up two-tone dial, stainless steel case, Ref. 6426, 10 x 33 mm, crown 6 mm

PRECISION / two-tone dial, freshened up, raised indices, stainless steel case, Ref. 6246, 10 x 33 mm

PRECISION / printed Rolex frown, freshened-up two-tone dial, stainless steel case, Ref. 6246, 10 x 33 mm

OYSTER / freshened-up dial with small second, 1960s, steel and gold bicolor case, Cal. 1225, Ref. 6426, 10 x 33.5 mm

OYSTER

OYSTER / freshened-up dial, 1960s, stainless steel case, Ref. 6426, 10 x 33 mm, crown 6 mm

PRECISION / 9 karat gold case, hand-wound, 1950, Ref. 6426, 10 x 33 mm

PRECISION / original dial, 1950s, stainless steel case, Ref. 6426, Cal. 1210, 10.5 x 32.5 mm

PRECISION / raised numerals and indices, freshened-up dial, Jubilee band, stainless steel case, Ref. 6426, 10.5 x 34.5 mm

PRECISION / hand-wound, Rolex crown on dial, 1970s, Ref. 6426, 9.6 x 36.4 mm

PRECISION / stainless steel case, hand-wound, 1970s, Ref. 6426, 10.6 x 35.4 mm

PRECISION / stainless steel case, hand-wound, 1960s, Ref. 6426, 10 x 33 mm

OYSTER / stainless steel case, hand-wound, 1970s, Ref. 6426, 10.1 x 32.7 mm

OYSTER / stainless steel case, hand-wound, 1970s, Ref. 6426, 10 x 30 mm

OYSTER / stainless steel case, hand-wound, 1970s, Ref. 6426, 10 x 34 mm

PRECISION / stainless steel case, hand-wound, 1950, Ref. 6426, 10 x 33 mm

OYSTER / stainless steel case, hand-wound, 1970s, Ref. 6426, 9 x 33 mm

OYSTER / stainless steel case, hand-wound, 1970s, Ref. 6426, 10 x 33 mm

OYSTER / Ref. 6426, hand-wound, 9 x 33 mm

PRECISION / simple black dial, freshened up, 1960s, Ref. 6426m 10 x 33 mm

PRECISION / stainless steel case, Ref. 6426, 10 x 33 mm

PRECISION / freshened-up black dial, raised indices, stainless steel case, Ref. 6246, 10 x 28 mm

PRECISION / raised gold indices with tritium plating, freshened-up dial, 1970s, Ref. 6426, 10 x 33 mm

PRECISION / hand-wound, old original Oyster band, 1965, stainless steel case, Ref. 6426, Cal. 1210, 10 x 34 mm

PRECISION / original dial and hands, 1970s, stainless steel case, Ref. 6426, 10.5 x 33 mm, crown 6 mm

OYSTER

PRECISION matte silver dial with bar indices, 1970s, stainless steel case, Ref. 6426, 11.5 x 33 mm

PRECISION / simple design, stainless steel case, Ref. 6426, 10.5 x 33 mm

OYSTER / medium size, original dial, Oyster band, 1960s, stainless steel case, Ref. 6426, 9 x 28 mm

ROYAL / printed Roman numerals, raised indices, medium size, 1960s, stainless steel case, Ref. 6426, 9 x 28 mm

ROYAL / bar indices, 1940s, plaque case, Ref. 6426, 10 x 33.5 mm, crown 6 mm

Ref. 6427

ROYAL / simple model, leaf hands, white original dial, raised indices, 1950s, Ref. 6426, 10.5 x 33 mm

DATE / faded date indication, freshened-up dial, 1970s, Ref. 6426, stainless steel case, 11.5 x 33.5 mm

DATE / freshened-up black dial, 1960s, Ref. 6426, 11.5 x 33.5 mm

OYSTER stainless steel case, hand-wound, 1960s, Ref. 6427, 10.2 x 32.7 mm

OYSTER / stainless steel case, hand-wound, 1982, Ref. 6427, 10.4 x 34.5 mm

OYSTER / stainless steel case, hand-wound, 1970s, Ref. 6427, 11 x 33 mm

OYSTER / stainless steel case, hand-wound, 1970s, Ref. 6427, 9 x 33 mm

PRECISION / fine bar indices, freshened-up dial, stainless steel case, 1950s, Ref. 6427, 10 x 33 mm

OYSTER, wedge indices, 1960s, stainless steel case, Ref. 6427, 11 x 33 mm

ROYAL / standard model, 1960s, stainless steel case, Ref. 6427, 9.5 x 33.5 mm

Ref. 6428

Ref. 6429

Ref. 6430

OYSTER / shock-resistant, stainless steel case, hand-wound, 1950s, Ref. 6428, 10.4 x 34 mm

PRECISION / 1950s, Rolex crown by 12, Ref. 6429, stainless steel case, 10 x 32.5 mm

SPEEDKING / freshened-up two-tone dial, stainless steel case, Ref. 6430, 10 x 29 mm, crown 5.5 mm

SPEEDKING / matte silver dial, raised numerals and indices, Ref. 6430m 9,.5 x 29 mm

SPEEDKING / rare model, freshened-up two-tone dial, 1960s, Ref. 6430, 9 x 28 mm

OYSTER

SPEEDKING / 1970s, good condition, original black dial, flexible band, Ref. 6430, 9 x 29 mm

SPEEDKING / glossy black original dial, raised silver indices, stainless steel case, 1960s, Ref. 6430, 9.5 x 29 mm

SPEEDKING / simple model, silver dial, signature "Speedking" in script, stainless steel case, Ref. 6430, 10 x 29 mm

SPEEDKING / freshened-up black dial, raised numerals and indices, 1967, stainless steel case, Ref. 6430, 9.5 x 28.5 mm

SPEEDKING / slightly faded original dial, Jubilee band, 1960s, hand-wound, stainless steel case, Ref. 6430, Cal. 1220, 9.5 x 29 mm

Ref. 6444

SPEEDKING / white dial, wedge indices, 1963, stainless steel case, Ref. 6430, 9.5 x 29 mm, crown 5.5 mm

SPEEDKING / original dial, 1960s, hand-wound, stainless steel case, Ref. 6430, Cal. 1220, 10 x 29 mm

ROYAL / two-tone original dial, central second, 1950s, stainless steel case, Ref. 6444, 9.5 x 31 mm

ROYAL / original dial, Explorer design, gold numerals, 1940s, stainless steel case, Ref. 6444, 10 x 31 mm

ROYAL / original dial, Explorer design, 1950s, stainless steel case, Ref. 6444, 10 x 31 mm

PRECISION / freshened-up matte silver Explorer dial, 1950s, stainless steel case, Ref. 6444, 9.5 x 31 mm

ROYAL / freshened-up dial, clear design, 1950s, stainless steel case, Ref. 6444, 11 x 31 mm

ROYAL / elaborate matte gold dial, freshened up, 1950s, stainless steel case, Ref. 6444, Cal. 1210, 10 x 31 mm

ROYAL / original dial, stainless steel case, Ref. 6444, 10 x 31 mm, crown 6 mm

OYSTER / central second, shock resistant, stainless steel case, hand-wound, 1950s, Ref. 6444, 10 x 32 ..

Ref. 6466

DATE / freshened-up dial, date indication, Ref. 6466, stainless steel case, 10.5 x 29 mm, 5 mm crown

DATE / freshened-up two-tone dial, medium size, Ref. 6466, 11.5 x 29 mm

DATE / raised gold indices, Ref. 6466, stainless steel case, 11.5 x 29 mm, 5.5 mm crown

DATE / freshened-up black dial, white railway minutery, Ref. 6466, stainless steel case, 11.5 x 29 mm, crown 5.5 mm

DATE / printed luminous numerals, 1960s, Ref. 6466, stainless steel case, 10.5 x 29 mm

OYSTER

DATE / medium size, stainless steel case, hand-wound, 1960s, Ref. 6466, 11 x 29 mm

DATE / stainless steel case, hand-wound, 1950s, Ref. 6466, 10 x 29 mm

DATE / stainless steel case, hand-wound, 1950s, Ref. 6466, 10 x 29 mm

SPEEDKING / freshened-up matte silver dial, bar indices, 1960s, stainless steel case, Ref. 6466, 9.5 x 29 mm

DATE / 1960s, gold numerals and indices, red date indication, 12 x 32 mm, 5 mm crown

DATE / 1960s, freshened-up dial, Ref. 6466, 11 x 29.5 mm, 5 mm crown

DATE / large hands, 1950s, Ref. 6466, stainless steel case, 10.5 x 29 mm

DATE / small date indication, 1945, Ref. 6646, gold and steel bicolor case, 11 x 29 mm, 6 mm crown

DATE / raised bar indices and luminous points, freshened-up dial, 1960s, hand-wound, Ref. 6466, Cal. 1210, stainless steel case, 11 x 29 mm

DATE / freshened-up dial, leaf hands, 1960s, Ref. 6466, hand-wound, Cal. 1210, stainless steel case, 11 x 29 mm

DATE wedge indices, red date indication, freshened-up dial, 1960s, Ref. 6466, stainless steel case, 11.5 x 29 mm

DATE / blue dial with raised indices, medium size, 1960s, Ref. 6466, stainless steel case, 11.5 x 29 mm

DATE / freshened-up white dial, 1960s, Ref. 6466, hand-wound, Cal. 1210, stainless steel case, 11 x 29 mm

DATE / two-tone dial, 1967, Ref. 6466, stainless steel case, medium size, 11 x 29 mm

DATE / medium size, simple model, gold case, bar indices, 1948, Ref. 6466, 11.5 x 29.5 mm, 5.5 mm crown

DATE / leaf hands, 1960s, Ref. 6466, stainless steel case, 11 x 29 mm

DATE / two-tone dial, date indication in red, Ref. 6466, stainless steel case, 10.5 x 28.5 mm, 5.5 mm crown

DATE / red date indication, 1960s, Ref. 6466, stainless steel case, 11 x 29 mm

DATE / medium size, black dial, 1973, stainless steel case, Oyster band, Ref. 6466, 10.5 x 29 mm, 5.5 mm crown

DATE / 1960s, medium size, small bar indices, Oyster band, Ref. 6466, 10.5 x 29 mm

OYSTER

DATE / stainless steel case, hand-wound, 1950s, Ref. 6466, 11 x 29 mm

DATE / original gold dial, medium size, stainless steel case, Ref. 6466, 11.5 x 29 mm, 5.5 mm crown

DATE / medium size, stainless steel case, 1960, Ref. 6466, 11 x 29 mm

DATE PRECISION / gilded stainless steel case, hand-wound, 1960s, Ref. 6466, 11.5 x 30.9 mm

DATE / freshened-up dial, raised gold bar indices, 1970s, stainless steel case, Ref. 6466, 12 x 29 mm

DATE / 1950s, rare model with gold plating, Ref. 6466, Cal. 1215, 11 x 29 mm

DATE / black dial, medium size, original band, 1960s, Ref. 6466, stainless steel case, 11 x 29.5 mm, 5.5 mm crown

DATE / black dial, raised indices, 1969, Ref. 6466, stainless steel case, medium size, 11 x 29 mm

DATE / black dial, damaged hour hand, 1950s, Ref. 6466, stainless steel case, 10.5 x 29 mm

DATE / original matte silver dial, gold Rolex crown, 1970s, Ref. 6466, stainless steel case, 11 x 29.5 mm

DATE / freshened-up white dial, raised gold indices, medium size, 1960s, Ref. 6466, stainless steel case, 12 x 29 mm

DATE / cream dial, leaf hands, 1970s, Ref. 6466, stainless steel case, 11 x 29 mm

DATE / black dial with raised gold indices, gold plated case, 1958, Ref. 6466, 11 x 29 mm

DATE / medium size, gold lunette, white dial, leaf hands, Ref. 6466, 10.5 x 29.5 mm

DATE / freshened-up black dial, 1960s, Ref. 6466, 11 x 29 mm

DATE / medium size, black dial with raised plaque indices, freshened up, 1965, Ref. 6466, 11 x 29 mm

DATE / medium size, black dial with raised gold indices, Ref. 6466, 11 x 29 mm

DATE / medium size, flat lunette, Ref. 6466, 11 x 29 mm

DATE / with guarantee document, date indication in red and black, 1956, Ref. 6466, 11 x 29 mm

DATE / medium size, simple dial, 1960s, Ref. 6466, 11 x 29.5 mm

OYSTER

DATE / black dial with raised gold indices, leather band, stainless steel case, 1973, Ref. 6466, 12 x 29 mm

Ref. 6480
OYSTER / stainless steel case, hand-wound, 1970s, Ref. 6480, 10 x 33 mm

OYSTER / guilloched dial, hand-wound, 1940s, stainless steel case, Ref. 6480, Cal. 1210, 10 x 33 mm

OYSTER / original black dial in good condition, hand-wound, shock resistant, stainless steel case, Ref. 6840, 10 x 33 mm

PRECISION / original dial, 1950s, stainless steel case, Cal. 1210, Ref. 6480, 10.5 x 33 mm

PRECISION / freshened-up dark blue dial, 1960s, stainless steel case, Ref. 6480, 10 x 33 mm, crown 6 mm

Ref. 6482
PRECISION / guilloched dial, raised gold indices, 1950s, Ref. 6482, 11 x 33 mm

Ref. 6494
DATE / two-tone dial with raised plaque numerals and indices, date indication in red, Ref. 6494, stainless steel case, 10.5 x 33.5 mm, 5.5 mm crown

DATE / striking gold indices, two-tone dial, 1956, Ref. 6494, stainless steel case, 10.5 x 33 mm

DATE / raised numerals and indices of 18 karat plaque, stainless steel case, Ref. 6494, 10.5 x 33 mm, 5.5 mm crown

Ref. 6496
Ref. 6506

DATE / early 1950s, red and black date indication, Ref. 6494, hand-wound, Cal. 1215, stainless steel case, 11 x33.5 mm

DATE / "ROLEX" signature in different type face, stamped numerals and indices, 1954, Ref. 6494, 10.5 x 33 mm

DATE / two-color date indication, Jubilee band, 1950s, Ref. 6494, 11 x 33 mm

DATE / raised gold numerals and indices, two-tone dial freshened up, 1960s, Ref. 6496, stainless steel case, 11 x 33 mm, 5.5 mm crown

SPEEDKING / large raised numerals and indices, 1952, Ref. 6056, 11.5 x 28 mm, crown 6 mm

Ref. 6548
Ref. 6694

SPEEDKING / gold bar indices, freshened-up two-tone dial, stainless steel case, Ref. 6548, 10.5 x 29 mm, crown 5.5 mm

OYSTER / freshened-up dial, 1950s, stainless steel case, Ref. 6548, 11 x 28.5 mm

DATE / freshened-up unique dial, luminous numerals, Ref. 6694, 11 x 33 mm

DATE / freshened-up dial with Roman and Arabic numerals, 1950s, Ref. 6694, stainless steel case, 11 x 33.5 mm, crown 5.5 mm

DATE / freshened-up Oysterdate model with unique dial, screwed-on crown, stainless steel case, Ref. 6694, 11 x 33.5 mm

OYSTER

DATE / striking numerals and indices, two-tone dial freshened up, Ref. 6694, stainless steel case, 11 x 33.5 mm, 5.5 mm crown

DATE / two-tone dial, freshened up, plaque case, 1970s, Ref. 6694, 12 x 33.5 mm

DATE / two-tone dial with raised gold indices, stainless steel case, Ref. 6694, 11.5 x 33.5 mm

DATE / freshened-up two-tone dial, raised indices and hands of plaque, Ref. 6694, stainless steel case, 11.5 x 33.5 mm, 5.5 mm crown

DATE / rare two-tone dial, 1970s, Ref. 6694, stainless steel case, 11.5 x 33.5 mm, 5.5 mm crown

DATE / freshened-up dial, raised numerals, Ref. 6694, stainless steel case, 12 x 33.5 mm, 5.5 mm crown

DATE / 1970s, Ref. 6694, hand-wound, 12 x 33 mm

DATE / printed Roman numerals, white dial, 1972, Ref. 6694, stainless steel case, 12 x 33 mm, 5 mm crown

DATE PRECISION / stainless steel case, hand-wound, 1970s, Ref. 6694, 11 x 33 mm

DATE PRECISION / stainless steel case, hand-wound, 1970s, Ref. 6694, 12 x 33 mm

DATE PRECISION / stainless steel case, hand-wound, 1970s, Ref. 6694, 11 x 33 mm

DATE PRECISION / stainless steel case, hand-wound, 1970s, Ref. 6694, 12 x 33 mm

DATE / stainless steel case, hand-wound, 1960, Ref. 6694, 12 x 33 mm

DATE / stainless steel case, hand-wound, 1974, Ref. 6694, 11 x 33 mm

DATE / stainless steel case, hand-wound, 1970s, Ref. 6694, 11 x 33 mm

DATE / dial with military background, stainless steel case, hand-wound, 1960-70s, Ref. 6694, 11.4 x 33.4 mm

DATE PRECISION / stainless steel case, hand-wound, 1970s, Ref. 6694, 10.9 x 33 mm

DATE PRECISION / stainless steel case, hand-wound, 1970s, Ref. 6694, 12.1 x 35.7 mm

DATE / stainless steel case, 1970s, Ref. 6694, 12 x 33 mm

DATE / stainless steel case, hand-wound, 1970s, Ref. 6694, 12 x 33 mm

OYSTER

DATE / stainless steel case, hand-wound, 1970s, Ref. 6694, 11 x 33 mm

DATE PRECISION / stainless steel case, hand-wound, 1970s, Ref. 6694, 11 x 33 mm

DATE / stainless steel case, hand-wound, 1970s, Ref. 6694, 11 x 33 mm

DATE / stainless steel case, hand-wound, 1970s, Ref. 6694, 11 x 33 mm

DATE / stainless steel case, hand-wound, 1970s, Ref. 6694, 12 x 33 mm

DATE / stainless steel case, hand-wound, 1977, Ref. 6604, 11 x 33 mm

DATE / stainless steel case, hand-wound, 1981, Ref. 6694, 11 x 33 mm

DATE / stainless steel case, hand-wound, 1950s, Ref. 6694, 11 x 33 mm

DATE / stainless steel case, hand-wound, 1970s, Ref. 6694, 11 x 33 mm

DATE / stainless steel case, hand-wound, 1981, Ref. 6694, 11 x 33 mm

DATE / stainless steel case, hand-wound, 1974, Ref. 6694, 11 x 33 mm

DATE / stainless steel case, hand-wound, 1974, Ref. 6694, 11 x 33 mm

DATE / stainless steel case, hand-wound, 1973, Ref. 6694, 11 x 33 mm

DATE / stainless steel case, hand-wound, 1950s, Ref. 6694, 11 x 33 mm

DATE / stainless steel case, hand-wound, 1950s, Ref. 6694, 11 x 33 mm

DATE / stainless steel case, hand-wound, 1960, Ref. 6694, 13 x 33 mm

DATE / stainless steel case, hand-wound, 1977, Ref. 6694, 11 x 33 mm

DATE / stainless steel case, 1978, Ref. 6694, 11 x 33 mm

DATE / stainless steel case, hand-wound 1972, Ref. 6694, 11 x 33 mm

DATE / stainless steel case, hand-wound, 1980, Ref. 6694, 11 x 33 mm

OYSTER

DATE / stainless steel case, hand-wound, 1978, Ref. 6694, 11 x 33 mm

DATE / hand-wound, original band, stainless steel case, Ref. 6694, 11 x 33,5 mm

DATE / typical Rolex model with date window (x 2.5), Ref. 6694, 11.5 x 33 mm

PRECISION / luxurious design, matte silver dial with raised indices, 1950s, stainless steel case, Ref. 6694, 10 x 33 mm

PRECISION / standard model, freshened-up black dial, 1970s, Ref. 6694, 10 x 32.5 mm

DATE / Oyster Date, Oyster band, Ref. 6694, 11 x 33 mm, 5 mm crown

DATE / simple model, stainless steel case, white dial, Rolex crown by the 12, Ref. 6694, 11 x 33 mm, 5 mm crown

DATE / 1960s, stainless steel Oyster case with 14 karat gold plating, Ref. 6694, 11.5 x 33.5 mm

DATE / stainless steel Oyster case, black dial, Ref. 6694, 11 x 33 mm

DATE / black dial, raised gold bar indices, Ref. 6694, 12 x 33.5 mm

DATE / 1950s, gold plated case, screwed stainless steel case bottom, Ref. 6694, 11 x 33.5 mm

DATE / black dial, 1960s, Ref. 6694, 11.5 x 33.5 mm, 5.5 mm crown

DATE / 1960s, Ref. 6694, 12 x 33.5 mm, 5.5 mm crown

DATE / 1960s, freshened-up black dial, Ref. 6694, 12 x 34 ,,

DATE / 1970s, gold dial, Oyster case, Ref. 6694, 11 x 33.5 mm

DATE / 1970s, freshened-up dial, original Oyster band, Ref. 6694, 11 x 33 mm, 5 mm crown

DATE / 1970s, leather band, Ref. 6694, 11 x 33.5 mm

DATE / 1970s, simple model, white dial, raised gold indices, Ref. 6694, 11 x 33 mm

DATE / 1970s, original white dial, raised gold indices, Ref. 6694, 11 x 33.5 mm, 6 mm crown

DATE / 1970s, freshened-up black dial, Oyster band, hand-wound, Ref. 6694, Cal. 1225, 11 x 33.5 mm, 5 mm crown

OYSTER

DATE / 1960s, wedge indices, Dauphin hands, original dial, Ref. 6694, Cal. 1215, 11 x 33.5 mm

DATE / 1970s, freshened-up dark blue dial, screwed-on crown, watertight, Ref. 6694, 11.5 x 32.5 mm

DATE / 1970s, black dial, Ref. 6694, 12 x 33 mm

DATE / black dial, raised gold indices, 1970s, stainless steel case, Ref. 6694, Cal. 1215, 11.5 x 33.5 mm

DATE / raised numerals and indices, 1950s, stainless steel case, Ref. 6694, 11.5 x 33.5 mm

DATE / matte silver dial, standard model, 1970s, hand-wound, stainless steel case, Ref. 6694, Cal. 1215, 12 x 33.5 mm

DATE / Oyster Date with date window, 1980s, hand-wound, stainless steel case, Ref. 6694, Cal. 1225, 11.5 x 33.5 mm

DATE / original dial, 1960s, hand-wound, Ref. 6694, Cal. 1215, 11 x 33.5 mm

DATE / black dial, raised bar indices, 1960s, Ref. 6694, stainless steel case, 11.5 x 33.5 mm

DATE / Rolex crown by the 12, freshened-up black dial, 1970s, Ref. 6694, stainless steel case, 12 x 33.5 mm, 5.5 mm crown

DATE / freshened-up dial, 1970s, Ref. 6694, stainless steel case, 11 x 33.5 mm, 5.5 mm crown

DATE / original black dial, raised bar indices, 1970s, Ref. 6694, stainless steel case, 11.5 x 33.5 mm

DATE / standard model, 1970s, Ref. 6694, stainless steel case, 12 x 33.5 mm

DATE /freshened-up dial, 1970s, Ref. 6694, stainless steel case, 11 x 33.5 mm, 5.5 mm crown

DATE / raised gold indices, white dial, 1950s, Ref. 6694, stainless steel case, 11.5 x 33.5 mm

DATE / bar hands, 1960s, Ref. 6694, stainless steel hands, 11.5 x 33.5 mm, 5.5 mm crown

DATE / freshened-up gold dial, bar hands, Ref. 6694, stainless steel case, 11.5 x 33.5 mm, 5.5 mm crown

DATE / bar indices, freshened-up gold dial, stainless steel case, 11.5 x 33.5 mm

DATE / freshened-up dial, Ref. 6694, stainless steel case, 11.5 x 33.5 ,,, 5.5 mm crown

DATE / original gold dial with central second, 1970s, Ref. 6694, stainless steel case, 11.5 x 33.5 mm

OYSTER

DATE / original gold dial, 1980s, Ref. 6694, stainless steel case, 11.5 x 33.5 mm, 5.5 mm crown

DATE / freshened-up dial, 1960s, Ref. 6694, stainless steel case, 11 x 33 mm, 5.5 mm crown

DATE / original gold dial, Ref. 6694, stainless steel case, 11.5 x 33 mm

DATE / freshened-up dial, Ref. 6694, stainless steel case, 11.5 x 33 mm, 5.5 mm crown

DATE / black dial, raised indices, leaf hands, Ref. 6694, stainless steel case, 11.5 x 33.5 mm, 5 mm crown

DATE original dark gray dial with raised indices, 1977, Ref. 6694, stainless steel case, 11.5 x 33 mm, 5 mm crown

DATE / white dial, "OYSTERDATE" in red, 1961, Ref. 6694, stainless steel case, 11 x 33.5 mm, 5 m crown

DATE / freshened-up dial with printed Arabic numerals, Ref. 6694, stainless steel case, 11 x 33.5 mm

DATE / original dial with Arabic army emblem, Ref. 6694, stainless steel case, 1.5 x 33.5 mm

DATE / original dial, Arabic army emblem, Ref. 6694, stainless steel case, 11.5 x 33.5 mm

DATE / raised indices, silver dial with Arabic army emblem, 1970s, Ref. 6694, stainless steel case, 11.5 x 33.5 mm

DATE / dial with raised indices and date window, hand-wound, Ref. 6694, Cal. 1225, stainless steel case, 11.5 x 33.5 mm

DATE / big striking indices, freshened-up dial, Ref. 6694, stainless steel case, 11 x 33.5 mm

DATE / simple model, 1967, Ref. 6694, stainless steel case, 11 x 32.5 mm, 5.5 mm crown

DATE / original dark blue dial, 1960s, Ref. 6694, stainless steel case, 11 x 33.5 mm

DATE / black dial, 1960s, faded date indication, Ref. 6694, stainless steel case, 11 x 33.5 mm

DATE / original black dial in good condition, Ref. 6694, stainless steel case, 11.5 x 33.5 mm, 5.5 mm crown

DATE / striking numerals and indices on original two-tone dial, red date indication, 1960s, Ref. 6694, stainless steel case, 11.5 x 33.5 mm

DATE / original blue dial, raised bar indices, Ref. 6694, stainless steel case, 12 x 33.5 mm, 5.5 mm crown

DATE / freshened-up black dial, 1960s, Ref. 6694, hand-wound, Cal. 1215, stainless steel case, 11.5 x 33.5 mm

OYSTER

DATE / freshened-up dial with star indices, 1960s, Ref. 6694, hand-wound, Cal. 1215, stainless steel case, 12 x 33.5 mm

DATE / freshened-up white dial, raised bar indices, 1970s, Ref. 6694, plaque hands and case, 12 x 33.5 mm

DATE / original dial, 1960s, Ref. 6694, stainless steel case, 12 x 33.5 mm

DATE / matte black dial with raised gold indices, 1980s, Ref. 6694, stainless steel case, 11 x 33.5 mm

DATE / white dial with raised bar indices, 1960s, Ref. 6694, stainless steel case, 5.5 mm crown

DATE / large raised bar indices, freshened-up black dial, 1970s, Ref. 6694, stainless steel case, 11.5 x 33.5 mm

DATE / nice two-tone dial with date loupe, Ref. 6694, stainless steel case, 11 x 33 mm

DATE / original black dial, Ref. 6694, stainless steel case, 12 x 33.5 mm

DATE / original champagne-colored dial, leather band, 1970s, Ref. 6694, stainless steel case, 11 x 33 mm

DATE / raised gold bar indices, original blue dial, 1970s, Ref. 6694, stainless steel case, 11 x 34 mm

DATE / silver dial, Oyster band, 1966, Ref. 6694, stainless steel case, 11.5 x 33.5 mm

DATE / hand-wound, Ref. 6694, gold plated case, 11 x 33 mm

DATE / black dial with raised gold bar indices, 1972, Ref. 6694, stainless steel case, 12 x 33 mm, 5 mm crown

DATE / gold dial with raised bar indices, 1970s, Ref. 6694, stainless steel case, 11.5 x 33.5 mm

DATE / original black dial with luminous points, 1970s, Ref. 6694, hand-wound, Cal. 1225, stainless steel case, 11 x 33.5 mm

DATE / original dial, 1970s, Ref. 6694, stainless steel case, 11.5 x 33.5 mm, 5.5 mm crown

DATE / freshened-up black dial, Rolex crown by the 12, Ref. 6694, stainless steel case, 11 x 33 mm, 5.5 mm crown

DATE / simple silver dial, 1960s, Ref. 6694, hand-wound, Cal. 1225, stainless steel case, 11 x 33.5 mm

DATE / freshened-up black dial, raised gold indices, original band, 1960s, Ref. 6694, stainless steel case, 11 x 34 mm

DATE / white dial with raised wedge indices, 1960s, Ref. 6694, 11 x 33 mm

OYSTER

DATE / thick raised bar indices, Oyster band in good condition, 1966, Ref. 6694, 11 x 34 mm

DATE / black dial with raised bar indices, 1970s, Ref. 6694, 11 x 33 mm

DATE / simple black dial, 1980s, Ref. 6694, 11 x 33.5 mm

DATE / freshened-up dark blue dial, 1970s, Ref. 6694, 11.5 x 33.5 mm, 5 mm crown

DATE / matte silver dial, raised bar indices, 1970s, Ref. 6694, 11 x 33 mm

DATE / matte silver dial with bar indices, stainless steel case, 1970s, Ref. 6694, 11.5 x 33 mm

DATE / freshened-up matte silver dial, 1970s, Ref. 6694, Cal. 1225, 11.5 x 33 mm

DATE / black dial with gold-edged numerals and indices, Ref. 6694, 10 x 33 mm

DATE / 14 karat gold lunette, matte black dial with raised gold indices, 1960s, Ref. 6694, 12.5 x 33.5 mm

DATE / matte gold dial, 1970s, Ref. 6694, 11.5 x 33.5 mm

Ref. 15200 **OTHER OYSTERS**

DATE / freshened-up black dial, stainless steel case, 1972, Ref. 6694, 11.5 x 33.5 mm

DATE / automatic, stainless steel case, 2000, Ref. 15200, 12 x 33 mm

OYSTER / steel case, original dial, hand-wound, 11.5 x 28.5 mm

SPEEDKING / original Roman and Arabic numerals and indices, Mercedes hands, 10.5 x 28.5 mm

SPEEDKING / red dial, Mercedes hands, stainless steel case, 10,5 x 28.5 mm

OYSTER / signed "Chronometer", striking second hand, hand-wound, stainless steel case, 10.5 x 27 mm

AIR-GIANT / simple stainless steel case, gold raised numerals, 11.5 x 32.5 mm

ROYAL / nice blue steel hands, matte white dial, hand-wound, shock resistance, stainless steel case, 11.5 x 31,5 mm

IMPERIAL / "Chronometre", stainless steel case, medium size, 11 x 27 mm, crown 5.5 mm

ROYAL / nice railway minutery, matte white dial, 1950s, stainless steel case, 12.5 x 28.5 mm, crown 5.5 mm

OYSTER

OYSTER / original matte white dial, small second, dealer's signature "P. Orr & Sons Ltd", pillow-shaped stainless steel case, 11 x 28.5 mm, crown 6 mm

OYSTER / raised numerals, freshened-up dial, small second, pillow-shaped stainless steel case

ROYAL / classic dial, railway minutery, also on small second, stainless steel case, 12 x 28 mm, crown 5.5 mm

ROYAL / dealer's signature "H. G. Bell Salisbury", raised numerals, small second, stainless steel case, 10.5 x 29 mm, crown 5.5 mm

ROYAL / raised Arabic numerals and railway minutery, stainless steel case, projecting crown, 10 x 28 mm, crown 5.5 mm

OYSTER / arched signature, projecting crown, stainless steel case, 10.5 x 28.5 mm

ROYAL / early model with no catalog number, original luminous numerals, stainless steel case, 10 x 28.5 mm

OYSTER / "ultra prima", blued steel hands, original dial, 1930s, stainless steel case, 11.5 x 28 mm

OYSTER / dealer's signature on original dial, stainless steel case, 11.5 x 27.5 mm

ROYAL original dial with small second, dealer's signature "Dorbies Ltd Nairobi", 1930s, stainless steel case, 11.5 x 28.5 mm

SPEEDKING / original dial with small second, 1940s, stainless steel case, 11 x 28 mm

FIREFLY / luminous hands, stainless steel case, lunette with raised indices, 12 x 27.5 mm

SPEEDKING / matte rose dial, Arabic numerals and indices, luminous hands, all original, 10.5 x 28.5 mm

ROYAL / two-tone dial with luminous numerals, steel and gold bicolor case, 10.5 x 32.5 mm, crown 5 mm

ROYALITE / original dial with large numerals, bar indices, luminous hands, stainless steel case, 12.5 x 29 mm

ROYAL / original dial, Roman numerals, decorative hands, stainless steel case, 11.5 x 30 mm, crown 6 mm

ROYAL / Oyster case with fine engraving, freshened-up dial, Roman numerals, 10 x 31 mm, crown 6 mm

PRECISION / original dial, raised numerals combined with dot and wedge indices, gold case, 11 x 28.5 mm, crown 6 mm

ROYAL GIANT / raised plaque numerals and indices, stainless steel case, 12 x 32.5 mm

SPEEDKING / original white dial, silver hands, stainless steel case, 10.5 x 29.5 mm

OYSTER

OYSTER / dealer's signature "Mappin" on original dial, rare model with covered band attachments, gold and steel bicolor case, 11.5 x 28.5 mm

OYSTER / stainless steel case, hand-wound, 10 x 33 mm

ROYAL / simple model, two-tone dial, small second, stainless steel case, 11 x 29 mm, crown 6 mm

ROYAL / original two-tone dial, bar hands, 14 karat plaque case, 12.5 x 28 mm

ROYAL / original dial, stainless steel case, 11.5 x 30 mm, crown 5.5 mm

DATE / guilloched dial, steel and gold bicolor case and band, 10.5 x 29 mm, 5 mm crown

ROYAL / stainless steel Oyster case, Super-Oyster crown, medium size, 10.5 x 30.5 mm, crown 6 mm

AQUA / Oyster Company model, original dial with dealer's signature "Lund & Blockley," stainless steel case, 11 x 30 mm, crown 5 mm

PRECISION / raised gold indices, Arabic 12, stainless steel case, 10.5 x 32.5 mm

PRECISION / dial guilloched only in the center, stainless steel case, 12 x 33 mm

OYSTER / matte gold dial with Arabic army emblem, original, stainless steel case, 10 x 33 mm, crown 6 mm

ROYAL / raised gold indices, freshened-up matte black dial, medium size, stainless steel case, 10 x 31 mm

OYSTER / stainless steel case, hand-wound, years not known, 10 x 33 mm

SPEEDKING / freshened-up green dial, medium size, skeletal case bottom, 9.5 x 28.5 mm

SPEEDKING / gold hands and raised indices, original black dial, 9.5 x 28.5 mm

DATE / original dial, date indication in red and black, steel bicolor case with gold lunette, 11 x 29.5 mm, 5.5 mm crown

DATE / simple model, original dial, 11.5 x 33.5 mm, 5.5 mm crown

DATE / freshened-up black case with raised gold indices, overhauled, Oyster band, stainless steel case, 11 x 33.5 mm

DATE / raised indices, original dial, 1960s, 11.5 x 33.5 mm, 5.5 mm crown

DATE / discolored original dial, medium size, plaque-plated case, 11 x 29.5 mm, 5 mm crown

OYSTER PERPETUAL

Rolex perfected automatic winding for an everyday useful watch and produced many models of this type:

The classic Oyster Perpetual is equipped with an automatic movement without date and a traditional dial. Other varieties with which it was placed on the market are Dauphin hands and dials with wedge indices.

The Oyster Perpetual "DATEJUST," expanded by various functions, has meanwhile become a Rolex standard. In 1945, when Rolex put the Oyster Perpetual "DATE" and "DATEJUST" models on the market, this was new to the world. These models are equipped with date indication in a small window with loupe glass of 2.5x magnification. "DATEJUST" means that the date is switched exactly at 12 o'clock midnight.

The Oyster Perpetual "DAY-DATE," with weekday and date indicators, was a new top-class model in the Oyster Perpetual series. In the Day-Date series there are no stainless steel cases, only 18-karat yellow, red, or white gold or platinum cases. The band for the "DAY-DATE" is the so-called Tricolor band, which consists of three different gold materials. In the luxury models not only is the case gold, but so are the bottom, the crown, and the spring step.

Old advertisement with Hans Wilsdorf, the inventor of the watertight wristwatch and pathfinder to the chronometer watch.

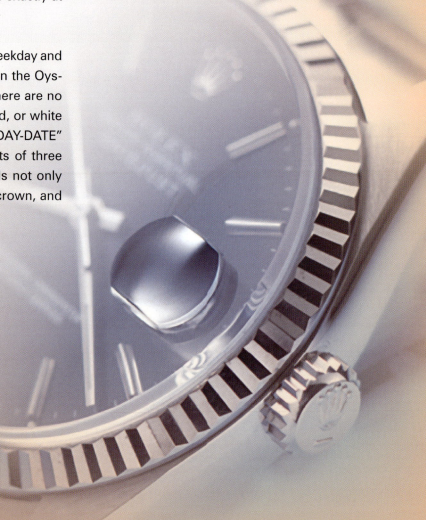

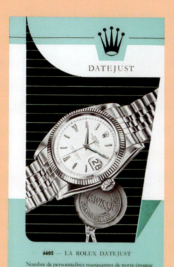
Advertisement from 1958.

Old advertisement.

This picture comes from a 1958 catalog.

Old Rolex advertisement.

Advertisement with David Plastow.

Rolex Catalog, 1966.

OYSTER PERPETUAL

OYSTER PERPETUAL 1940s

CHRONOMETER / automatic, stainless steel case, 1940s, 14 x 31 mm

OYSTER PERPETUAL / "Zephyr" model, 1940s, 12 x 34 mm

OYSTER PERPETUAL 1950s

DATE / early model with red date indication, channeled lunette, silver dial, 1950s, 15 x 33.5 mm

OYSTER PERPETUAL / 18 karat yellow gold case, medium size, original band, 1950s, 11 x 28.5 mm

OYSTER PERPETUAL / medium size, Cal. 1130, 1950s, 11 x 29 mm

OYSTER PERPETUAL / 14 karat yellow gold case, guilloched dial, raised indices, 1950s, 13 x 31.5 mm

OYSTER PERPETUAL / modern leaf hands, 18 karat yellow gold case and Oyster band, 1955, 11.5 x 34.5 mm

OYSTER PERPETUAL / bicolor model, champagne-colored dial, gilded case, Oyster band, 1954, 10.5 x 29 mm

OYSTER PERPETUAL / bicolor case, raised wedge indices, black dial, 195,3, 11.5 x 32.5 mm

DATEJUST / red and black date indication, nicely freshened-up dial, 1950s, 14 x 34 mm

DATEJUST / slightly bowed case bottom, medium size, freshened-up dial with red signature "Chronometre", 1954, 14 x 34 mm

DATEJUST / stainless steel case, 1950s, 14 x 34 mm

DATEJUST / alternating red and black date indication, stainless steel case, freshened-up dial, 1950s, 14.5 x 34.5 mm

DATEJUST / stainless steel and white gold bicolor case, black dial, gold bar indices, 1956, 11 x 34.5 mm

DATE / earlier model, date indication with loupe, stainless steel case, 1950s, 12 x 33.5 mm, 6 mm crown

OYSTER PERPETUAL / original piece, gold plated dial, raised numerals 3, 6, 9 and indices, 1950s, 13 x 34 mm

OYSTER PERPETUAL / lunette with raised indices, 18 karat gold case, guilloched dial, 1950s, 13 x 32.5 mm

DATEJUST / day indication in red and black, 1950s, 9 karat gold case, hand-wound, 10.5 x 34 mm

OYSTER PERPETUAL 1960s

OYSTER PERPETUAL / automatic, stainless steel case, 1960s, 13 x 33 mm

OYSTER PERPETUAL / "Zephyr" model, only for the American market, dial with dot indices, 1960s, 12 x 33 mm

OYSTER PERPETUAL

OYSTER PERPETUAL / yellow gold and stainless steel bicolor case, modern leaf hands, 1963, 12 x 33 mm

OYSTER PERPETUAL / certificate and box, modern leaf hands, 1960s, 12 x 32.5 mm

DATEJUST / stainless steel and gold bicolor case, gold dial with wedge indices, 1960s, 11.5 x 35.5 mm

OYSTER PERPETUAL / blued central second, dial with Arabic numerals, 1960s, 14.5 x 32.5 mm

OYSTER PERPETUAL / lunette with raised indices, stainless steel case, original white dial, 1960s, 11.5 x 33 mm

DATE / stainless steel case, classic leaf hands, discolored dial, 1963, 11 x 33 mm, 6.5 mm crown

OYSTER PERPETUAL / 14 karat yellow gold case and crown, matte gold dial, 1960s, 11.5 x 32 mm

DATEJUST / early model, original white gold lunette, 1960s, 14 x 34 mm

DATEJUST / white gold lunette, stainless steel case, original silver dial, 1960s, 12 x 33,5 mm

DATEJUST / 18 karat yellow gold case, original black dial, 1960s, 12 x 34.5 mm, 6 mm crown

OYSTER PERPETUAL 1970s

DATEJUST / 14 karat massive gold case, dealer's signature "Tiffany & Co" on original black dial, 1967, 11.5 x 33.5 mm, 5.5 mm crown

DAY DATE / 18 karat gold case and band, blue enamel dial, 1964, 12.5 x 34.5 mm, 6 mm crown

OYSTER PERPETUAL / gilded case, matte silver dial, 1970s, 11.5 x 33 mm

OYSTER PERPETUAL / medium size, 14 karat yellow gold case, raised indices in matte silver dial, 1970s, 10.5 x 28.5 mm, 5 mm crown

DATE / stainless steel case, rose dial, 1970s, 12.5 x 33.5 mm

DATE / stainless steel case, freshened-up dial with raised bar indices, 1970s. 12.5 x 33.5 mm

DATE / stainless steel case, blue dial with raised bar indices, 1970s, 12.5 x 34 mm, 6 mm crown

DATE / original band, overhauled, freshened-up dial, 1970s, 12.5 x 33.5 mm

DATE / simple model, matte silver dial, gold bar indices, Cal. 1565, 1970s, 12 x 34 mm, Ref. 1501

DATE / polished band. Lunette with raised indices, gold and stainless steel bicolor case, 1870s, 12 x 34 mm, 6 mm crown

OYSTER PERPETUAL

DATE / lunette with raised indices, stainless steel case, black dial;, 1970s, 11.5 x 34 mm.

OYSTER PERPETUAL / :1974: engraved on case bottom, 14 karat yellow gold case, 1970s, 12.5 x 32.5 mm

OYSTER PERPETUAL / raised bar indices, stainless steel and gold bicolor case, 1970s, 12.5 x 33 mm

OYSTER PERPETUAL / stainless steel and gold bicolor case, raised bar indices, matte silver dial, 1970s, 12.5 x 33 mm

DATE / 14 karat yellow gold case, original dial, 1970s, 12 x 33 mm, 5 mm crown

DATEJUST / older model, plastic crystal, overhauled, stainless steel and white gold bicolor case, freshened-up dial, 1970s, 12.5 x 34.5 mm

DATEJUST / channeled lunette, stainless steel case, 1970s, 12.5 x 34 mm

DATEJUST / slim lunette with raised indices, stainless steel case, blue dial, 1970s, 12 x 34.5 mm

DATEJUST / stainless steel and 14 karat yellow gold bicolor case, silver dial, raised bar indices, 1970s, 12 x 34.5 mm

DATEJUST / stainless steel and gold bicolor case, original gold dial, 1970s, 12.5 x 34.5 mm

DATEJUST / original Jubilee band, stainless steel and white gold bicolor case, 1970s, 12.5 x 34.5 mm

DAY-DATE / overhauled, 18 karat yellow gold, 10 indices set with diamonds on green dial, 1972, 12.5 x 34.5 mm, 6 mm crown

DAY-DATE / overhauled, 18 karat gold case and band, gold dial, 1970s, 12.5 x 34.5 mm

DAY-DATE / 18 karat white gold case, black dial, 1975, 12.5 x 34.5 mm

OYSTER PERPETUAL 1980s

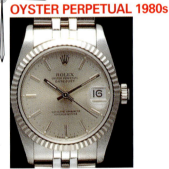
DATEJUST / medium size, white gold lunette, 1985, 11 x 29.5 mm

Ref. 1002

OYSTER PERPETUAL / two-tone dial with inside minutery, 1950s, 13 x 33 mm, Ref. 1002

OYSTER PERPETUAL / two-tone dial, 1960s, 12.5 x 33 mm, Ref. 1002

OYSTER PERPETUAL / automatic, stainless steel case, 1960s, Ref. 1002, 13 x 33 mm

OYSTER PERPETUAL / automatic, stainless steel case, 1970s, Ref. 1002, 13 x 33 mm

OYSTER PERPETUAL / simple lunette, beige dial, raised bar indices, 1960s, 11.5 x 32 mm. Ref. 1002

OYSTER PERPETUAL

OYSTER PERPETUAL / silver indices on pressed dial, 1950s, 12 x 34 mm, Ref. 1002

OYSTER PERPETUAL / 1960s, 11.5 x 33, Ref. 1002

OYSTER PERPETUAL / stainless steel case, silver dial, 1970s, 11.5 x 33 mm, Ref. 1002

OYSTER PERPETUAL / stainless steel case, original dial, wedge indices, 12 x 33 mm, Ref. 1002

OYSTER PERPETUAL /14 karat yellow gold case, raised bar indices on golden dial, 1960s, 11.5 x 32.5 mm, Ref. 1002

OYSTER PERPETUAL / automatic, stainless steel case, 1989, Ref. 1002, 12 x 32 mm

OYSTER PERPETUAL / stainless steel case, raised bar indices on gray dial, 1960s, 11.5 x 33 mm, 5.5 mm crown, Ref. 1002

DATE / automatic, stainless steel case, 1970s, Ref. 1002, 13 x 35 mm

Ref. 1005

OYSTER PERPETUAL / automatic, 18 karat yellow gold bicolor case, 1970s, Ref. 1005, 12 x 35 mm

OYSTER PERPETUAL / bicolor case, blue dial, 1980s, 12 x 33 mm, 5 mm crown, Ref. 1005

OYSTER PERPETUAL / 18 karat gold case, original gold dial, Cal. 1560, 1970s, 12 x 32,5 mm, Ref. 1005

Ref. 1006

OYSTER PERPETUAL / 18 karat gold and stainless steel bicolor case, original dial with gold indices, 1980s, 12 x 33 mm, Ref. 1006

Ref. 1007

OYSTER PERPETUAL / automatic, stainless steel case, 1970s, Ref. 1007, 13 x 33 mm

OYSTER PERPETUAL / Oyster case, lunette with raised indices, stainless steel case and band, 12 x 33 mm, Ref. 1007

OYSTER PERPETUAL / lunette with raised indices, Cal. 1560, 1960s, 12 x 32.5 mm, Ref. 1007

OYSTER PERPETUAL / silver dial with raised bar indices, stainless steel case, 12 x 32 mm, Ref. 1007

Ref. 1008

OYSTER PERPETUAL / "Zephyr" model for the American market, very nice lunette, 1950s, 12 x 33 mm, Ref. 1008

OYSTER PERPETUAL / "Zephyr" model for American market, Cal. 1560, 1950s, 12x 34 mm, Ref. 1008

Ref. 1010

OYSTER PERPETUAL / 14 karat yellow gold Bombay case, 11 x 32.5 mm, Ref. 1010

Ref. 1014

OYSTER PERPETUAL / original band, 14 karat gold case, silver dial, 1960s, 11.5 x 33 mm, Ref. 1014

OYSTER PERPETUAL

 **Ref. 1018**
 **Ref. 1019**

OYSTER PERPETUAL / gilded case, Cal. 1560, 1960s, 11.5 x 33 mm, Ref. 1014

OYSTER PERPETUAL / Jubilee band, stainless steel case, 1970s, 12 x 35 mm, Ref. 1018

MILGAUSS / anti-magnetic, second stop, 12 x 37 mm, Ref. 1019

MILGAUSS / original dial, Cal. 1580, 1960s, 12.5 x 37.5 mm, Ref. 1019

MILGAUSS / second Milgauss model with straight second hand, original dial, 1966, 14 x 37.5 mm, Ref. 1019

MILGAUSS / original silver dial, 1960s, 13.5 x 37.5 mm, Ref. 1019

MILGAUSS / rare model with dealer's signature "Tiffany & Co", stainless steel case, original dial, 14 x 37 mm

MILGAUSS / overhauled, original white dial, 1960s, 12.5 x 37 mm, Ref. 1019

MILGAUSS . / original white dial, Cal. 1580, 1970s, 13 x 37 mm, Ref. 1019

MILGAUSS / overhauled, with box and certificate, 1979, 13.5 x 37 mm, Ref. 1019

 **Ref. 1023**
 **Ref. 1024**

MILGAUSS / in new condition, original dial, 1970s, 12.5 x 37 mm, Ref. 1019

MILGAUSS / silver dial, 1960s, 14 x 37.5 mm, Ref. 1019

OYSTER PERPETUAL / finely rippled lunette and case of 18 karat gold, 1960s, 12 x 32.5 mm, Ref. 1023

OYSTER PERPETUAL / automatic, gold-filled case, 1960s, Ref. 1024, 12 x 32.8 mm

OYSTER PERPETUAL / gilded case, gold dial, 12 x 33 mm, Ref. 1024

 **Ref. 1025**
 **Ref. 1030**

OYSTER PERPETUAL / 14 karat gold case and lunette, 1957, 12 x 32 mm, Ref. 1024

OYSTER PERPETUAL / case with gold hood, sold in America, Cal. 1560, 11 x 33 mm, Ref. 1024

OYSTER PERPETUAL / case with gold hood, raised bar indices on gold dial, 1970s, 12 x 33 mm, Ref. 1024

OYSTER PERPETUAL / gold case and band, Cal. 1570, 12 x 33 mm, Ref. 1025

OYSTER PERPETUAL / lunette with raised indices of 14 karat gold, wedge indices, 12 x 32,5 mm, Ref. 1030

OYSTER PERPETUAL

Ref. 1038    **Ref. 1090**    **Ref. 1109**    **Ref. 1500**

OYSTER PERPETUAL / automatic, 18 karat yellow gold and stainless steel bicolor case, 1986, Ref. 1038G, 12 x 34.2 mm

OYSTER PERPETUAL / "Zephyr" model, bicolor case, dial with dot indices, 1960s, 12 x 34 mm, Ref. 1038

MILGAUSS / anti-magnetic, stainless steel case, 1970s, 13.5 x 37.5 mm, Ref. 1090

MILGAUSS / anti-magnetic, rare model with black dial, 1960s, 13.5 x 37.5 mm, Ref. 1019

DATE / automatic, stainless steel case, 1970s, Ref. 1500, 12 x 35 mm

DATE / automatic, stainless steel case, 1970s, Ref. 1500, 12 x 34 mm

DATE / automatic, stainless steel case, 1970s, Ref. 1500G, 11 x 33 mm

DATE / automatic, stainless steel case, 1970s, Ref. 1500m 13 x 33 mm

DATE / automatic, stainless steel case, 1970s, Ref. 1500, 13 x 33 mm

DATE / automatic, stainless steel case, 1970s, Ref. 1500, 12 x 33 mm

DATE / automatic, stainless steel case, 1970s, Ref. 1500, 12 x 33 mm

DATE / automatic, stainless steel case, 1970s, Ref. 1500, 12 x 33 mm

DATE / automatic, stainless steel case, 1970s, Ref. 1500, 12 x 33 mm

DATE / automatic, stainless steel case, 1970s, Ref. 1500, 12 x 33 mm

DATE / automatic, stainless steel case, 1970s, Ref. 1500, 13 x 34 mm

DATE / automatic, stainless steel case, 1970s, Ref. 1500, 12 x 34 mm

DATE / automatic, stainless steel case, 1970s, Ref. 1500, 12 x 33 mm

DATE / automatic, stainless steel case, 1970s, Ref. 1500, 12 x 33 mm

DATE / automatic, stainless steel case, 1970s, Ref. 1500, 13 x 33 mm

DATE / automatic, stainless steel case, 1970s, Ref. 1500, 12 x 33 mm

OYSTER PERPETUAL

DATE / automatic, stainless steel case, 1970s, Ref. 1500, 12 x 33 mm

DATE / automatic, stainless steel case, 1960s, Ref. 1500, 12 x 33 mm

DATE / automatic, stainless steel case, 1972, Ref. 1500m 12 x 33 mm

DATE / automatic, stainless steel case, 1967, Ref. 1500, 12 x 33 mm

DATE / automatic, stainless steel case, 1977, Ref. 1500, 11 x 33 mm

DATE / automatic, stainless steel case, 1977, Ref. 1500, 11 x 33 mm

DATE / automatic, stainless steel case, 1969, Ref. 1500, 12 x 33 mm

DATE / automatic, stainless steel case, 1968, Ref. 1500, 11 x 33 mm

DATE / automatic, stainless steel case, 1953, Ref. 1500, 12 x 33 mm

DATE / automatic, stainless steel case, 1970, Ref. 1500, 11 x 33 mm

DATE / stainless steel case, raised bar indices on blue dial, 1970s, 12 x 33.5 mm, 6 mm crown, Ref. 1500

DATE / stainless steel case, 1950s, 12 x 33 mm, 6 mm crown, Ref. 1500

DATE / stainless steel case, original dial, 12 x 33 mm, 6 mm crown, Ref. 1500

DATE / stainless steel case, original blue dial, 12 x 33 mm, 6 mm crown, Ref. 1500

DATE / lunette with raised indices, 1970s, 11.5 x 34 mm, 6 mm crown, Ref. 1500

DATE / stainless steel case, raised short bar indices, 1960s, 12.5 x 33.5 mm, Ref. 1500

DATE / stainless steel case, Dauphin hands, original white dial, 1960s, 12.5 x 33.5 mm, 6 mm crown, Ref. 1500

DATE / original band, 18 karat yellow gold case, raised indices and printed Roman numerals, 1970s, 1 x 33.5 mm, Ref. 1500

DATE lunette with raised indices, stainless steel case, 1970s, Cal. 1565, 12.5 x 34 mm, Ref. 1500

DATE / stainless steel case, 1960s, 11.5 x 32.5 mm, Ref. 1500

OYSTER PERPETUAL

DATE / raised gold indices on black dial, stainless steel dial, Cal. 1570, 1965, 12.5 x 33.5 mm, Ref. 1500

DATE / stainless steel case, matte gold dial, 12 x 33 mm, Ref. 1500

DATE / medium size, stainless steel case, Cal. 1575, 1970s, 12 x 33.5 mm, Ref. 1500

DATE / in good condition, 14 karat yellow gold case, Cal. 1565, 1960s, 11 x 33 mm, Ref. 1500

DATE / lunette with raised indices, stainless steel case, 1970s, 12 x 33.5 mm, Ref. 1500

DATE / stainless steel case, freshened-up rose dial, 1971, 12 x 33.5 mm, 6 mm crown, Ref. 1500

DATE / bicolor model, medium size, Cal. 1570, 1960s, 12 x 33.5 mm, 6 mm crown, Ref. 1500

DATE / stainless steel case, 1973, 12.5 x 33 mm, Ref. 1500

DATE / stainless steel case, Cal. 1560, 1965, 13 x 33 mm, 6 mm crown, Ref. 1500

DATE / stainless steel case, freshened-up blue dial, Cal. 1560, 1960s, 11.5 x 33.5 mm, 6 mm crown, Ref. 1500

DATE / sky-blue dial, stainless steel case, 1970s, 12.5 x 33.5 mm, 6 mm crown, Ref. 1500

DATE / original matte silver dial and band, stainless steel case, Cal. 1570, 1960s, 12.5 x 33.5 mm, 6 mm crown, Ref. 1500

DATE / bicolor case, matte gold dial, Cal. 1570, 1960s, 12 x 33.5 mm, 6 mm crown, Ref. 1500

DATE / stainless steel case, 1970s, 11.5 x 33.5 mm, 6 mm crown, Ref. 1500

DATE / freshened-up dial in stepped blue, stainless steel case, 1970s, 12.5 x 33.5 mm, 6 mm crown, Ref. 1500

DATE / bicolor case, channeled lunette, 1978, 12 x 33 mm, 6 mm crown, Ref. 1500

DATE / original band, matte silver dial, Cal. 1560, 1970s, 12.5 x 33.5 mm, 6 mm crown, Ref. 1500

DATE / small bar indices, stainless steel case, 1970s, 11.5 x 33.5 mm, 6 mm crown, Ref. 1500

DATE / Cal. 5035, 1980s, 13 x 33.5 mm, Ref. 1500

DATE / second stop, stainless steel case, original dial, Cal. 1570, 1970s, 11.5 x 33.5 mm, Ref. 1500

OYSTER PERPETUAL

DATE / simple design, dark blue dial, Cal. 1570, 11 x 33.5 mm, Ref. 1500

DATE / freshened-up light blue dial, stainless steel case, 1970s, 12 x 33.5 mm, Ref. 1500

DATE / stainless steel case, raised silver indices on black dial, 12 x 33.5 mm, 6 mm crown, Ref. 1500

DATE / original dial, Cal. 1570, 1960s, 12 x 33.5 mm, Ref. 1500

DATE / stainless steel case, raised indices, 1970s, 12 x 33.5 mm, Ref. 1500

Ref. 1501

DATE / Jubilee band, stainless steel case, original blue dial, Cal. 1570, 1970s, 13.5 x 33.5 mm, Ref. 1500

DATE / black dial, second stop, Oyster band, stainless steel case, Cal. 1570, 12 x 33.5 mm, Ref. 1500

DATE, original Oyster band, lunette with raised indices, matte silver dial, 1970s, 12 x 34 mm, Ref. 1500

DATE / automatic, stainless steel case, 1974, Ref. 1501, 11 x 34 mm

DATE / automatic, stainless steel case, 1970s, Ref. 1501, 12 x 34 mm

DATE / automatic, stainless steel case, 1970s, Ref. 1501, 12 x 34 mm

DATE / automatic, stainless steel case, 1971, Ref. 1501, 12 x 33 mm

DATE / automatic, stainless steel case, 1967, Ref. 1501, 12 x 34 mm

DATE / automatic, stainless steel case, 1960s, Ref. 1501, 12 x 34 mm

DATE / automatic, stainless steel case, 1969, Ref. 1501, 12 x 34 mm

DATE / automatic, stainless steel case, 1977, Ref. 1501, 12 x 34 mm

DATE / lunette with raised indices, matte silver dial, stainless steel case, 1970s, 12.5 x 34 mm, Ref. 1501

DATE / stainless steel case, original white dial with Roman numerals, 1980s, 12.5 x 34 mm, 6 mm crown, Ref. 1501

DATE / lunette with raised indices, original dial, stainless steel case, 1960s, 12.5 x 34.5 mm, Ref. 1501

DATE / lunette with raised indices, stainless steel case, Cal. 1570, 1960s, 11 x 34 mm, 6 mm crown, Ref. 1501

OYSTER PERPETUAL

DATE / lunette with raised indices, stainless steel case, 1970s, Ref. 1501, 12 x 34 mm

DATE / lunette with raised indices, black dial, stainless steel case, 12 x 34 mm, 6 mm crown, Ref. 1501

DATE lunette with raised indices, stainless steel case, 1969, 12 x 33 mm, 6 mm crown, Ref. 1501

DATE / lunette with raised indices, stainless steel case, late 1960s, 12 x 34 mm, 6 mm crown, Ref. 1501

DATE / lunette with raised indices, stainless steel case, freshened-up light blue dial, 13 x 33 mm, Ref. 1501

Ref. 1503
Ref. 1505

DATE / lunette with raised indices, original dial, Cal. 1570, 1965, 12 x 34 mm, Ref. 1501

DATE / lunette with raised indices, stainless steel case, Oyster band, 12 x 34 mm, Ref. 1501

DATE / lunette with raised indices, original dial, 12.5 x 34 mm, Ref. 1501

DATE / 18 karat gold case and band, original gold dial, 1970s, 11.5 x 32 mm, Ref. 1503

DATE / automatic, stainless steel case, 1972, Ref. 1505, 12 x 35 mm

Ref. 1512
Ref. 1550
Ref. 1560

DATE / stainless steel and gold bicolor case, freshened-up brown dial, gold indices, 1980s, 12 x 33.5 mm, Ref. 1505

DATE / "Zephyr" model, automatic, 18 karat yellow gold and stainless steel bicolor case, 1960s, Ref. 1512, 12 x 33 mm

DATE / automatic, gold case, 1979, Ref. 1550, 12 x 34 mm

DATE / 14 karat gold-coated case, Cal. 1560, 1970s, 12 x 33 mm, Ref. 1550

DATE / with second stop, 18 karat yellow gold case, 1970s, 12.5 x 32.5 mm, 5 mm crown, Ref. 1560

Ref. 1600
Ref. 1601

DATEJUST / automatic, stainless steel case, 1981, Ref. 1600, 13.1 x 34.4 mm

DATEJUST / stainless steel and yellow gold bicolor case, original dial, raised indices, 12 x 34.5 mm, Ref. 1600

DATEJUST / stainless steel and 14 karat gold bicolor model, dial with gold indices. 1970s, 12 x 34.5 mm, Ref. 1600

DATEJUST / channeled lunette, silver dial, 12.5 x 34.5 mm, 6 mm crown, Ref. 1600

DATEJUST / automatic, white gold and stainless steel bicolor case, 1970s, Ref. 1601, 12 x 34 mm

OYSTER PERPETUAL

DATEJUST / automatic, white gold and stainless steel bicolor case, 1960, Ref. 1601, 12.4 x 34.9 mm

DATEJUST / automatic, red gold and stainless steel bicolor case, 1970, Ref. 1601, 12.4 x 34.3 mm

DATEJUST / automatic, white gold and stainless steel bicolor case, 1980s, Ref. 1601, 13.2 x 35 mm

DATEJUST / automatic, 14 karat yellow gold and stainless steel bicolor case, 1970s, Ref. 1601, 12 x 36 mm

DATEJUST / automatic, 18 karat yellow gold and stainless steel bicolor case, 1960s, Ref. 1601, 12 x 34 mm

DATEJUST / automatic, stainless steel case, 1970s, Ref. 1601, 12 x 32 mm

DATEJUST / automatic, stainless steel case, 1970s, Ref. 1601, 13 x 35 mm

DATEJUST / automatic, stainless steel case, 1970, Ref. 1601, 12 x 34 mm

DATEJUST / automatic, white gold and stainless steel bicolor case, 1970s, Ref. 1601, 13 x 33 mm

DATEJUST / automatic, 18 karat yellow gold and stainless steel bicolor case, 1970s, Ref. 1601, 12 x 34 mm

DATEJUST / automatic, 18 karat yellow gold and stainless steel bicolor case, 1970s, Ref. 1601, 13 x 34 mm

DATEJUST / automatic, stainless steel case, 1970s, Ref. 1601, 12 x 34 mm

DATEJUST / automatic, stainless steel case, 1970s, Ref. 1601, 12 x 34 mm

DATEJUST / automatic, white gold and stainless steel bicolor case, 1977, Ref. 1601, 12 x 34 mm

DATEJUST / automatic, white gold and stainless steel bicolor case, 1968, Ref. 1601, 12 x 34 mm

DATEJUST / automatic, stainless steel case, 1967, Ref. 1601, 12 x 35 mm

DATEJUST / automatic, 18 karat yellow gold and stainless steel bicolor case, 1965, Ref. 1601, 12 x 34 mm

DATEJUST / automatic, white gold and stainless steel bicolor case, 1979, Ref. 1601, 12 x 34 mm

DATEJUST / automatic, 14 karat yellow gold and stainless steel bicolor case, 1970s, Ref. 1601SY, 12 x 34 mm

DATEJUST / red gold and stainless steel bicolor case, 1983, Ref. 1601, 12 x 35 mm

OYSTER PERPETUAL

DATEJUST / automatic, 18 karat white gold and stainless steel bicolor case, 1973, Ref. 1601, 12 x 34 mm

DATEJUST / automatic, red gold and stainless steel bicolor case, 1970, Ref. 1601, 12 x 34 mm

DATEJUST / automatic, stainless steel case, 1971, Ref. 1601, 12 x 34 mm

DATEJUST / white gold and stainless steel bicolor case, 1971, Ref. 1601, 12.5 x 34.5 mm

DATEJUST / freshened-up white dial with gold indices and numerals, Cal. 1570, 12.5 x 34.5 mm, Ref. 1601

DATEJUST / white gold lunette, original dial, 12 x 34.5 mm, Ref. 1601

DATEJUST / 18 karat gold lunette, raised indices, Cal. 1560, 12 x 34.5 mm, Ref. 1601

DATEJUST / white gold and stainless steel bicolor model, 12 x 34 mm, Ref. 1601

DATEJUST / 14 karat white gold lunette, original black dial, Cal. 1570, 12.5 x 34.5 mm, Ref. 1601

DATEJUST / gold and stainless steel bicolor model, 12 x 34 mm, Ref. 1601

DATEJUST / channeled white gold lunette, silver dial, 1970s, 12.5 x 34.5 mm, Ref. 1601

DATEJUST / white gold and stainless steel bicolor model, 1968, 13 x 34 mm, Ref. 1601

DATEJUST / 18 karat yellow gold and stainless steel bicolor case, brown dial, 1970s, 12 x 34.5 mm, Ref. 1601

DATEJUST / stainless steel and 18 karat gold bicolor model, original dial and Dauphin hands, 1960s, 11.5 x 34.5 mm, Ref. 1601

DATEJUST / plastic crystal, white gold and stainless steel bicolor case, 1977, 12 x 34.5 mm, 6 mm crown, Ref. 1601

DATEJUST / all original except Jubilee band, white gold and stainless steel bicolor case, 1970s, 12 x 34.5 mm, Ref. 1601

DATEJUST / stainless steel case, freshened-up carmine red dial, 1970s, 12.5 x 34.5 mm, Ref. 1601

DATEJUST / 14 karat and stainless steel bicolor case, original dial, large Roman numerals, 1965, 11.5 x 34.5 mm, Ref. 1601

DATEJUST / stainless steel case, freshened-up green dial, 1970s, 12.5 x 34.5 mm, 6 mm crown, Ref. 1601

DATEJUST / stainless steel and 18 karat yellow gold bicolor case, original gold dial, 1970s, 13 x 35 mm, 6 mm crown, Ref. 1601

OYSTER PERPETUAL

DATEJUST / stainless steel and 18 karat gold bicolor case, freshened-up blue dial, gold indices, 1970s, 12 x 34.5 mm, Ref. 1601

DATEJUST / stainless steel case, 1970s, 12.5 x 34.5 mm, Ref. 1601

DATEJUST / stainless steel case, original dial, 1965, 12 x 34.5 mm, 6 mm crown, Ref. 1601

DATEJUST / 18 karat gold case, original dial, raised indices, 1950s, 11.5 x 34.5 mm, Ref. 1601

DATEJUST / 14 karat yellow gold and stainless steel bicolor case, Cal. 1570, 1970s, 12.5 x 34.5 mm, Ref. 1601

DATEJUST / raised bar indices on black dial, stainless steel and white gold bicolor case, 1970s, 12.5 x 34 mm, Ref. 1601

DATEJUST / stainless steel case, freshened-up rose dial, 1978, 12.5 x 34.5 mm, 6 mm crown, Ref. 1601

DATEJUST / stainless steel case, freshened-up carmine red dial, 1970s, 12.5 x 33.5 mm, Ref. 1601

DATEJUST / gold and stainless steel bicolor case, freshened-up blue dial, 1970s, 12.5 x 34.5 mm, Ref. 1601

DATEJUST / stainless steel and white gold bicolor case, leaf hands. Raised bar indices, 1950s, 11.5 x 34.5 mm, Ref. 1601

DATEJUST / stainless steel and 14 karat gold bicolor case, discolored original dial, early 1960s, 12.5 x 34.5 mm, Ref. 1601

DATEJUST / 18 karat gold case, 12 x 34 mm, Ref. 1601

DATEJUST / stainless steel and yellow gold bicolor case, raised bar indices, 1970s, 12.5 x 34 mm, Ref. 1601

DATEJUST / stainless steel and white gold bicolor case, Cal. 1565, 1960s, 12 x 34.5 mm, Ref. 1601

DATEJUST / rare model, freshened-up dial with red signature "DateJust", Cal. 1560, 1960s, 12 x 34 mm, Ref. 1601

DATEJUST / 18 karat gold, original dial in good condition, 1950s, 12 x 34.5 mm, Ref. 1601

DATEJUST / Jubilee band, white gold lunette, original blue dial, 12 x 34.5 mm, Ref. 1601

DATEJUST / white gold lunette, stainless steel case, 12.5 x 34.5 mm, Ref. 1601

DATEJUST / stainless steel and yellow gold bicolor case, metal band replaced by leather one, Cal. 1570, 1960s, 12 x 34.5 mm, Ref. 1601

DATEJUST / stainless steel and 14 karat gold bicolor model, freshened-up black dial, 1970s, 12.5 x 34 mm, Ref. 1601

OYSTER PERPETUAL

DATEJUST / raised bar indices, 12 x 34.5 mm, Ref. 1601

DATEJUST / 1970s, 12.5 x 34.5 mm, Ref. 1601

DATEJUST / 14 karat yellow gold and stainless steel bicolor case, striking gray dial, Cal. 1570, 1970s, 12 x 34 mm, Ref. 1601

DATEJUST / polished lunette, freshened-up green dial, Cal. 1560, 1970s, 12 x 35 mm, Ref. 1601

DATEJUST / with box and certificate, 18 karat yellow gold lunette, dial with raised indices, Cal. 1575, 1960s, 12 x 34 mm, Ref. 1601

DATEJUST / freshened-up blue dial, Cal. 1570, 1970s, 12 x 34 mm, Ref. 1601

DATEJUST / plastic crystal, 12 x 34.5 mm, Ref. 1601

DATEJUST / Jubilee band, 18 karat white gold lunette, 1970s, 12 x 34.5 mm, Ref. 1601

DATEJUST / stainless steel and 18 karat yellow gold bicolor case, freshened-up brown dial, Cal. 1570, 1970s, 12 x 34.5 mm, Ref. 1601

DATEJUST / stainless steel case, blue dial, Cal. 1570, 1970s, 12 x 34.5 mm, Ref. 1601

DATEJUST / rare 18 karat gold model, 1970s, 12 x 34.5 mm, Ref. 1601

DATEJUST / white gold lunette, Cal. 1575, 1970s, 13 x 34.5 mm, Ref. 1601

DATEJUST / second stop, stainless steel and 14 karat gold bicolor case, golden brown dial, 1970s, 12.5 x 34.5 mm, Ref. 1601

DATEJUST / stainless steel and white gold bicolor case, 1960s, 12.5 x 34.5 mm, 6 mm crown, Ref. 1601

DATEJUST / channeled lunette, stainless steel and 18 karat gold bicolor case, 1980s, 11.5 x 34.5 mm, Ref. 1601

DATEJUST / stainless steel case, matte silver dial, raised bar indices, 1960s, 11.5 x 35 mm, 6 mm crown, Ref. 1601

DATEJUST / stainless steel and white gold bicolor case, blue dial, slim bar indices, 1970s, 12.5 x 34.5 mm, Ref. 1601

DATEJUST / stainless steel and 14 karat yellow gold bicolor case, Cal. 1570, 1970s, 12.5 x 34.5 mm, Ref. 1601

DATEJUST / 18 karat white gold case, original black dial, Cal. 1575, 1970s, 11.5 x 34.5 mm, 6 mm crown, Ref. 1601

DATEJUST / stainless steel and white gold bicolor case, freshened-up green dial, bar indices, 12.5 x 34.5 mm, Ref. 1601

OYSTER PERPETUAL

DATEJUST / stainless steel and 14 karat gold bicolor case, 12 x 34.5 mm, 6 mm crown, Ref. 1601

DATEJUST / stainless steel and white gold bicolor case, original brown dial, 1970s, 12.5 x 34.5 mm, Ref. 1601

DATEJUST / "Thunderbird" model with 60-minute markings on lunette, stainless steel case, Ref. 1560, 1970s, 13 x 36.5 mm, 6 mm crown, Ref. 1601

DATEJUST / stainless steel case, original gray dial, bar indices, 1977, 12.5 x 34 mm, 6 mm crown, Ref. 1601

DATEJUST / automatic, white gold and stainless steel bicolor case, 1970s, Ref. 1601, 12 x 34 mm

Ref. 1603

DATE / automatic, 18 karat yellow gold and stainless steel bicolor case, 1973, Ref. 1603, 12 x 33 mm

DATEJUST / automatic, stainless steel case, 1970, Ref. 1603, 13 x 34 mm

DATEJUST / automatic, stainless steel case, 1970s, Ref. 1603, 12 x 34 mm

DATEJUST / automatic, stainless steel case, 1970s, Ref. 1603, 12 x 34 mm

DATEJUST / automatic, stainless steel case, 1978, Ref. 1603, 13 x 25 mm

DATEJUST / automatic, stainless steel case, 1967, Ref. 1603, 12 x 35 mm

DATEJUST / automatic, stainless steel case, 1970s, Ref. 1603, 11 x 35 mm

DATEJUST / automatic, 18 karat yellow gold and stainless steel bicolor case, 1973, Ref. 1603, 12 x 33 mm

DATEJUST / stainless steel Jubilee band and case, 12 x 35 mm, Ref. 1603

DATEJUST / blue dial with 10 indices set with diamonds, 1970s, 12.5 x 34.5 mm, Ref. 1603

DATEJUST / second stop, stainless steel case and band, well-preserved blue dial, Cal. 1570, 1970s, 12 x 35 mm Ref. 1603

DATEJUST / stainless steel lunette, Jubilee band, freshened-up dial, late 1960s, 12 x 35 mm, Ref. 1603

DATEJUST / classic guilloched dial, 11.5 x 34.5 mm, Ref. 1603

DATEJUST / stainless steel case, freshened-up black dial, 1960s, 12.5 x 34.5 mm, Ref. 1603

DATEJUST / older model, lunette with raised indices, black Roman numerals on white dial, 1948, 12 x 34.5 mm, Ref. 1603

OYSTER PERPETUAL

 **Ref. 1625**

DATEJUST / stainless steel case, matte silver dial with raised bar indices, 1970s, 13 x 35 mm, Ref. 1603

THUNDERBIRD / red gold and stainless steel bicolor case, 1971, Ref. 1625, 12.8 x 36.4 mm

THUNDERBIRD / automatic, 18 karat white gold and stainless steel bicolor case, 1970s. Ref. 1625, 12.3 x 35.4 mm

THUNDERBIRD / automatic, 18 karat yellow gold and stainless steel bicolor case, 1960s, Ref. 1625, 11.8 x 36 mm

THUNDERBIRD / automatic, 18 karat yellow gold and stainless steel bicolor case, 1970s, Ref. 1625, 12 x 35 mm

    **Ref. 1630**

THUNDERBIRD / automatic, yellow gold and stainless steel bicolor case, 1968, Ref. 1625, 12 x 35 mm

THUNDERBIRD / automatic, 14 karat yellow gold and stainless steel bicolor case, 1962, Ref. 1625, 12 x 35 mm

DATEJUST / "Turn-O-Graph" with turning lunette, 12 x 35.5 mm, Ref. 1625

DATEJUST / stainless steel and 14 karat yellow gold bicolor case, Cal. 1570, 1960s, 11.5 x 35.5 mm, Ref. 1625

DATEJUST / case for model with quartz movement, yellow gold and stainless steel bicolor case, 1970s, 12 x 34 mm, Ref. 1630

Ref. 1803

DAY-DATE / automatic, 18 karat white gold case, 1965, Ref. 1803, 12 x 34 mm

DAY-DATE / automatic, red gold case, 1973, Ref. 1803, 12 x 34 mm

DAY-DATE / automatic, 18 karat red gold case, 1970, Ref. 1803, 12.4 x 35 mm

DAY-DATE / automatic, 18 karat yellow gold case, 1968, Ref. 1803, 12 x 34 mm

DAY-DATE / automatic, 18 karat yellow gold case, 1968, Ref. 1803, 13 x 34 mm

DAY-DATE / day and weekday indications, President band and case of 18 karat gold, 12.5 x 34.5 mm, Ref. 1803

DAY-DATE / 18 karat gold case, original peppermint green enamel dial, 14x 34.5 mm, 6 mm crown, Ref. 1803

DAY-DATE / original condition, black dial with gold indices, 1955, 12 x 34.5 mm, 6 mm crown, Ref. 1803

DAY-DATE / rare model with unusual gold dial, gold band, 18 karat massive gold case, 12.5 x 34.5 mm, Ref. 1803

DAY-DATE / 18 karat gold case, freshened-up gold dial, 13.5 x 34.5 mm, Ref. 1803

OYSTER PERPETUAL

Ref. 1807

Ref. 3131

Ref. 3496

DAY-DATE / leather band, 18 karat yellow gold case, original dial, 1970s, 12.5 x 34.5 mm, Ref. 1803

DAY-DATE / 18 karat white gold case, freshened-up dial with raised Roman numerals, 1970s, 13 x 34,5 mm, Ref. 1803

DAY-DATE / 18 karat yellow gold case, 1966, 12.5 x 34 mm, 6 mm crown, Ref. 1807

OYSTER PERPETUAL / automatic, 18 karat yellow gold case, 1950s, Ref. 3131, 12.8 x 29.9 mm

OYSTER PERPETUAL / wide lunette, Arabic numerals, AR movement, 1939, 11.5 x 28.5 mm, Ref. 3496

Ref. 3536

Ref. 3772

Ref. 4846

Ref. 4857

Ref. 5075

OYSTER PERPETUAL / flexible band, hidden attachments, stainless steel case, late 1940s, 13.5 x 32 mm, Ref. 3536

OYSTER PERPETUAL / medium size, automatic, yellow gold and stainless steel bicolor case, 1940s, Ref. 3772, 13.2 x 27.6 mm

OYSTER PERPETUAL / rare AR movement, 1940s, steel case, 13.5 x 29 mm, Ref. 4846

OYSTER PERPETUAL / AR model, large wedge indices, 18 karat gold and steel bicolor case, original dial, 13 x 28 mm, Ref. 4857

DATE / older model without date loupe, turning gold lunette, stainless steel and gold case, 16 x 33.5 mm, Ref. 5075

Ref. 5500

Ref. 6062

OYSTER PERPETUAL / automatic, stainless steel case, 1970s, Ref. 5500, 11 x 33 mm

OYSTER PERPETUAL / small raised Roman numerals, freshened-up two-tone dial, 11 x 32.5 mm, Ref. 5500

OYSTER PERPETUAL / stainless steel and 18 karat yellow gold bicolor case, original dial with mosaic pattern, 1970s, 11.5 x 33 mm, Ref. 5500

TRIPLE CALENDAR / very rare model with full calendar and moon phase, star indices, 1950s, Ref. 6002

TRIPLE CALENDAR / full calendar with moon phase, stainless steel case, 1950s, 14 x 33 mm, Ref. 6062

Ref. 6085

Ref. 6103

DATE / early model with date indication, stainless steel and 14 karat gold bicolor case, signature "DATE", 1950s, 14.5 x 33.5 mm, Ref. 6075

OYSTER PERPETUAL / automatic, 18 karat yellow gold case, 1950s, Ref. 6085, 11 x 32 mm

OYSTER PERPETUAL / stainless steel Super Oyster case without screwed crown, 1950s, 13.5 x 32.5 mm, Ref. 6085

OYSTER PERPETUAL / leaf hands, yellow gold case, 1950s, 13 x 33 mm, Ref. 6085

OYSTER PERPETUAL stainless steel and gold bicolor case and band, raised indices on white dial, 12 x 32 mm, Ref. 6103

OYSTER PERPETUAL

OYSTER PERPETUAL / older model with gold lunette, guilloched dial, 1950s, 13.5 x 33 mm, Ref. 6117

TURN-O-GRAPH / lunette with raised indices as in earlier Submariner models, 1954, 12 x 36 mm, Ref. 6202

TURN-O-GRAPH / stainless steel case, 13.5 x 35 mm, 5 mm crown, Ref. 6202

TURN-O-GRAPH / nice gold lunette, stainless steel and gold bicolor case, 1954, 13 x 35.5 mm, 5.5 mm crown, Ref. 6202

OYSTER PERPETUAL / stainless steel case, guilloched dial, wedge indices, 1950s, 12.5 x 32.5 mm. Ref. 6284

OYSTER PERPETUAL / stainless steel case, guilloched dial, 1956, 11.5 x 33 mm, Ref. 6284

OYSTER PERPETUAL / stainless steel case, original dial, wedge indices, 1950s, 13 x 33 mm, Ref. 6284

OYSTER PERPETUAL / stainless steel case, freshened-up guilloched dial, 1950s, 12.5 x 32.5 mm, Ref. 6284

DATEJUST / freshened-up dial, 1950s, 13.5 x 34.5 mm, Ref. 6305

DATEJUST / slightly bowed case bottom, black dial, 1960s, 14 x 34.5 mm, Ref. 6305

DATEJUST / stainless steel and white gold bicolor case, guilloched dial, signature "Datejust" in lower part of dial (added later?), 1950s, 13.5 x 34.5 mm, Ref. 6305

DATE / automatic, 14 karat yellow gold and stainless steel bicolor case, 1960s, Ref. 6517, 11.5 x 25 mm

DATEJUST / automatic, 18 karat yellow gold case, 1970s, Ref. 6517, 9 x 21 mm

OYSTER PERPETUAL / stainless steel case, gold wedge indices and Arabic numerals on guilloched dial, 12 x 33 mm, Ref. 6518

DATE / stainless steel case, guilloched dial, raised gilded indices, 1960s, 12.5 x 33.5 mm, Ref. 6518

DATE / stainless steel case, matte white dial, raised wedge indices, 1950s, 13.5 x 33 mm, Ref. 6518

DATE / guilloched two-tone dial, wedge indices, stainless steel case, 13 x 33 mm, 6 mm crown, Ref. 6518

DATE / red date indication, stainless steel case, 1954, 12.5 x 33 mm, 6 mm crown, Ref. 6518

DATEJUST / older model without date loupe, stainless steel case, white dial with red signature "Datejust", 1950s, 13 x 33 ,,, Ref. 6518

DATE / automatic, stainless steel case, 1960s, Ref. 6518, 13 x 33 mm

OYSTER PERPETUAL

Ref. 6530

DATE / raised gold indices and numerals, freshened up, stainless steel case, 1950s, 12.5 x 32.5 mm, Ref. 6530

Ref. 6532

OYSTER PERPETUAL / stainless steel case, slightly discolored original white dial, 1960s, 11.5 x 33.5 mm, Ref. 6532

Ref. 6534

DATE / stainless steel case, 11.5 x 33.5 mm, Ref. 6534

DATE / stainless steel case, Cal. 1030, 1960s, 12 x 33 mm, Ref. 6534

DATE / date indication with gold frame, wedge indices, freshened-up dial, 1960s, 12 x 32.5 mm, Ref. 6534

Ref. 6541

MILGAUSS / early model with turning lunette, anti-magnetic, stylized lightning-bolt second hand, 1950s, 13 x 37 mm, Ref. 6541

Ref. 6546

OYSTER PERPETUAL / watertight to 50 meters, stainless steel case, freshened-up dial, 1958, 12 x 33 mm, 5 mm crown, Ref. 6546

Ref. 6548

OYSTER PERPETUAL / medium size, Oyster band, simple black dial, 1955, 11.5 x 29 mm, Ref. 6548

OYSTER PERPETUAL / stainless steel case, original dial, 1940s, 11.5 x 29.5 mm, 5.5 mm crown, Ref. 6548

OYSTER PERPETUAL / medium size, stainless steel case, gold indices, 11 x 29 mm, 5.5 mm crown, Ref. 6548

Ref. 6549

OYSTER PERPETUAL / original case and band of 18 karat red gold, 11 x 28 mm, Ref. 6549

OYSTER PERPETUAL / medium size, Jubilee band, stainless steel case, freshened-up dial, 1960s, 10 x 28.5 mm, Ref. 6549

OYSTER PERPETUAL / stainless steel and 14 karat gold bicolor case, raised bar indices on silver dial, 1966, Ref. 6549

Ref. 6551

OYSTER PERPETUAL / small model, black dial, 18 karat gold case, 1950s, 11 x 28.5 mm, Ref. 6551

Ref. 6552

OYSTER PERPETUAL / stainless steel case, matte white dial with raised gold indices, 1950s, Ref. 6552, 12.5 x 33.5 mm

Ref. 6556

TRUE BEAT / stainless steel case, automatic movement, springing second, original dial, 1960s, 12.5 x 33 mm, Ref. 6556

Ref. 6564

OYSTER PERPETUAL / automatic, stainless steel case, 1950s, Ref. 6564, 11.6 x 32.3 mm

OYSTER PERPETUAL / discolored dial with raised indices, Cal. 1030, 1960s, 12 x 33 mm, Ref. 6564

OYSTER PERPETUAL / stainless steel case, raised gold indices on black dial, 12 x 33 mm, Ref. 6564

OYSTER PERPETUAL / very well-freshened dial, raised silver indices, 1960s, 12 x 33 mm, Ref. 6564

OYSTER PERPETUAL

Ref. 6565

OYSTER PERPETUAL /gold wedge indices on white dial, 1940s, 11.5 x 32.5 mm, Ref. 6564

OYSTER PERPETUAL / automatic, stainless steel case, 1950s, Ref. 6564, 12 x 33 mm

OYSTER PERPETUAL / stainless steel case, freshened-up dial, 12 x 32 mm, 5.5 mm crown, Ref. 6565

OYSTER PERPETUAL / lunette with raised indices, Cal. 1030, 12 x 32.5 mm, Ref. 6565

OYSTER PERPETUAL / lunette with raised indices, 18 karat gold case, wedge indices, 1955, 11.5 x 32.5 mm, 5 mm crown, Ref. 6565

Ref. 6567

OYSTER PERPETUAL / automatic, 14 karat red gold case, 1960s, Ref. 6567, 12.5 x 34 mm

OYSTER PERPETUAL / automatic, 14 karat yellow gold and stainless steel bicolor case, 1960s, Ref. 6567, 11.7 x 32.6 mm

OYSTER PERPETUAL / 18 karat yellow gold case, raised gold indices, leaf hands, 1960s, 12 x 32.5 mm, Ref. 6567

OYSTER PERPETUAL / 14 karat yellow gold case, wedge indices, leaf hands, 12 x 32.5 mm, Ref. 6567

OYSTER PERPETUAL / channeled white gold lunette, original matte white dial, 12 x 33 mm, 5 mm crown, Ref. 6567

Ref. 6569

Ref. 6580

OYSTER PERPETUAL / stainless steel case, gold wedge indices, 12 x 32 mm, Ref. 6567

OYSTER PERPETUAL / freshened-up dial, discolored hands and case, Cal. 1030, 1960s, 12 x 33 mm, Ref. 6569

OYSTER PERPETUAL / lunette with raised indices, stainless steel case, white dial, 1956, 12 x 32.5 mm, Ref. 6569

OYSTER PERPETUAL / bicolor model with polished lunette, discolored dial, 1950s, 12 x 33 mm, Ref. 6580

OYSTER PERPETUAL / gold and stainless steel bicolor case, faded dial, 11 x 33 mm, Ref. 6580

Ref. 6584

Ref. 6590

Ref. 6604

OYSTER PERPETUAL / stainless steel case, raised indices, Cal. 1030, 1960s, 12 x 33 mm, Ref. 6582

OYSTER PERPETUAL / "Zephyr" model, stainless steel and yellow gold bicolor case, 1950s, 12.5 x 33.5 mm, Ref. 6582

OYSTER PERPETUAL / 14 karat yellow gold Jubilee band and case, Cal. 1030, 1950s, 11 x 32 mm, Ref. 6584

OYSTER PERPETUAL / lunette with raised indices, Cal. 1030, 1950s, 12 x 33 mm, Ref. 6590

DATEJUST / early model with red date indication, freshened-up dial, Cal. 1065, 1950s, 13 x 34.5 mm, Ref. 6604

OYSTER PERPETUAL

Ref. 6605

OYSTER PERPETUAL / with chronometer certificate, lunette with raised indices, gold and stainless steel bicolor case, 1972, 13 x 32 mm, Ref. 6605

DATE / stainless steel case with 14 karat white gold lunette, original white dial with bar indices, 1950s, 13 x 33.5 mm, 6 mm crown, Ref. 6605

DATEJUST / white gold lunette, 1956, 12.5 x 34.5 mm, Ref. 6605

DATEJUST / older model, stainless steel and gold bicolor case, discolored dial, 1959, 12 x 34.5 mm, Ref. 6605

DATEJUST / 18 karat yellow gold case, original dial, raised wedge indices, 1960s, 12.5 x 34.5 mm, Ref. 6605

Ref. 6623

DATEJUST / leather band, 14 karat yellow gold case, freshened-up dial, 1960s, 12 x 35 mm, Ref. 6605

DATEJUST / 14 karat gold and stainless steel bicolor case, Cal. 1065, 1960s, 12 x 34.5 mm, Ref. 6605

DATEJUST / early model with raised wedge indices, stainless steel and gold bicolor case, 1959, 13 x 34.5 mm, Ref. 6005

DATEJUST / stainless steel and white gold bicolor case, original dial, Dauphin hands, 13 x 34.5 mm, 6 mm crown, Ref. 6605

OYSTER PERPETUAL / medium size, 18 karat yellow gold and stainless steel bicolor case, 1970s, 12 x 29 mm, Ref. 6623

Ref. 6627

Ref. 6634

DATE / automatic, 18 karat red gold case, 1970, Ref. 6627, 11 x 29 mm

DATE / medium size, 18 karat yellow gold case, 1965, 11 x 29 mm, 5 mm crown, Ref. 6627

OYSTER PERPETUAL / bicolor model, stainless steel, 18 karat yellow gold lunette, gold wedge indices, 12 x 33 mm, Ref. 6634

OYSTER PERPETUAL / gold case, 1942, 12 x 33 mm, Ref. 6634

OYSTER PERPETUAL / gilded case, wedge indices and Dauphine hands ion gold dial, 1960s, 12 x 33 mm, Ref. 6634

Ref. 6827

OYSTER PERPETUAL / with original band and bicolor case of stainless steel and gold, 1960s, 12 x 33 mm, Ref. 6634

DATEJUST / automatic, yellow gold and stainless steel bicolor case, 1970s, Ref. 6827, 12 x 33 mm

DATEJUST / automatic, stainless steel case, 1970s, Ref. 6827, 11 x 29 mm

DATEJUST / automatic, 18 karat yellow gold case, 1980, Ref. 6827, 11 x 30 mm

DATEJUST / medium size, rose dial, 1977, 11 x 29 mm, Ref. 6827

OYSTER PERPETUAL

DATEJUST / automatic, yellow gold and stainless steel bicolor case, 1970, Ref. 6827, 11 x 29 mm

Ref. 8074
OYSTER PERPETUAL / large indices on original white dial, gold case, 13/5 x 31.5 mm, Ref. 8074

Ref. 14203
OYSTER PERPETUAL / automatic, yellow gold and stainless steel bicolor case, 2003, Ref. 14203M, 11 x 33 mm

Ref. 14233
OYSTER PERPETUAL / automatic, 18 karat yellow gold and stainless steel bicolor case, 2000, Ref. 14233M, 11.4 x 33.5 mm

OYSTER PERPETUAL / automatic, 18 karat gold and stainless steel bicolor case, 2000, Ref. 14233, 11.4 x 33.5 mm

OYSTER PERPETUAL / automatic, yellow gold and stainless steel bicolor case, 1991, Ref. 14233, 11 x 33 mm

Ref. 15000
DATE / automatic, 1970s, Ref. 15000, 12 x 34 mm

DATE / automatic, stainless steel case, 1980s, Ref. 15000, 13 x 34 mm

DATE / automatic, stainless steel case, 1988, Ref. 15000, 12 x 34 mm

DATE / automatic, stainless steel case, 1987, Ref. 15000, 13 x 34 mm

DATE / automatic, stainless steel case, 1980, Ref. 15000, 12 x 33 mm

DATE / United Arab Emirates Army emblem, stainless steel case, Cal. 3035, 1980s, 13 x 33.5 mm, Ref. 15000

DATE / dealer's signature "Tiffany & Co", stainless steel case, 13 x 33.5 mm, 5 mm crown, Ref. 15000

Ref. 15001
DATE / automatic, stainless steel case, 1970s, Ref. 15001, 13 x 33 mm

Ref. 15010
DATE / United Arab Emirates Army emblem on dial, stainless steel case, Cal. 3035, 1980s, 12 x 33.5 mm

DATE United Arab Emirates Army emblem, lunette with raised indices, stainless steel case, Cal. 3035, 1980s, 13 x 34 mm, Ref. 15010

Ref. 15053
DATE / automatic, 18 karat yellow gold and stainless steel bicolor case, 1987, Ref. 15053, 13 x 34.3 mm

DATE / 14 karat gold and stainless steel bicolor model, United Arab Emirates Army emblem, Cal. 3035, 1980s, 13 x 33.5 mm, Ref. 15053

Ref. 15200
DATE automatic, stainless steel case, 1999, Ref. 15200, 11.9 x 13.5 mm

DATE / automatic, stainless steel case, 1999, Ref. 15200, 11.8 x 33.5 mm

OYSTER PERPETUAL

DATE / automatic, stainless steel case, 1999, Ref. 15200, 11.9 x 33.5 mm

DATE / automatic, stainless steel case, 2000, Ref. 15200, 12 x 33.5 mm

DATE / automatic, stainless steel case, 2000, Ref. 15200, 11.6 x 33.4 mm

DATE / automatic, stainless steel case, 2000, Ref. 15200, 11.8 x 33.5 mm

DATE / automatic, stainless steel case, 1996, Ref. 15200, 12 x 33 mm

DATE / automatic, stainless steel case, 2001, Ref. 15200M 12 x 34 mm

DATE / automatic, stainless steel case, 1990, Ref. 15200, 12 x 34 mm

DATE / automatic, stainless steel case, 1990, Ref. 15200, 12 x 34 mm

DATE / automatic, stainless steel case, 1992, Ref. 15200, 12 x 34 mm

DATE / automatic, stainless steel case, 2003, Ref. 15200, 12 x 33 mm

DATE / stainless steel case, 2003, Ref. 15200, 12 x 33 mm

DATE / automatic, stainless steel case, 1996, Ref. 15200, 12 x 34 mm

DATE / automatic, stainless steel case, 1994, Ref. 15200, 12 x 33 mm

DATE / automatic, stainless steel case, 1998, Ref. 15200, 12 x 33 mm

DATE / automatic, stainless steel case, 1998, Ref. 15200, 12 x 34 mm

Ref. 15203

DATE / automatic, 18 karat yellow gold and stainless steel bicolor case, 1998, Ref. 15203, 12 x 34 mm

Ref. 15210

DATE / automatic, stainless steel case, 1999, Ref. 15210, 11.8 x 33.6 mm

DATE / automatic, stainless steel case, 1997, Ref. 15210, 12 x 34 mm

Ref. 15238

DATE / 18 karat yellow gold case, 1991, Ref. 15238, 11.7 x 33.6 mm

Ref. 15505

DATE / case coated with yellow gold, black dial, 1980s, 13 x 13.5, 5 mm crown, Ref. 15505

OYSTER PERPETUAL DATEJUST

The Oyster Perpetual DateJust has become a Rolex standard. The development of the quick-change mechanism for the date was sensational in its time.

OYSTER PERPETUAL

Ref. 16013

DATEJUST / automatic, 18 karat yellow gold and stainless steel bicolor case, 1981, Ref. 16013, 13 x 34 mm

DATEJUST / automatic, 18 karat yellow gold and stainless steel bicolor case, 1985, Ref. 16013, 13 x 34 mm

DATEJUST / automatic, 18 karat yellow gold and stainless steel bicolor case, 1987, Ref. 16013, 13 x 34 mm

DATEJUST / 18 karat gold and stainless steel bicolor model, original dial, Cal. 3035, 1980s, 12.5 x 34.5 mm, Ref. 16013

DATEJUST / original dial with 10 indices set with diamonds, 1970s, 12.5 x 34.5 mm, Ref. 16013

DATEJUST / plastic crystal, stainless steel and 18 karat yellow gold bicolor case, 1980s, 13 x 34.5 mm, Ref. 16013

DATEJUST / Oyster band, United Arab Emirates Army emblem, stainless steel and gold bicolor case, 1980s, 13 x 34 mm, 6 mm crown, Ref. 16013

DATEJUST / stainless steel and 18 karat yellow gold bicolor case, original gold dial, 1980s, 13 x 34 mm, Ref. 16013

DATEJUST / stainless steel and yellow gold bicolor case, original dial, Cal. 3035, 1980s, 13 x 34.5 mm, Ref. 16013

DATEJUST / stainless steel and 14 karat yellow gold bicolor case, 13 x 34.5 mm, Ref. 16013

DATEJUST / striking freshened-up dial, Cal. 3035, 1980s, 12 x 34 mm, Ref. 16013

DATEJUST / dial with United Arab Emirates emblem, Cal. 3035, 1980s, 13 x 35 mm, Ref. 16013

DATEJUST / stainless steel and gold bicolor case, 13 x 34.5 mm, 6 mm crown, Ref. 16013

DATEJUST 10 indices set with diamonds, stainless steel and gold bicolor case, 1970s, 12.5 x 34,5 mm, Ref. 16013

DATEJUST / Thunderbird model, stainless steel and yellow gold bicolor case, Cal. 3135, 1980s, 11.5 x 36.5 mm, 6 mm crown, Ref. 16013

Ref. 16014

DATEJUST / older model with plastic crystal, stainless steel and 18 karat yellow gold bicolor model, 1980s, 12.5 x 34.5 mm, Ref. 16013

DATEJUST / automatic, white gold and stainless steel bicolor case, 1970s, Ref. 16014, 12 x 34 mm

DATEJUST / automatic, stainless steel case, 1980, Ref. 16014, dial with 10 indices set with diamonds, 13 x 35 mm

DATEJUST / automatic, stainless steel case, 1970s, Ref. 16014, dial with 10 indices set with diamonds, 13 x 35 mm

DATEJUST / automatic, stainless steel case, 1980s, Ref. 16014, 12 x 34 mm

OYSTER PERPETUAL

DATEJUST / automatic, stainless steel case, 1980s, Ref. 16014, 13 x 34 mm

DATEJUST / automatic, stainless steel case, 1980s, Ref. 16014G, 13 x 34 mm

DATEJUST / automatic, stainless steel case, 1980s, Ref. 16014, 12 x 34 mm

DATEJUST / automatic, white gold and stainless steel bicolor case, 1985, Ref. 16014, 13 x 34 mm

DATEJUST / automatic, white gold and stainless steel bicolor case, 1980s, Ref. 16014, 12 x 34 mm

DATEJUST / automatic, white gold and stainless steel bicolor case, 1978, Ref. 16014, 13 x 34 mm

DATEJUST / automatic, white gold and stainless steel bicolor case, 1983, Ref. 16014, 13 x 34 mm

DATEJUST / plastic crystal, 18 karat white gold and stainless steel bicolor case, 1980s, 11.5 x 34.5 mm, Ref. 16014

DATEJUST / stainless steel case, original silver dial with mosaic pattern, 1984, 12.5 x 34.5 mm, Ref. 16014

DATEJUST / plastic crystal, box and certificate, silver dial with 10 indices set with diamonds, 12.5 x 34.5 mm, Ref. 16014

Ref. 16030

DATEJUST / stainless steel case, freshened-up rose dial, raised Roman numerals, 1970s, 13 x 34 mm, Ref. 16014

DATEJUST / stainless steel and 18 karat white gold bicolor case, United Arab Emirates Army emblem, 1980s, 13 x 34.5 mm, Ref. 16014

DATEJUST / automatic, stainless steel case, 1985, Ref. 16030, 12 x 35 mm

DATEJUST / automatic, stainless steel case, 1989, Ref. 16030, 12 x 35

DATEJUST / automatic, 18 karat yellow gold and stainless steel bicolor case, 1981, Ref. 16030, 13 x 35 mm

Ref. 16200

DATEJUST / stainless steel case, 1980s, 12 x 34.5 mm, Ref. 16030

DATEJUST / rippled lunette, matte silver dial, 1980s, 12.5 x 35 mm, Ref. 16030

DATEJUST / stainless steel case, 1980s, 12.5 x 35 mm, Ref. 16030

DATEJUST / automatic, stainless steel case, 2000, Ref. 16200, 11.8 x 34.3 mm

DATEJUST / automatic, stainless steel case, 2000, Ref. 16200, 11.9 x 34.2 mm

OYSTER PERPETUAL

DATEJUST / automatic, stainless steel case, 1999, Ref. 16200, 12.2 x 34.3 mm

DATEJUST / automatic, stainless steel case, 2000, Ref. 16200, 12.3 x 34.3 mm

DATEJUST / automatic, stainless steel case, 2001, dial with 10 indices set with diamonds, Ref. 16200G, 12 x 34 mm

DATEJUST / automatic, stainless steel case, 2001, Ref. 16200, 12 x 34 mm

DATEJUST / automatic, stainless steel case, 1990s, Ref. 16200, 12 x 34 mm

DATEJUST / automatic, stainless steel case, 2000, Ref. 16200, 12 x 34 mm

DATEJUST / automatic, stainless steel case, 2000, Ref. 16200, 12 x 34 mm

DATEJUST / automatic, stainless steel case, 2000, Ref. 16200, 12 x 34 mm

DATEJUST / automatic, stainless steel case, 1998, Ref. 16200, 12 x 34 mm

DATEJUST / good condition, automatic, stainless steel case, 2003, Ref. 16200, 12 x 34 mm

DATEJUST / good condition, automatic, stainless steel case, 2003, Ref. 16200, 12 x 34 mm

DATEJUST /automatic, stainless steel case, 2000, Ref. 16200, 11 x 29 mm

Ref. 16203

DATEJUST / automatic, 18 karat yellow gold and stainless steel bicolor case, 1990, Ref. 16203, 12 x 34 mm

DATEJUST / automatic, yellow gold and stainless steel bicolor case, 1995, Ref. 16203, 12 x 34 mm

DATEJUST / automatic, 18 karat yellow gold and stainless steel bicolor case, 1994, Ref. 16203G, dial with 10 indices set with diamonds, 12 x 34 mm

Ref. 16220

DATEJUST / automatic, white gold and stainless steel bicolor case, 1993, Ref. 16220, 12.1 x 34.4 mm

DATEJUST / automatic, white gold and stainless steel bicolor case, 1996, Ref. 16220, 12.1 x 34.3 mm

DATEJUST / automatic, white gold and stainless steel bicolor case, 1990, Ref. 16220, 11.7 x 34.4 mm

DATEJUST / automatic, white gold and stainless steel bicolor case, 2000, Ref. 16220, 11.5 x 34.3 mm

DATEJUST automatic, stainless steel case, 1990s, Ref. 16220, 12 x 34 mm

OYSTER PERPETUAL

Ref. 16233

DATEJUST / automatic, stainless steel case, 1990s, Ref. 16220, 12 x 34 mm

DATEJUST / automatic, stainless steel case, 1990, Ref. 16220, 12 x 34 mm

DATEJUST / yellow gold and stainless steel bicolor case, 1992, Ref. 16233, 12 x 34 mm

DATE / automatic, yellow gold and stainless steel bicolor case, 1998, Ref. 16233, 12 x 33 mm

DATEJUST/ 18 karat yellow gold and stainless steel bicolor case, 1990, Ref. 16233, 12 x 34.4 mm

DATEJUST / automatic, 18 karat yellow gold and stainless steel bicolor case, 1991, Ref. 16233, 12 x 34.4 mm

DATEJUST / automatic, 18 karat yellow gold and stainless steel bicolor case, 1996, Ref. 16233G, dial with 10 indices set with diamonds, 11.8 x 34.4 mm

DATEJUST / automatic, 18 karat yellow gold and stainless steel bicolor case, 1996, Ref. 16233G, dial with 10 indices set with diamonds, 11.9 x 34.4 mm

DATEJUST / yellow gold and stainless steel bicolor case, 2000, Ref. 16233, 12 x 34.5 mm

DATEJUST / automatic, 18 karat yellow gold and stainless steel bicolor case, 1997, Ref. 16233, 12.1 x 34.5 mm

DATEJUST / automatic, 18 karat yellow gold and stainless steel bicolor case, 1994, Ref. 16233, 12 x 34.5 mm

DATEJUST / automatic, 18 karat yellow gold and stainless steel bicolor case, 1990, Ref. 16233, 12 x 34.3 mm

DATEJUST / automatic, 18 karat yellow gold and stainless steel bicolor case, 1994, Ref. 16233G, dial with 10 indices set with diamonds, 12.1 x 34.5 mm

DATEJUST / automatic, 18 karat yellow gold and stainless steel bicolor case, 1994, Ref. 16233G, dial with 10 indices set with diamonds, 12.3 x 34.3 mm

DATEJUST / automatic, 18 karat yellow gold and stainless steel bicolor case, 1998, Ref. 16233, 12.3 x 34.3 mm

DATEJUST / automatic, 18 karat yellow gold bicolor case, 1993, Ref. 16233, 11.9 x 34.3 mm

DATEJUST / automatic, 18 karat yellow gold and stainless steel bicolor case, 1999, Ref. 16233, 12.2 x 34.5 mm

DATEJUST / automatic, 18 karat yellow gold and stainless steel bicolor case, 1996, Ref. 16233, 12 x 34.4

DATEJUST / automatic, 18 karat yellow gold and stainless steel bicolor case, 2000, Ref. 16233, 11.9 x 34.3 mm

DATEJUST / automatic, 18 karat yellow gold and stainless steel bicolor case, 1998, Ref. 16233G, 12 x 34 mm

Oyster Perpetual

OYSTER PERPETUAL

DATEJUST / automatic, 18 karat yellow gold and stainless steel bicolor case, 1999, Ref. 16233, 12 x 34 mm

DATEJUST / automatic, 18 karat yellow gold and stainless steel case, 1994, Ref. 16233, 12 x 34 mm

DATEJUST / automatic, 18 karat yellow gold and stainless steel, 1992, Ref. 16233, 12 x 34 mm

DATEJUST / automatic, 18 karat yellow gold and stainless steel bicolor case, 1990, Ref. 16233, 12 x 34 mm

DATEJUST / automatic, 18 karat yellow gold and stainless steel bicolor case, 2000s, Ref. 16233, 12 x 34 mm

DATEJUST / automatic, yellow gold and stainless steel bicolor case, 1991, Ref. 16233G, 12 x 34 mm

DATEJUST / automatic, yellow gold and stainless steel bicolor case, 1994, Ref. 16233, 12 x 34 mm

DATEJUST / automatic, yellow gold and stainless steel bicolor case, 1992, Ref. 16233, 12 x 34 mm

DATEJUST / automatic, yellow gold and stainless steel bicolor case, 1991, Ref. 16233, 12 x 34 mm

DATEJUST / yellow gold and stainless steel bicolor case, 1995, Ref. 16233, 12 x 34 mm

Ref. 16234

DATEJUST / automatic, yellow gold and stainless steel bicolor case, 1996, Ref. 16233, 12 x 34 mm

DATEJUST / stainless steel and 18 karat gold bicolor case, guilloched dial with dealer's signature "Tiffany & Co". 1980s, 12 x 34.5 mm, Ref. 16233

DATEJUST / automatic, stainless steel case, 1996, Ref. 16234NA, 12 x 34 mm

DATEJUST / automatic, white gold and stainless steel bicolor case, 2000, Ref. 16234, 12 x 34 mm

DATEJUST / automatic, white gold and stainless steel bicolor case, 1992, Ref. 16234, 12 x 34 mm

DATEJUST / automatic, white gold and stainless steel bicolor case, 1995, Ref. 16234, 12 x 34 mm

DATEJUST / stainless steel case, 1991m Ref. 16234, 12 x 34 mm

DATEJUST / automatic, white gold and stainless steel bicolor case, 1991, Ref. 16234, 12 x 34 mm

DATEJUST / automatic, stainless steel case, 1993, Ref. 16234, 12 x 34 mm

DATEJUST / automatic, white gold and stainless steel bicolor case, 1993, Ref. 16234, 12 x 34 mm

OYSTER PERPETUAL

DATEJUST / 18 karat white gold and stainless steel bicolor case, 1992, Ref. 16234, 12 x 34 mm

DATEJUST / 18 karat white gold and stainless steel bicolor case, 1988, Ref. 16234, 12 x 34 mm

DATEJUST / automatic, white gold and stainless steel bicolor case, 2003, Ref. 16234, 12 x 34 mm

DATEJUST / good condition, white gold and stainless steel bicolor case, 2003, Ref. 16234, 13 x 35 mm

DATEJUST / automatic, stainless steel case, 2000, Ref. 16234, 12 x 34 mm

DATEJUST / automatic, white gold and stainless steel bicolor case, 1994, Ref. 16234, 12 x 34 mm

DATEJUST / 1996, automatic, 18 karat white gold case, Ref. 16234, dial with 10 indices set with diamonds, 12 x 34 mm

DATEJUST / automatic, white gold and stainless steel bicolor case, 1995, Ref. 16234G, 12.1 x 34.5 mm

DATEJUST / automatic, white gold and stainless steel bicolor case, 2000, Ref. 16234G, 12.3 x 34.6 mm

DATEJUST / automatic, white gold and stainless steel bicolor case, 1991, Ref. 16243G, dial with 10 indices set with diamonds, 12 x 34.4 mm

DATEJUST / automatic, white gold and stainless steel bicolor case, 1995, Ref. 16234, dial with 10 indices set with diamonds, 12 x 34 mm

DATEJUST / automatic, stainless steel case, 1990s, Ref. 16234G, 11 x 39 mm

DATEJUST / automatic, white gold and stainless steel bicolor case, 1994, Ref. 16243G, dial with 10 indices set with diamonds, 12 x 34 mm

DATEJUST / automatic, white gold and stainless steel bicolor case, 1991, Ref. 16234G, dial with 10 indices set with diamonds, 12.2 x 34.3 mm

DATEJUST / automatic, white gold and stainless steel bicolor case, 2000, Ref. 16234G, dial with 10 indices set with diamonds, 12 x 34.5 mm

DATEJUST / automatic, white gold and stainless steel bicolor case, 1998, Ref. 16234G, 12 x 34 mm

Ref. 16238

DATEJUST / automatic, 18 karat yellow gold case, 1990, Ref. 16238G, dial with 10 indices set with diamonds, 12 x 34 mm

DATEJUST / automatic, 18 karat yellow gold, Ref. 16238, 12 x 34 mm

Ref. 16250

DATEJUST / white gold "Turn-O-Graph" lunette, Cal. 3035, 1980s, 12.5 x 36.5 mm, Ref. 16250

DATEJUST / stainless steel and white gold bicolor case, dealer's signature "Tiffany & Co" on original gray dial, 1980s, 13.5 x 37 mm, Ref. 16250

THUNDERBIRD

The DateJust with turning lunette was nicknamed "Thunderbird." This name comes from the U.S. Air Force's Air Demonstration Squadron.

OYSTER PERPETUAL

Ref. 16253

THUNDERBIRD / automatic, 18 karat yellow gold and stainless steel bicolor case, 1987, Ref. 16253, 13 x 37 mm

THUNDERBIRD / automatic, 18 karat yellow gold and stainless steel bicolor case, 1980s, Ref. 16253, 12 x 36 mm

THUNDERBIRD / automatic, yellow gold and stainless steel bicolor case, 1985, Ref. 16253, 13 x 36 mm

Ref. 16263

THUNDERBIRD / automatic, yellow gold and stainless steel bicolor case, 1998, Ref. 16263, 12 x 37 mm

THUNDERBIRD / automatic, yellow gold and stainless steel bicolor case, 1990, Ref. 16263, 12 x 37 mm

THUNDERBIRD / automatic, yellow gold and stainless steel bicolor case, 1998, Ref. 16263, 11.9 x 36.5 mm

THUNDERBIRD / automatic, 18 karat white gold and stainless steel bicolor case, 1991, Ref. 16263, 12 x 37 mm

THUNDERBIRD / Thunderbird model, lunette with 60-minute divisions, stainless steel and yellow gold bicolor case, Ref. 16263, 13 x 36.5 mm, 6 mm crown

Ref. 16264

THUNDERBIRD / automatic, 18 karat white gold and stainless steel bicolor case, mother-or-pearl color dial, 2001, Ref. 16264, 12 x 36 mm

THUNDERBIRD / automatic, white gold and stainless steel bicolor case, 2003, mother-of-pearl color dial, Ref. 16264, 12 x 37 mm

THUNDERBIRD / automatic, 18 karat white gold and stainless steel bicolor case, 1999, Ref. 16264, 12 x 37 mm

THUNDERBIRD / white gold and stainless steel bicolor case, 2003, Ref. 16264, 12 x 37 mm

THUNDERBIRD / automatic, white gold and stainless steel bicolor case, 2003, Ref. 16264, 12 x 37 mm

THUNDERBIRD / automatic, 18 karat white gold and stainless steel bicolor case, 1996, Ref. 16264, 12.3 x 36.8 mm

THUNDERBIRD / automatic, white gold and stainless steel bicolor case, 2000, Ref. 16264, 13 x 36 mm

Ref. 16283

THUNDERBIRD / automatic, 18 karat white gold and stainless steel bicolor case, 1992, Ref. 16264, 12 x 37 mm

THUNDERBIRD / automatic, 18 karat white gold and stainless steel bicolor case, 1999, Ref. 16262, 12 x 37 mm

THUNDERBIRD / automatic, white gold and stainless steel bicolor case, 1995, Ref. 16264, 12 x 36 mm

THUNDERBIRD / good condition, white gold and stainless steel bicolor case, 2003, Ref. 16264, 12 x 37 mm

DATEJUST / automatic, yellow gold and stainless steel bicolor case, 1991, Ref. 16283G, 12 x 34 mm

OYSTER PERPETUAL

Ref. 17000
DATEJUST / quartz movement, stainless steel case, 1978, Ref. 17000, 13 x 34 mm

Ref. 17013
DATEJUST / quartz movement, 18 karat yellow gild and stainless steel bicolor case, 1979, Ref. 17013, 13 x 34 mm

DATEJUST / quartz movement, 18 karat yellow gold and stainless steel bicolor case, 1991, Ref. 17013, 12.5 x 34.2 mm

Ref. 18033
DAY-DATE / automatic, 18 karat yellow gold case, 1980, Ref. 18033, 13 x 34 mm

Ref. 18038
DAY-DATE / automatic, yellow gold case, 1986, Ref. 18038, 13 x 34 mm

DAY-DATE / automatic, 18 karat yellow gold case, 1986, Ref. 18038, 13 x 34 mm

DAY-DATE / Jubilee band, 18 karat yellow gold case, 12.5 x 34.5 mm, Ref. 18038

DAY-DATE / "President" model, 18 karat yellow gold case and band, 10 indices set with diamonds, 13 x 34.5 mm, Ref. 18038

Ref. 18039
DAY-DATE / automatic, 18 karat yellow and white gold bicolor case, Ref. 18039, dial with 10 indices set with diamonds, 12.8 x 34.2 mm

DAY-DATE / automatic, yellow gold and stainless steel bicolor case, 1987, Ref. 18039BIC, 12 x 35 mm

Ref. 18078
DAY-DATE / automatic, 18 karat yellow gold case, 1986, Ref. 18078, 12.5 x 34.1 mm

Ref. 18108
DAY-DATE / automatic, 18 karat yellow gold case, 12 diamond on the lunette, 1986, Ref. 18108, 12.6 x 35 mm

Ref. 18206
DAY-DATE / automatic, platinum case, 1996, Ref. 18206A, 12.4 x 34.9 mm

Ref. 18238
DAY-DATE / automatic, 18 karat yellow gold case, 1989, Ref. 18238, 12.1 x 34.3 mm

DAY-DATE / automatic, 18 karat yellow gold case, 1991, Ref. 18238, mother-of-pearl color dial, 12 x 34 mm

DAY-DATE / automatic, 18 karat yellow gold case, Ref. 18238G, dial with 10 indices set with diamonds, 12.3 x 34.4 mm

DAY-DATE / automatic, 18 karat yellow gold case, 1990, Ref. 18238, 12 x 34 mm

DAY-DATE / automatic, yellow gold case, 1993, Ref. 18238, 12 x 34 mm

DAY-DATE / automatic, 18 karat yellow gold case, Ref. 18238, 12,3 x 34.3 mm

DAY-DATE / automatic, 18 karat yellow gold case, 1988, Ref. 18238A, dial with 10 indices set with diamonds, 12.1 x 34.5 mm

OYSTER PERPETUAL

DAY-DATE / automatic, 18 karat yellow gold case, 1987, Ref. 18238, 12.2 x 34.4 mm

DAY-DATE / automatic, 18 karat yellow gold case, 1993, Ref. 18238, 12.2 x 34.4 mm

DAY-DATE / automatic, 18 karat yellow gold case, 1991, Ref. 18238, 12 x 34 mm

DAY-DATE / automatic, 18 karat yellow gold case, 1995, 18238A, dial with 10 indices set with diamonds, 13 x 34 mm

DAY-DATE / automatic, 18 karat yellow gold case, 1991, Ref. 18238, 12 x 34 mm

Ref. 18239

DAY-DATE / automatic, white gold case, 1989, Ref. 18239, 12 x 34 mm

DAY-DATE / automatic, 18 karat white gold case, 1993, Ref. 18239, 12.2 x 34.4 mm

DAY-DATE / automatic, 18 karat white gold case, 1991, Ref. 18239, 12 x 34.2 mm

DAY-DATE / automatic, 18 karat white gold case, 1989, Ref. 18239, 12.3 x 34.5 mm

DAY-DATE / automatic, 18 karat yellow gold and stainless steel; bicolor case, 1990, Ref. 18239, dial with 10 indices set with diamonds, 12.2 x 34.3 mm

Ref. 18248   **Ref. 18348**

DAY-DATE / automatic, 18 karat yellow and white gold, 1989, Ref. 18239, dial with 10 indices set with diamonds, 12.1 x 34.4 mm

DAY-DATE / automatic, 18 karat yellow gold case, 1993, Ref. 18248, 12.2 x 34.3 mm

DAY-DATE / automatic, 18 karat yellow gold case, 1988, Ref. 18248, 12.1 x 34.4 mm

DAY-DATE / automatic, platinum case, diamond lunette, 1988, Ref. 18348A, 12.2 x 35 mm

DAY-DATE / automatic, 18 karat yellow gold case, diamond lunette, 1995, Ref. 18348A, 12.3 x 35.2 mm

Ref. 18388   **Ref. 19018**   **Ref. 50006**

DAY-DATE / automatic, 18 karat yellow gold case, 1991, Ref. 18348A, diamond lunette and 10 indices set with diamonds, 12.1 x 35.1 mm

DAY-DATE / automatic, 18 karat yellow gold case, case and dial set with diamonds, 1990, Ref. 18388, 12.1 x 35.4

DAY-DATE / quartz movement, 18 karat yellow gold case, 1986, Ref. 19018N, 12.9 x 34.9 mm

DAY-DATE / quartz movement, 18 karat yellow gold case, 1985, Ref. 19018, 12.8 x 34 mm

OYSTER PERPETUAL PRECISION / automatic, stainless steel case, 1950s, Ref. 50006, 13 x 29 mm

OYSTER PERPETUAL

Ref. 67180

OYSTER PERPETUAL / automatic, stainless steel case, 1993, Ref. 67180, 10 x 24 mm

Ref. 67480

OYSTER PERPETUAL / automatic, stainless steel case, 1990s, Ref. 67840, 11 x 29 mm

OYSTER PERPETUAL / medium size, automatic, stainless steel case, 1996, Ref. 67480, 10.3 x 29.3 mm

OYSTER PERPETUAL / medium size, automatic, stainless steel case, 1990s, Ref. 67480, 10.3 x 29.2 mm

OYSTER PERPETUAL / medium size, automatic, stainless steel case, 1996, Ref. 67480, 10.4 x 30.2 mm

OYSTER PERPETUAL / automatic, stainless steel case, 1990s, Ref. 67840, 11 x 30 mm

OYSTER PERPETUAL / medium size, automatic, stainless steel case, 1998, Ref. 67480, 10 x 29 mm

OYSTER PERPETUAL / medium size, automatic, stainless steel; case, 1996, Ref. 67480, 10 x 29 mm

OYSTER PERPETUAL / automatic, stainless steel case, 1990s, Ref. 67480, 10 x 29 mm

OYSTER PERPETUAL / automatic, stainless steel case, 1990, Ref. 67480, 10 x 29 mm

OYSTER PERPETUAL / automatic, stainless steel case, 1990s, Ref. 67480, 10 x 29 mm

OYSTER PERPETUAL / automatic, stainless steel case, 1993, Ref. 67480, 10 x 29 mm

Ref. 67483

OYSTER PERPETUAL / automatic, yellow gold and stainless steel bicolor case, 1991, Ref. 67483, 10 x 29 mm

Ref. 67513

OYSTER PERPETUAL / medium size, automatic, 18 karat yellow gold and stainless steel bicolor case, 1996, Ref. 67513, 10.3 x 29.1 mm

OYSTER PERPETUAL / medium size, automatic, 18 karat yellow gold and stainless steel bicolor case, 1991, Ref. 67513, 10.1 x 29.1 mm

Ref. 67514

OYSTER PERPETUAL / medium size, automatic, 18 karat white gold and stainless steel bicolor case, 1993, Ref. 67514, 10.2 x 29 mm

Ref. 68233

DATEJUST / automatic, 18 karat yellow gold and stainless steel bicolor case, 1996, Ref. 16233, 12.1 x 34.4 mm

Ref. 68240

DATEJUST / medium size, automatic, stainless steel case, 1998, Ref. 68240, 11 x 29.2 mm

DATEJUST / medium size, automatic, stainless steel case, 197, Ref. 68240, 10.9 x 29.2 mm

DATEJUST / automatic, stainless steel case, 1980s, 68240, 11 x 29 mm

OYSTER PERPETUAL

Ref. 68258

DATEJUST / automatic, 18 karat yellow gold case, 1995, Ref. 68258NGR, 11 x 30 mm

Ref. 68273

DATEJUST / medium size, automatic, 18 karat yellow gold and stainless steel case, 1985, Ref. 68273, 10.9 x 28.9 mm

DATEJUST / medium size, automatic, 18 karat yellow gold and stainless steel bicolor case, 1993, Ref. 68273, 10.9 x 29.1 mm

DATEJUST / medium size, automatic, 18 karat yellow gold and stainless steel bicolor case, 1998, Ref. 68273, 10.8 x 29.2 mm

DATEJUST / medium size, automatic, 18 karat yellow gold and stainless steel bicolor case, 1987, Ref. 68273G, dial with 10 indices set with diamonds, 10.8 x 29.2 mm

DATEJUST / medium size, automatic, 18 karat yellow gold and stainless steel bicolor case, Ref. 68273G, dial with 10 indices set with diamonds, 11 x 29 mm

DATEJUST / medium size, automatic, 18 karat yellow gold and stainless steel bicolor case, Ref. 68273G, dial with 10 indices set with diamonds, 10.5 x 29 mm

DATEJUST / medium size, automatic, 18 karat yellow gold and stainless steel bicolor case, 1994, Ref. 68273G, dial with 10 indices set with diamonds, 10.9 x 29 mm

DATEJUST / medium size, automatic, 18 karat yellow gold and stainless steel case, 1993, Ref. 68273G, dial with 10 indices set with diamonds, 10.8 x 29.5 mm

DATEJUST / medium size, automatic, 18 karat yellow gold and stainless steel bicolor case, 1988, Ref. 68273G, dial with 10 indices set with diamonds, 10.7 x 29 mm

DATEJUST / medium size, automatic, 18 karat yellow gold and stainless steel bicolor case, 1994, Ref. 68273G, dial with 10 indices set with diamonds, 10.7 x 29.1 mm

DATEJUST / automatic, 18 karat yellow gold and stainless steel bicolor case, 1993, Ref. 68273G, 11 x 29 mm

DATEJUST / automatic, 18 karat yellow gold and stainless steel bicolor case, 1995, Ref. 68273G, 11 x 29 mm

DATEJUST / automatic, yellow gold and stainless steel bicolor case, 1987, Ref. 68273G, 11 x 29 mm

DATEJUST / medium size, automatic, 18 karat yellow gold and stainless steel bicolor case, 1994, Ref. 68273, 11.1 x 29.2 mm

DATEJUST / medium size, automatic, 18 karat yellow gold and stainless steel bicolor case, 1986, Ref. 68273, 10.9 x 28.9 mm

DATEJUST / medium size, automatic, 18 karat yellow gold and stainless steel bicolor case, 1994, Ref. 68273, 10.8 x 29.2 mm

DATEJUST / medium size, automatic, 18 karat yellow gold and stainless steel bicolor case, 1991, Ref. 68273, 10.9 x 29.2 mm

DATEJUST / medium size, automatic, 18 karat yellow gold and stainless steel bicolor case, 1993, Ref. 68273, 10.8 x 29.1 mm

DATEJUST / medium size, automatic, 18 karat yellow gold and stainless steel bicolor case, 1987, Ref. 68273, 10.9 x 29.8 mm

OYSTER PERPETUAL

DATEJUST / medium size, automatic, 18 karat yellow gold and stainless steel bicolor case, 1988, Ref. 68273, 10.7 x 29.1 mm

DATEJUST / automatic, yellow gold and stainless steel bicolor case, 1990s, Ref. 68273, 11 x 29 mm

DATEJUST / automatic, yellow gold and stainless steel bicolor case, 1980s, Ref. 68273, 11 x 29 mm

DATEJUST / automatic, yellow gold and stainless steel bicolor case, 1990s, Ref. 68273, 11 x 29 mm

DATEJUST / automatic, yellow gold and stainless steel bicolor case, 1994, Ref. 68273, 11 x 29 mm

DATEJUST / automatic, white gold and stainless steel bicolor case, 1987, Ref. 68274, 11 x 29 mm

DATEJUST / medium size, automatic, white gold and stainless steel bicolor case, 1996, Ref. 68274, 10.7 x 29.2 mm

DATEJUST / medium size, automatic, 19 karat white gold and stainless steel bicolor case, 1996, Ref. 68274, 10.9 x 29 mm

DATEJUST / medium size, automatic, 18 karat white gold and stainless steel bicolor case, 1993, Ref. 68274G, dial with 10 indices set with diamonds, 10.9 x 29.1 mm

DATEJUST / automatic, white gold and stainless steel bicolor case, 1993, Ref. 68274, 11 x 29 mm

Ref. 68278

DATEJUST / medium size, automatic, 18 karat yellow gold case, dial with diamond ring, 11 x 29 mm

DATEJUST / automatic, 18 karat yellow gold case, Ref. 68278G, 11 x 35 mm

DATEJUST / automatic, 18 karat yellow gold case, 1990, Ref. 68278G, 11 x 29 mm

DATEJUST / automatic, 18 karat yellow gold case, 1980, Ref. 68278, 11 x 29 mm

DATEJUST / automatic, yellow gold case, 1985, Ref. 68278, 11 x 30 mm

Ref. 68279

DATEJUST / automatic, yellow gold case, 1986, Ref. 68278, 11 x 29 mm

DATEJUST / automatic, 18 karat white gold case, 1991, Ref. 68279, 11 x 29 mm

DATEJUST / automatic, gold case, 1985, Ref. 68279BICG, 11 x 29 mm

DATEJUST / automatic, yellow gold and stainless steel bicolor case, 1993, Ref. 68279BICG, dial with 10 indices set with diamonds, 11 x 30 mm

DATEJUST / 1988, Ref. 68279BICG, 11 x 29 mm

OYSTER PERPETUAL

Ref. 68519 | Ref. 69160 | Ref. 69173 | Ref. 69174

DATEJUST / automatic, white gold case, 2000, Ref. 68279, 11 x 29 mm

DATEJUST / automatic, 18 karat white gold case set with diamonds, 1991, Ref. 68519, diamond lunette, blue dial, 11 x 30 mm

DATE / automatic, stainless steel case, 1993, Ref. 69160, 11 x 25 mm

DATEJUST / automatic, yellow gold and stainless steel bicolor case, 1991, Ref. 69173, 11 x 25 mm

DATEJUST / automatic / white gold and stainless steel bicolor case, 1996, Ref. 69174, 11 x 25 mm

Ref. 69179

DATEJUST / automatic, white gold and stainless steel bicolor case, 1995, Ref. 69174, 11 x 29 mm

DATEJUST / automatic, white gold and stainless steel bicolor case, 1995, Ref. 69174G, 11 x 25 mm

DATEJUST / automatic, white gold and stainless steel bicolor case, 1998, Ref. 69174G, 11 x 23 mm

DATEJUST / automatic, white gold and stainless steel bicolor case, 1997, Ref. 69174, 11 x 24 mm

DATEJUST / automatic, yellow gold and stainless steel bicolor case, 1994, Ref. 69179BIC, 11 x 26 mm

Ref. 77080

OYSTER PERPETUAL / automatic, stainless steel case, 2003, Ref. 77080, 11 x 39 mm

OYSTER PERPETUAL / automatic, stainless steel case, 1999, Ref. 77080, 10 x 29 mm

OYSTER PERPETUAL / automatic, stainless steel case, 1990s, Ref. 77080, 10 x 29 mm

OYSTER PERPETUAL / automatic, stainless steel case, 2001, Ref. 77080, 10 x 29 mm

OYSTER PERPETUAL / automatic, stainless steel case, 2001, Ref. 77080, 10 x 29 mm

OYSTER PERENNIAL / automatic, stainless steel case, 2001, Ref. 77080, 10 x 29 mm

OYSTER PERPETUAL / good condition, automatic, stainless steel case, 1990s, Ref. 77080, 10 x 29 mm

OYSTER PERPETUAL / good condition, automatic, stainless steel case, 2003, Ref. 77080, 11 x 30 mm

OYSTER PERPETUAL / good condition, automatic, 2003, Ref. 77080, 11 x 30 mm

OYSTER PERPETUAL / good condition, automatic, stainless steel case, 2003, Ref. 77080, 11 x 30 mm

OYSTER PERPETUAL

Ref. 77483 **Ref. 78240** **Ref. 78274**

OYSTER PERPETUAL / good condition, automatic, stainless steel case, 2003, Ref. 77080, 11 x 30 mm

OYSTER PERPETUAL / medium size, automatic, 18 karat yellow gold and stainless steel bicolor case, 1999, Ref. 77483, 10.3 x 29.1 mm

DATEJUST / automatic, stainless steel case, 2001, Ref. 78240, 11 x 29 mm

DATEJUST / automatic, stainless steel case, 2003, Ref. 78240, 11 x 29 mm

DATEJUST / medium size, automatic, white gold and stainless steel bicolor case, 2001, Ref. 78274G, dial with 10 indices set with diamonds. 10.9 x 29.3 mm

Ref. 79174

DATEJUST / medium size, automatic, white gild and stainless steel bicolor case, 1999, Ref. 78274G, dial with 10 indices set with diamonds, 10.8 x 29.1 mm

DATEJUST / medium size, automatic, white gold and stainless steel bicolor case, 1990, Ref. 68274G, dial with 10 indices set with diamonds, 10.8 x 29.2 mm

DATEJUST / automatic, 18 karat white gold and stainless steel bicolor case, 2000, Ref. 79174, mother-of-pearl colored dial, 11 x 25 mm

DATEJUST / automatic, 18 karat white gold and stainless steel bicolor case, 2003, Ref. 79174, 11 x 25 mm

DATEJUST / automatic, 18 karat white gold and stainless steel bicolor case, 2003, Ref. 79174, 11 x 25 mm

Ref. 79179 **Ref. 81209** **Ref. 88239** **Ref. 118205**

DATEJUST / automatic, 18 karat white gold and stainless steel case, 2003, Ref. 79179, mother-of-pearl colored dial, 11 x 25 mm

DATEJUST / medium size, automatic, 18 karat white gold case, 2000, Ref. 81209, 11.4 x 32.3 mm, dial with 10 indices set with diamonds

DAY-DATE / automatic, 18 karat white and yellow gold bicolor case, dial with 10 indices set with diamonds, 1988, Ref. 88239, 12 x 34.4 mm

DAY-DATE / automatic, 18 karat red gold case, 2001, Ref. 118205, 12.5 x 35.3 mm

DAY-DATE / automatic, 18 karat yellow gold case, 2001, Ref. 11823G, dial with 10 indices set with diamonds, 12.3 x 35 mm

Ref. 118238 **Ref. 118239** **OTHER OYSTER PERPETUALS**

DAY-DATE / automatic, 18 karat red gold case, 2001, Ref. 118205, dial with 10 indices set with diamonds, 13 x 35 mm

DAY-DATE / automatic, red gold case, 2003, Ref. 118205A, dial with 10 indices set with diamonds, 13 x 40 mm

DAY-DATE / automatic, 18 karat yellow gold case, Ref. 118238A, dial with 10 indices set with diamonds, 13.3 x 35 mm

DAY-DATE / automatic, 18 karat white gold case, dial with 10 indices set with diamonds, 2001, Ref. 118239A, 12.4 x 36 mm

OYSTER PERPETUAL / stainless steel case, freshened-up dial, 11.5 x 33 mm

OYSTER PERPETUAL

OYSTER PERPETUAL / dealer's signature "Tiffany & Co", medium size, 11 x 28.5 mm

OYSTER PERPETUAL / stainless steel case, original matte white dial, gold indices, 12 x 33 mm

OYSTER PERPETUAL / very rare model with star indices, 18 karat yellow gold case

OYSTER PERPETUAL / 14 karat gold case, raised indices on black dial, 12 x 33 mm, 5 mm crown

OYSTER PERPETUAL / "Zephyr" model, simple dial with luminous dot indices, 13 x 33 mm

DATE / early model, band 20 mm wide, white dial, gilded indices and hands, 12.5 x 33.5 mm, 6 mm crown

DATEJUST / finely engraved case and band, guilloched black dial, 12 x 37 mm, 6 mm crown

DATE / older band, stainless steel and 14 karat yellow gold bicolor case, Dauphin hands, original dial, 12.5 x 33.5 mm

DATE / red date indication, stainless steel case, freshened-up dial, Cal. 6534, 1960s, 13 x 33 mm, 6 mm crown

DATE / 50th Anniversary model, case for quartz watches, 12.5 x 34.5 mm

DATEJUST / channeled lunette, stainless steel case and band, 12.5 x 34.5 mm

DATEJUST / with box and certificate, original dial with dealer's signature "Tiffany & Co", stainless steel case, 11 x 29.5 mm

DATEJUST / Thunderbird model, stainless steel and white gold bicolor case, 12 x 35 mm, 5 mm crown

DAY-DATE / very finely chased band attachments, raised bar indices, 12 x 34.5 mm, 6 mm crown

DAY-DATE / certificate, gold case, red dealer's signature "Tiffany & Co" on black dial, 13.5 x 34 mm

SUBMARINER

The Rolex watch with the Oyster case, developed in 1926, is absolutely and lastingly watertight. The next request was to improve it even more. After many experiments it was possible in 1953 to produce a high-value diver's watch, the so-called OYSTER SUBMARINER.

Its watertightness was then guaranteed to a depth of 100 meters, but had risen by 1954 to 200 meters. With Mercedes hands it was also clearly easier to read. The SEA-DWELLER of 1971 is watertight even to 610 meters; this was improved in the 1980s to a sensational 1220 meters. To this day the Submariner enjoys great popularity among watch fans and collectors.

Advertisement

Submariner catalog from 1958

SUBMARINER

Ref. 5508

SUBMARINER / automatic, stainless steel case, 1950s, Ref. 5508, 13 x 37.2 mm

SUBMARINER / automatic, stainless steel case, 1960, Ref. 5508, 13 x 37 mm

SUBMARINER / automatic, stainless steel case, 1960s, Ref. 5508, 13 x 37 mm

SUBMARINER / automatic, stainless steel case, Ref. 5508, 13 x 37 mm

SUBMARINER / automatic, stainless steel case, 1961, Ref. 5508, 13 x 37 mm

SUBMARINER / automatic, stainless steel case, 1950s, Ref. 5508, 12 x 37 mm

SUBMARINER / automatic, stainless steel case, 1950, Ref. 5508, 13 x 37 mm

SUBMARINER / Cal. 1530 adjusted in 5 positions, 18,000 half-swings, no date indication 1958, Ref. 5508, 13 x 37 mm

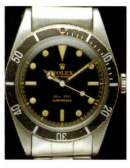

SUBMARINER / flatter than later model, for Italian market, no date indication, since 1958, Ref. 5508, 13 x 37 mm

SUBMARINER / no date indication or crown guard, watertight to 100 meters, made since 1958, Ref. 5508, 13 x 37 mm

SUBMARINER / lunette in good condition, no crown guard, watertight to 100 meters, 1950s, Ref. 5508, 12.5 x 37 mm

SUBMARINER / first model from 1950s, no crown guard, like-new case, Ref. 5508, Cal. 1530, 12.5 x 37.5 mm

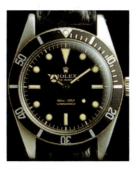

SUBMARINER / non-triplock crown, lunette without grooves, 1958, Ref. 5508, 12 x 37 mm

SUBMARINER / early model, no crown guard, watertight to 100 meters, original dial, 6 mm crown, 1950s, Ref. 5508. 13 x 37.5 mm

SUBMARINER / early model, watertight to 100 meters, case in like-new condition, 6 mm crown, 1950s, Ref. 5508, 12.5 x 37.5 mm

Ref. 5512

SUBMARINER / automatic, stainless steel case, 1970s, Ref. 5512, 15.4 x 39.1 mm

SUBMARINER / automatic, stainless steel case, 1970s, Ref. 5512, 14 x 39 mm

SUBMARINER / automatic, stainless steel case, 1972, Ref. 5512, 14 x 39 mm

SUBMARINER / automatic, stainless steel case, 1963, Ref. 5512, 15 x 39 mm

SUBMARINER / automatic, stainless steel case, 1963, Ref. 5512, 14 x 39 mm

SUBMARINER

SUBMARINER / automatic, stainless steel case, 1968, Ref. 5512, 13 x 40 mm

SUBMARINER / automatic, stainless steel case, 1964, Ref. 5512, 13.5 x 39 mm

SUBMARINER / automatic, stainless steel case, 1968, Ref. 5512, 14 x 38 mm

SUBMARINER / automatic, stainless steel case, 1950s, Ref. 5512, 15 x 38 mm

SUBMARINER / automatic, stainless steel case, 1970s, Ref. 5512, 15 x 38 mm

SUBMARINER / automatic, stainless steel case, 1961, Ref. 5512, 13 x 39 mm

SUBMARINER / automatic, stainless steel case, 1978, Ref. 5512, 13 x 40 mm

SUBMARINER / dealer's signature "Tiffany", chronometer without date indication, 1965, Ref. 5512, 14 x 39.5 mm

SUBMARINER / early model with crown guard, chronometer, no date indication, 1960s, Ref. 5512, 14 x 39.5 mm

SUBMARINER / chronometer without date indication, original dial, 1960s, Ref. 5512, 14 x 39.5 mm

Ref. 5513

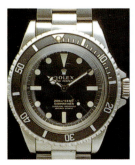    

SUBMARINER / Cal. 1570, chronometer version of Cal. 1520, 1960-77, Ref. 5512, 14.5 x 39.5 mm

SUBMARINER / chronometer, no date indication, "Tiffany" on the dial, Ref. 5512, 15 x 39.5 mm

SUBMARINER / automatic, stainless steel case, 1960s, Ref. 5513, 15.4 x 39.4 mm

SUBMARINER / automatic, stainless steel case, 1960s, Ref. 5513, 13 x 39 mm

SUBMARINER / automatic, stainless steel case, 1970, Ref. 5513, 13 x 39 mm

    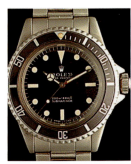

SUBMARINER / automatic, stainless steel case, 1985, Ref. 5513, 14 x 39 mm

SUBMARINER / automatic, stainless steel case, 1964, Ref. 5513, 14 x 39 mm

SUBMARINER / automatic, stainless steel case, 1988, Ref. 5513, 14 x 39 mm

SUBMARINER / automatic, stainless steel case, 1967, Ref. 5513, 14 x 39 mm

SUBMARINER / automatic, 1965, Ref. 5513, 13 x 40 mm

SUBMARINER

SUBMARINER / automatic, stainless steel case, 1978, Ref. 5513, 15 x 39 mm

SUBMARINER / automatic, stainless steel case, 1965, Ref. 5513, 14 x 39 mm

SUBMARINER / automatic, stainless steel case, 1964, Ref. 5513, 14 x 39 mm

SUBMARINER / automatic, stainless steel case, 1983, Ref. 5513, 14.5 x 39 mm

SUBMARINER / automatic, stainless steel case, 1980, Ref. 5513, 14.5 x 39 mm

SUBMARINER / automatic, stainless steel case, 1987, Ref. 5513, 14 x 39 mm

SUBMARINER / automatic, stainless steel case, 1970s, Ref. 5513, 15 x 38

SUBMARINER / automatic, stainless steel case, 1965, Ref. 5513, 13 x 39 mm

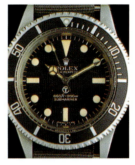
SUBMARINER / British Navy model, very legible tritium indices, "Broad Arrow" stamped on case bottom, Ref. 5513, 13 x 40 mm

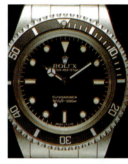
SUBMARINER / first model with triplock crown, arched plastic crystal, 1970s, Ref. 5513, 14 x 39.5 mm

SUBMARINER / chronometer without date indication, presumably 1960s, Ref. 5513, 14 x 39.5 mm

SUBMARINER / arched crystal, nicely overhauled, 1980s, Ref. 5513, 14 x 39.5 mm

SUBMARINER / "Comex" version has become very rare, arched plastic crystal, Ref. 5513, 14 x 39.5 mm

SUBMARINER / model with crown guard, no date indication, 1965-1970, Ref. 5513, 14.5 x 39.5 mm

SUBMARINER / no date indication, dealer's signature "Tiffany", arches crystal, Ref. 5513, 14.5 x 40 mm

SUBMARINER / Cal. 1520, no date indication, Ref. 5513, 1970s, 14.5 x 39.5 mm

SUBMARINER / arched crystal, no date indication, stainless steel case, 1981, Ref. 5513, 14 x 239.5 mm

SUBMARINER / plastic crystal, lunette turns to both sides, watertight to 300 meters, ca. 1985, Ref. 5513, 14 x 39.5 mm

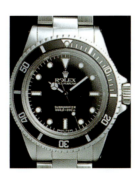
SUBMARINER / very good condition, no date indication, arched crystal, stainless steel case and band, 1968, Ref. 5513, 14 x 39.5 mm

SUBMARINER / circa 1985, Ref. 5513, 15 x 39.5 mm

SUBMARINER

SUBMARINER / no date indication, arched plastic crystal, Cal. 1520, late 1960s, Ref. 5513, 14 x 39.5 mm

SUBMARINER / early model, no depth indication, probably late 1950s, stainless steel case and band, Ref. 5513, 14.5 x 39.5 mm

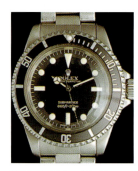

SUBMARINER / model without date indication, with arched crystal, original, 1960s, Cal. 1530, Ref. 5513, 14 x 39.5 mm

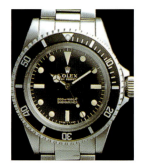

SUBMARINER / case and lunette in very good condition, stainless steel case and band, 1970s, Ref. 5513, 14.5 x 39 mm

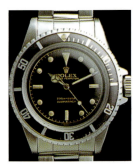

SUBMARINER / presumably 1960s, Ref. 5513, 15 x 39.5 mm

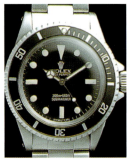

SUBMARINER / earlier model, watertight to 200 meters, freshened-up dial, stainless steel case, 1970s, Ref. 5513, 14.5 x 39 mm

SUBMARINER / arched crystal, 1967, Ref. 5513, a4 x 39.5 mm, stainless steel case

SUBMARINER / arched crystal, 1970s, Cal. 1520, Ref. 5513, 15 x 40 mm

SUBMARINER / luminous indices rimmed, Caliber 1520, 1970s, Ref. 5513, 15 x 39.5 mm

SUBMARINER / arched crystal, 1980s, Ref. 5513, 14.5 x 39.5 mm

SUBMARINER / luminous indices not rimmed, stainless steel case and band, original dial, Ref. 5513, 14 x 39.5 mm

SUBMARINER / original dial bears chronometer certificate, 1960s, Ref. 5513, 14 x 39.5 mm

SUBMARINER / arched crystal, 7 mm crown, Cal. 1570, Ref. 5513, 1970s, 14 x 39 mm

SUBMARINER / last model with Cal. 1520, arched crystal, 7 mm triplock crown, 18\980s, Ref. 5513, 15 x 39 mm

Ref. 5514

SUBMARINER / automatic, stainless steel case, 1969, Ref. 5514, 13 x 39 mm

Ref. 6200

SUBMARINER / early Comex version, no date indication, watertight to 200 meters, helium vent, Ref. 5514, 14 x 39.5 mm

SUBMARINER / very rare model with indices like Explorer I, characteristic red triangle by 12 in lunette, Ref. 6200, 1958, 16 x 37.5 mm

Ref. 6205

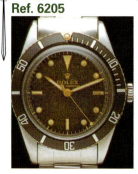

SUBMARINER / second model, built from 1953 to 1956, no crown guard, 6 mm crown, Cal A2 60, Ref. 6205, 13 x 38 mm

Ref. 6536

SUBMARINER / automatic, stainless steel case, 1957, Ref. 6536-1, 13 x 36 mm

SUBMARINER / automatic, stainless steel case, 1959, Ref. 6536-1, 13 x 37 mm

SUBMARINER

Ref. 6538

SUBMARINER / automatic, stainless steel case, 1950, Ref. 6536, 13 x 37 mm

SUBMARINER / automatic, stainless steel case, date indication with loupe, 1950s, Ref. 6536, 12 x 38 mm

SUBMARINER / second model, watertight to 100 meters, Cal. 1030, 1950s, 13 x 37.5 mm

SUBMARINER / early model, new caliber 1030 installed later, original box, made since 1957, Ref. 6536, 13 x 37 mm

SUBMARINER / automatic, stainless steel case, 1956, Ref. 6538, 15 x 37 mm

Ref. 14060

SUBMARINER / so-called "James Bond" model without crown guard, very rare early model, bicolor case, Ref. 6538, 15 x 37.5 mm

SUBMARINER / no crown guard, so-called "James Bond model", lunette with fine grooves, 1958, Ref. 6538, 16 x 37 mm

SUBMARINER / original crown 8 mm, no crown guard, watertight to 200 meters, 1950s, Cal. 1030, Ref. 6538, 15 x 37 mm

SUBMARINER / automatic, stainless steel case, 1994, Ref. 14060, 11 x 40 mm

SUBMARINER / automatic, stainless steel case, 1991, Ref. 14060, 13 x 39 mm

SUBMARINER / automatic, stainless steel case, 1999, Ref. 14060, 13 x 39 mm

SUBMARINER / automatic, stainless steel case, good condition, 2003, Ref. 14060M, 13 x 40 mm

SUBMARINER / automatic, stainless steel case, 1998, Ref. 14060, 11 x 39 mm

SUBMARINER DATE

SUBMARINER DATE

Ref. 1680

SUBMARINER / automatic, stainless steel case, 1971, Ref. 1680, 14.4 x 39.6 mm

SUBMARINER / automatic, stainless steel case, 1971, Ref. 1680, 14 x 38.4 mm

SUBMARINER / automatic, stainless steel case, 1980, Ref. 1680, 14 x 39.4 mm

SUBMARINER / automatic, stainless steel case, 1970s, Ref. 1680, 14 x 39.6 mm

SUBMARINER / automatic, stainless steel case, so-called "Red Sub", 1970, Ref. 1680, 13 x 39 mm

SUBMARINER / automatic, stainless steel case, 1969, Ref. 1680, 14 x 39 mm

SUBMARINER / automatic, stainless steel case, 1978, Ref. 1680, 14 x 39 mm

SUBMARINER / automatic, stainless steel case, 1970, Ref. 1680, 14 x 39 mm

SUBMARINER / automatic, stainless steel case, 1970, Ref. 1680, 14 x 39 mm

SUBMARINER / automatic, stainless steel case, 1980, Ref. 1680, 14 x 39 mm

SUBMARINER / automatic, stainless steel case, 1967, Ref. 1680, 14 x 39 mm

SUBMARINER / automatic, stainless steel case, date indication with loupe, Ref. 1680, 13 x 39 mm

SUBMARINER / automatic, stainless steel case, so-called "Red Sub", 1969, Ref. 1680, 14 x 39 mm

SUBMARINER / date indication with loupe, triplock crown, red Submariner signature, early 1970s, Ref. 1680, 14 x 39.5 mm

SUBMARINER / red Submariner signature, date indication with loupe, triplock crown, early 1970s, Ref. 1680, 14 x 39.5 mm

SUBMARINER / dealer's signature "Tiffany", date indication with loupe and triplock crown, Ref. 1680, 14 x 39.5 mm

SUBMARINER / chronometer model with date indication, original dial with dealer's signature "Tiffany", 1970s, Ref. 1680, 14 x 39 mm

SUBMARINER / "AMERICA CUP 1980 A.P. de YOUNG" engraved on case bottom, 1970s, Ref. 1680, 14.5 x 39.5 mm

SUBMARINER / red Submariner signature, triplock crown, Cal. 1570, stainless steel case, 1970s, Ref. 1680, 14 x 39 mm

SUBMARINER / red Submariner signature, date indication, Cal. 1570, chronometer, stainless steel case and band, 1970s, Ref. 1680, 14 x 39.5 mm

SUBMARINER DATE

SUBMARINER / red Submariner signature, same model as 7 but with original box and instructions, 1970s, Ref. 1680, 14 x 40 mm

SUBMARINER / red Submariner signature, in good condition, Cal. 1550, 1970s, Ref. 1680, original dial, 14 x 39.5 mm

SUBMARINER / red Submariner signature, with certificate and box, early 1970s, Ref. 1680, 14 x 39.5 mm

SUBMARINER / indices without rim, chronometer model with Cal. 1570, watertight to 200 meters, made until the seventies, Ref. 1680, 15 x 39.5 mm

SUBMARINER / red Submariner signature, indices without rim, Mercedes hands, original dial, 1970s, Ref. 1680, 14 x 39.5 mm

SUBMARINER / red Submariner signature, indices without rim, Mercedes hands, 1973, Ref. 1680, 13.5 x 39.5 mm

SUBMARINER / chronometer version with Cal. 1520, dealer's signature "Tiffany", 1960s, Ref. 1680, 14 x 39.5 mm

SUBMARINER / red Submariner signature, date indication with loupe, made from 1970 to 1974, Cal. 1575. Ref. 1680, 14 x 39.5 mm

SUBMARINER / original in good condition, 1980s, Cal. 1570, Ref. 1680, 14 x 39.5 mm

SUBMARINER / red Submariner signature, 1970s, Cal. 1570, date indication with loupe, stainless steel case, Ref. 1680, 14 x 39 mm

SUBMARINER / black dial, date indication with loupe, original stainless steel case, 1977, Ref. 1680, 14 x 39.5 mm

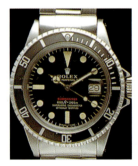
SUBMARINER / red Submariner signature, 1970s, Cal. 1575, Ref. 1680, 13 x 39.5 mm

SUBMARINER model with date indication and loupe, 1970s, Cal. 1570, Ref. 1680, 15 x 39.5 mm

SUBMARINER / red Submariner signature, dial in good condition, 1970s, Ref. 1680, 14 x 39.5 mm

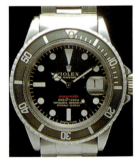
SUBMARINER / red Submariner signature, date indication, Cal. 1570, dial in good condition, 1968, Ref. 1680, 14 x 39.5 mm

SUBMARINER / red Submariner signature, original 1970s dial, Ref. 1680, stainless steel case, 14 x 39.5 mm

SUBMARINER / red Submariner signature, stainless steel case and band, Cal. 1570, Ref. 1680, 14 x 39.5 mm

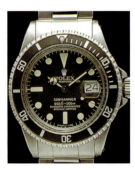
SUBMARINER / model with date indication and loupe, stainless steel case and band, 1970s, Cal. 1575, Ref. 1680, 14 x 39.5 mm

SUBMARINER / original dial, red Submariner signature, watertight to 200 meters, triplock crown, 1970s, Cal. 1570, Ref. 1680, 14.5 x 39.5 mm

SUBMARINER / date indication with loupe, triplock crown, watertight to 200 meters, 1973, Ref. 1680, 14 x 39.5 mm

SUBMARINER DATE

Ref. 16610

SUBMARINER / original dial with dealer's signature "Tiffany", triplock crown, late 1970s, Ref. 1680, 14.5 x 39.5 mm

SUBMARINER / presumably made for a client, blue dial, 18 karat white gold case, 1970s, Ref. 1680, 14.5 x 39.5 mm, 7 mm crown

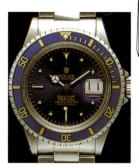
SUBMARINER / original light blue dial, blue lunette. Chronometer movement with Cal. 1570, 1970s, Ref. 1680, 14 x 39.5 mm

SUBMARINER / automatic, stainless steel case, 1988, Ref. 16610, 13 x 40 mm

SUBMARINER / automatic, stainless steel case, 1990s, Ref. 16610, 13 x 40 mm

SUBMARINER / automatic, stainless steel case, 1990s, Ref. 16610, 13 x 40 mm

SUBMARINER / automatic, date indication with loupe, 1996, Ref. 16610, 11 x 40 mm

SUBMARINER / automatic, stainless steel case, 2001, Ref. 16610, 13 x 41 mm

SUBMARINER / automatic, 2000, Ref. 16610, 13 x 40 mm

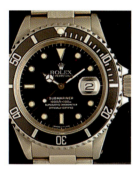
SUBMARINER / automatic, stainless steel case, 2001, Ref. 16610, 13 x 41 mm

SUBMARINER / automatic, stainless steel case, 1989, Ref. 16610, 13 x 40 mm

SUBMARINER / automatic, stainless steel case, 1999, Ref. 16610, 13 x 40 mm

SUBMARINER / automatic, stainless steel case, date indication with loupe, 1996, Ref. 16610, 13 x 40 mm

SUBMARINER / good condition, stainless steel case, date indication with loupe, 2003, Ref. 16610, 13 x 40 mm

SUBMARINER / automatic, stainless steel case, 1991, Ref. 16610, 13 x 40 mm

SUBMARINER / automatic, stainless steel case, 1992, Ref. 16610, 13 x 40 mm

SUBMARINER / automatic, stainless steel case, 2000, Ref. 16610, 13 x 40 mm

SUBMARINER / automatic, stainless steel case, date indication with loupe, 1998, Ref. 16610, 13 x 40 mm

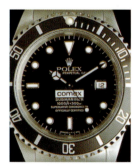
SUBMARINER / signed "Comex" (a French diving equipment firm) on dial, with box and certificate, 1990s, Ref. 16610, 13 x 40 mm

SUBMARINER / signed "Cartier", lapis lazuli dial, stainless steel case, 1980s, Ref. 16610, 13 x 40 mm

SUBMARINER DATE

Ref. 16613

SUBMARINER / date indication with loupe, dealer's signature "Tiffany", Ref. 16610, 12 x 40 mm

SUBMARINER / automatic, bicolor yellow gold and stainless steel case, 1990a, Ref. 16613, 13 x 40 mm

SUBMARINER / automatic, yellow gold and stainless steel bicolor case, date indication with loupe, 993, Ref. 16613, 11 x 40 mm

SUBMARINER / automatic, yellow gold and stainless steel bicolor case, date indication with loupe, Ref. 16613SG, dial with 8 indices set with diamonds, 11 x 41 mm

SUBMARINER / automatic, yellow gold and stainless steel bicolor case, date indication with loupe, 2000, Ref. 16613, 11 x 41 mm

SUBMARINER / automatic, 18 karat yellow gold and stainless steel bicolor case, 1990, Ref. 16613, 13 x 40 mm

SUBMARINER / automatic, 18 karat yellow gold and stainless steel bicolor case, 2001, Ref. 16613, 13 x 40 mm

SUBMARINER / automatic, 18 karat yellow gold and stainless steel bicolor case, 1988, Ref. 16613, 13 x 40 mm

SUBMARINER / automatic, 18 karat gold and stainless steel bicolor case, 1993, Ref. 16613, 13 x 40 mm

SUBMARINER / automatic, yellow gold and stainless steel bicolor case, date indication with loupe, 1990, Ref. 16613, 13 x 40 mm

Ref. 16618

SUBMARINER / automatic, 18 karat yellow gold and stainless steel bicolor case, 1991, Ref. 16613, 13 x 40 mm

SUBMARINER / automatic, 18 karat yellow gold and stainless steel bicolor case, date indication with loupe, 1994, Ref. 16613, 13 x 40 mm

SUBMARINER / automatic, 18 karat yellow gold and stainless steel bicolor case, date indication with loupe, 1995, Ref. 16613, 13 x 40 mm

SUBMARINER / automatic, 18 karat yellow gold case, Ref. 16618, 12.5 x 40 mm

SUBMARINER / automatic, yellow gold case, date indication with loupe, 1993, Ref. 16618, 11 x 40 mm

Ref. 16800

SUBMARINER / automatic, yellow gold case, date indication with loupe, 1991, Ref. 16618, 11 x 40 mm

SUBMARINER / automatic, 18 karat yellow gold case, 1991, Ref. 16618, 13 x 40 mm

SUBMARINER / automatic, 18 karat yellow gold case, date indication with loupe, 1991, Ref. 16618, 12 x 40 mm

SUBMARINER / automatic, stainless steel case, 1982, Ref. 16800, 12.8 x 40 mm

SUBMARINER/ automatic, stainless steel case, 1980s, Ref. 16800, 13 x 40 mm

SUBMARINER DATE

SUBMARINER / automatic, stainless steel case, 1980s, Ref. 16800, 13 x 40 mm

SUBMARINER / automatic, stainless steel case, 1981, Ref. 16800, 13 x 39 mm

SUBMARINER / automatic, stainless steel case, 1986, Ref. 16800, 13 x 40 mm

SUBMARINER / automatic, stainless steel case, 1983, Ref. 16800, 13 x 40 mm

SUBMARINER / automatic, stainless steel case, 1985, Ref. 16800, 13 x 37 mm

SUBMARINER / automatic, stainless steel case, 1987, Ref. 16800, 13 x 40 mm

SUBMARINER / automatic, stainless steel case, 1983, Ref. 16800, 13 x 40 mm

SUBMARINER / automatic, stainless steel case, 1987, Ref. 16800, 13 x 40 mm

SUBMARINER / automatic, stainless steel case, 1980s, Ref. 16800, 12 x 40 mm

Ref. 16808

SUBMARINER / automatic, 18 karat yellow gold case, 1980, Ref. 16808, 12.4 x 40 mm

OTHER SUBMARINERS

SUBMARINER / chronometer with rimless indices, no date indication, dealer's signature "Tiffany", 1960s, 14.5 x 39.5 mm

SUBMARINER / standard model, no date indication, with triplock crown and crown guard, watertight to 200 meters, 1970s, 14 x 39.5 mm

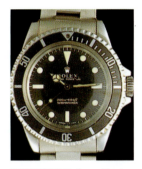
SUBMARINER / indices without frames, stainless steel case and band, original dial, 1960s, 14.5 x 39 mm

SUBMARINER / standard model, date indication with loupe, watertight to 200 meters, stainless steel case, 1970s, 14.5 x 39.5 mm

SUBMARINER / in good condition, date indication, original dial, stainless steel case, 15 x 39.5 mm

SUBMARINER / early model, no date indication, arched crystal, original dial, stainless steel case and band, watertight to 200 meters, 14 x 39.5 mm

SUBMARINER, first model with crown guard, very rare model, chronometer, no date indication, dealer's signature "Tiffany", 13.5 x 40 mm

SUBMARINER / stainless steel, 1960s, 13 x 39.5 mm

SEA-DWELLER

The Sea-Dweller Submariner, developed for deep-sea divers, is filled with helium gas. The reason is that until 1964 the glass was often damaged by overly high air pressure.

Rolex catalog from 1996

SEA-DWELLER

Ref. 1665

First SEA-DWELLER of the 1980s, no loupe, but a helium vent. Ref. 1665 Cal. 1570 1980s.

SEA-DWELLER / automatic, stainless steel case, 1970s, Ref. 1665, 16 x 39 mm

SEA-DWELLER / automatic, stainless steel case, 1977, Ref. 1665, 17 x 39 mm

SEA-DWELLER / automatic, stainless steel case, 1979, Ref. 1665, 17 x 39.3 mm

SEA-DWELLER / automatic, stainless steel case, 1970s, Ref. 1665, 17.5 x 39.5 mm

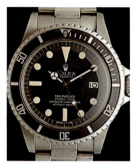
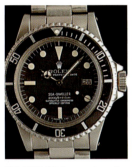

SEA-DWELLER / automatic, stainless steel case, 1970, Ref. 1665, 16 x 39 mm

SEA-DWELLER / automatic, stainless steel case, 1970s, Ref. 1665, 16 x 39 mm

SEA-DWELLER / automatic, stainless steel case, 1970s, Ref. 1665, 15 x 39 mm

SEA-DWELLER / automatic, stainless steel case, 1979, Ref. 1665, 17 x 39 mm

SEA-DWELLER / automatic, stainless steel case, 1978, Ref. 1665, 16 x 39 mm

SEA-DWELLER / automatic, stainless steel case, 1968, Ref. 1665, 16 x 39 mm

SEA-DWELLER / automatic, stainless steel case, 1977, Ref. 1665, 17 x 35 mm

SEA-DWELLER / automatic, stainless steel case, 1974, Ref. 1665, 17 x 39 mm

SEA-DWELLER / automatic, stainless steel case, 1980s, Ref. 1665, 17 x 39 mm

SEA-DWELLER / automatic, stainless steel case, 1981, Ref. 1665, 17 x 39 mm

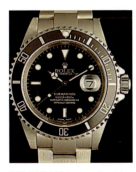

SEA-DWELLER / automatic, stainless steel case, 1970s, Ref. 1665, 15 x 39 mm

SEA-DWELLER / automatic, stainless steel case, 1979, Ref. 1665, 16 x 39 mm

SEA-DWELLER / automatic, stainless steel case, 1977, Ref. 1665, 15 x 39 mm

SEA-DWELLER / automatic, stainless steel case, 1978, Ref. 1665, 15 x 40 mm

SEA-DWELLER / automatic, stainless steel case, so-called "Red Sea D", 1979, Ref. 1665, 15 x 39 mm

SEA-DWELLER

SEA-DWELLER / relatively flat case, watertight to 500 meters, prototype, 1960s, Ref. 1665, 15 x 39.5 mm

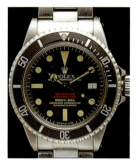
SEA-DWELLER / original dial, red Sea-Dweller and Submariner signature, Cal. 1575, Ref. 1665, 1970s, 17 x 39.5 mm

SEA-DWELLER / original dial, stainless steel case and band, arched crystal, 7 mm crown, Ref. 1665, 17 x 39.5 mm

SEA-DWELLER / red Sea-Dweller and Submariner signature, hands replaced, 1979, Ref. 1665, 17 x 39.5 mm

SEA-DWELLER / arched crystal, original dial, stainless steel case and band, 1980s, Ref. 1665, 15 x 39.5 mm

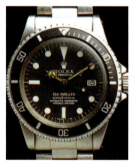
SEA-DWELLER / early model with arched crystal, 1970s, Ref. 1665, 7 mm crown, 17.5 x 39.5 mm

SEA-DWELLER / date indication, no loupe, with certificate, 1970s, Ref. 1665, 16.5 x 39.5 mm

SEA-DWELLER / 7 mm triplock crown, 1970s, Ref. 1665, 17 x 38.5 mm

SEA-DWELLER / red Sea-Dweller and Submariner signature, original dial, hands replaced, 1970s, Ref. 1665, 12 x 39.5 mm

SEA-DWELLER / flat crystal, 1980, Ref. 1665, 12 x 39.5 mm

SEA-DWELLER / 1960s, Ref. 1665, 17 x 40 mm

SEA-DWELLER / red Sea-Dweller and Submariner signature, made only briefly, 7 mm crown, 1970s, Ref. 1665, 17 x 39.5 mm

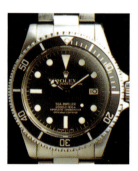
SEA-DWELLER / last Ref. 1665 model, watertight to 610 meters, stainless steel case and band, 7 mm crown, 1980s, 16.5 x 39.5 mm

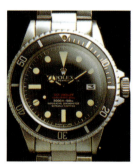
SEA-DWELLER / red Sea-Dweller and Submariner signature, original dial, 1970s, Ref. 1665, 17.5 x 39.5 mm

SEA-DWELLER / red Sea-Dweller and Submariner signature, produced only briefly, completely original, 1975, Ref. 1665, 16.5 x 39.5 mm

SEA-DWELLER / luminous tritium indices, 7 mm triplock crown, Ref. 1665, 17.5 x 39.5 mm

SEA-DWELLER / early model with Cal. 1570, Ref. 1665, 1970s, 16.5 x 39.5 mm

SEA-DWELLER / original dial with dealer's signature "Tiffany", 1970s, Cal. 1570, Ref. 1665, 16.5 x 39.5 mm

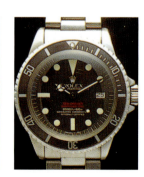
SEA-DWELLER / red Sea-Dweller and Submariner signature, Cal. 1575, 17 x 39.5 mm

SEA-DWELLER / additionally signed "submariner", typical earlier model, 1970s, Ref. 1665, 16.5 x 39.5 mm

SEA-DWELLER

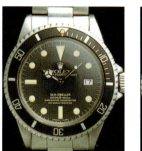

Ref. 16600

SEA-DWELLER / early model, watertight to 610 meters, helium vent on left side, 1970s, Ref. 1665, 17.5 x 39.5 mm

SEA-DWELLER / arched crystal, dealer's signature "Tiffany", 1960s, 16.5 x 37 mm

SEA-DWELLER / automatic, stainless steel case, 1999, Ref. 16600, 15 x 39 mm

SEA-DWELLER / automatic, stainless steel case, 1994, Ref. 16600, 14.7 x 39.4 mm

SEA-DWELLER / automatic, stainless steel case, 1990s, Ref. 16600, 15 x 39 mm

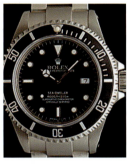

SEA-DWELLER / automatic, stainless steel case, 1990s, Ref. 16600, 15 x 39 mm

SEA-DWELLER / automatic, stainless steel case, 1980s, Ref. 16600, 15 x 39 mm

SEA-DWELLER / automatic, stainless steel case, 1990s, Ref. 16600, 15 x 39 mm

SEA-DWELLER / automatic, stainless steel case, 1996, Ref. 16600, 13 x 39 mm

SEA-DWELLER / automatic, stainless steel case, 2001, Ref. 16600, 12 x 36 mm

SEA-DWELLER / automatic, stainless steel case, 2001, Ref. 16600, 15 x 39 mm

SEA-DWELLER / automatic, stainless steel case, 1991, Ref. 16600, 15 x 39 mm

SEA-DWELLER / automatic, stainless steel case, 1999, Ref. 16600, 14 x 39 mm

SEA-DWELLER / automatic, stainless steel case, 1994, 16600, 14 x 39 mm

SEA-DWELLER / automatic, stainless steel case, 1998, Ref. 16600, 14 x 39 mm

Ref. 16660

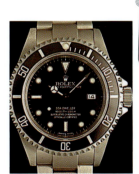
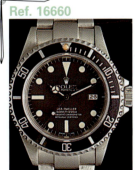

SEA-DWELLER / automatic, stainless steel case, 2003, Ref. 16600, 15 x 39 mm

SEA-DWELLER / automatic, stainless steel case, 2000, Ref. 16600, 15 x 40 mm

SEA-DWELLER / automatic, stainless steel case, 1968, Ref. 16660, 15 x 39 mm

SEA-DWELLER / automatic, stainless steel case, 1986, Ref. 16660, 15 x 39 mm

SEA-DWELLER / Comex model No. 3155, with box and certificate, 1983, Ref. 16660, 15 x 39.5 mm

YACHT-MASTER

The Yacht-Master came onto the market in 1992. In 1999 the Yacht-Master "ROLESIUM", fitted with a platinum lunette, was introduced at the Basel Fair.

YACHT-MASTER

Ref. 16622

Ref. 16628

YACHT-MASTER / so-called "Rolesium", automatic, platinum and stainless steel bicolor case, 2001, Ref. 16622, 12 x 40 mm

YACHT-MASTER / so-called "Rolesium", automatic, platinum and stainless steel bicolor case, 2003, Ref. 16622, 12 x 40 mm

YACHT-MASTER / so-called "Rolesium", automatic, platinum and stainless steel bicolor case, 1997, Ref. 16622, 12 x 40 mm

YACHT-MASTER / automatic, platinum and stainless steel bicolor case, 2000, Ref. 16622, 12 x 40 mm

YACHT-MASTER / automatic, 18 karat yellow gold case, 1994, 16628, 11.8 x 40 mm

Ref. 68628

YACHT-MASTER / automatic, yellow gold case, 1997, Ref. 16628B, 11 x 40 mm

YACHT-MASTER / automatic, yellow gold case, 1994, Ref. 16628, 11 x 40 mm

YACHT-MASTER / automatic, 18 karat yellow gold case, 1994, Ref. 16628, 12 x 40 mm

YACHT-MASTER / medium size, automatic, 18 karat yellow gold case, 1995, Ref. 68628, 10.9 x 34 mm

YACHT-MASTER / medium size, automatic, 18 karat yellow gold case, 1996, Ref. 68628, 11 x 25 mm

Ref. 69623

Ref. 168622

Ref. 168623

YACHT-MASTER / automatic, yellow gold and stainless steel bicolor case, 1997, Ref. 69623, 10 x 28 mm

YACHT-MASTER / medium size, automatic, 18 karat yellow gold and stainless steel bicolor case, Ref. 69623, 12 x 40 mm

YACHT-MASTER / medium size, automatic, 18 karat yellow gold and stainless steel bicolor case, 1998, Ref. 69623, 11 x 28 mm

YACHT-MASTER / so-called "Rolesium", medium size, automatic, platinum and stainless steel bicolor case, Ref. 168622, 11 x 33 mm

YACHT-MASTER / 18 karat yellow gold and stainless steel bicolor case, 1999, Ref. 168623, 11 x 34 mm

EXPLORER

When one hears the word "EXPLORER", one immediately thinks of the "EXPLORER I". But there are other models that bear the "EXPLORER" name. In general, the different varieties of the Explorer are much desired in the used-watch market. The Explorer with the fixed lunette, that came on the market in 1953, was then the only model in the Rolex sport-watch category. The Boy's Size with black or ivory dial, made for the North American market, is a rarity. The standard model has a black dial and Mercedes hand, and was made without a date until 1971. In 1972 there came the Explorer II, which had been fitted with date indication, 14-hour hand and a turning lunette. The Explorer II was made with an ivory dial only in 1988 and 1989.

Advertisement

EXPLORER

EXPLORER I
Ref. 1016

EXPLORER / good condition, automatic, stainless steel case, 1970s, Ref. 1016, 13 x 34.8 mm

EXPLORER / automatic, stainless steel case, 1960s, Ref. 1016, 12.9 x 35.1 mm

EXPLORER / automatic, stainless steel case, 1970s, Ref. 1016, 12.5 x 36 mm

EXPLORER / automatic, stainless steel case, 1979, Ref. 1016, 12.4 x 34.7 mm

EXPLORER / automatic, stainless steel case, 1960s, Ref. 1016, 12 x 35 mm

EXPLORER / automatic, stainless steel case, 1972, Ref. 1016, 13 x 35 mm

EXPLORER / automatic, stainless steel case, 1950s, Ref. 1016, 12 x 35 mm

EXPLORER / automatic, stainless steel case, 1984, Ref. 1016, 12 x 35 mm

EXPLORER / automatic, stainless steel case, 1973, Ref. 1016, 12 x 35 mm

EXPLORER / automatic, stainless steel case, 1989, Ref. 1016, 12 x 35 mm

EXPLORER / automatic, stainless steel case, 1964, Ref. 1016, 13 x 35 mm

EXPLORER / automatic, stainless steel case, 1956, Ref. 1016, 13 x 35 mm

EXPLORER / automatic, stainless steel case, 1974, Ref. 1610, 9 x 32 mm

EXPLORER / automatic, stainless steel case, 1970, Ref. 1016, 11.5 x 35 mm

EXPLORER / automatic, stainless steel case, 1965, Ref. 1016, 12 x 35 mm

EXPLORER / automatic, stainless steel case, 1966, Ref. 1016, 12 x 35 mm

EXPLORER / automatic, stainless steel case, 1971, Ref. 1016, 12 x 35 mm

EXPLORER I / index without rim, large Arabic numerals, 1980s, Ref. 1016, 12.5 x 35.5 mm

EXPLORER I / late model, 1984-85, Ref. 1016, 12 x 35 mm

EXPLORER I / watertight to 10 atm., Cal. 1560, Ref. 1016, 12.5 x 35 mm

EXPLORER I

EXPLORER I / Mercedes hands, black dial, luminous paint, 1960s, Ref. 1016, 13 x 35 mm

EXPLORER I / last Ref. 1016 model, 1980s, Cal. 1575, 12 x 35 mm

EXPLORER I / second stop, 1970s, Ref. 1016, 12 x 35 mm

EXPLORER I / dealer's signature "Tiffany", rare model, 1970s, Ref. 1016, 13.5 x 35.5 mm

EXPLORER I / white numerals and indices, 1964, Ref. 1016, 12.5 x 35 mm

EXPLORER I / signed "Cartier", very rare model, Ref. 1016, 12.5 x 35 mm

EXPLORER I / arched plastic crystal, 1960s, Cal. 1560, Ref. 1016, 12 x 35 mm

EXPLORER I / original certificate and box, 1970s, Cal. 1570, Ref. 1016, 13 x 35 mm

EXPLORER I / 1970s, Cal. 1560, Ref. 1016, 12 x 35 mm

EXPLORER I / 1964, Cal. 1560, Ref. 1016, 12 x 35 mm

EXPLORER I / special fine regulation, 1960s, Ref. 1016, 12 x 35 mm

EXPLORER I / second stop, stainless steel case, 1960s, Cal. 1570, Ref. 1016, 12 x 35 mm

EXPLORER I / early model, enlarged dial, 1960s, Ref. 1016, 12 x 35 mm

EXPLORER I / later model with second stop, watertight to 10 atm., Cal. 1570, 1970s, Ref. 1016, 12 x 35.5 mm

EXPLORER I / last model with Cal. 1575 and Ref. 1016, original box and certificate, 1985, 12.5 x 35 mm

EXPLORER I / "T < 25" means little tritium in the luminous matter, 1960s, Ref. 1016, 12.5 x 35 mm

EXPLORER I / faded indices, 1961, Ref. 1016, 12 x 35 mm

EXPLORER I / case kept in faultless condition with new parts, 1970s, Ref. 1016, 12.5 x 35.5 mm

EXPLORER I / early model, Ref. 1016, faded indices, 1964, 12 x 35 mm

EXPLORER I / second stop, 1970s, Cal. 1570, Ref. 1016, 12 x 35 mm

EXPLORER I

EXPLORER I / last Ref. 1016 model, perfect condition, with box and certificate, 1980s, 12 x 35 mm

EXPLORER I / last Ref. 1016 model, simple dial, with certificate, 1986, 12.5 x 35 mm

EXPLORER I / stainless steel case and lunette, made between 1960s and 1980s, Ref. 1016, 12.5 x 35 mm

EXPLORER I / last Ref. 1016 model, very good condition, 1988, 12 x 35 mm

EXPLORER I / Cal. 1560 without second stop, dial in good condition, 1960s, Ref. 1016, 12 x 35 mm

EXPLORER I / combination of gold indices and Jubilee band, 1960s, Ref. 1016, 12 x 35 mm

EXPLORER I / with box and certificate, 1960s, Ref. 1016, 12.5 x 35 mm

SPACE DWELLER / Explorer model, signed "Space Dweller", sold to test the market in Japan, 1960s, Ref. 1016, 12.5 x 35 mm

EXPLORER I / dealer's signature "Tiffany & Co", stainless steel case, 1960s, Ref. 1016, 12 x 35 mm

EXPLORER I / dealer's signature "Tiffany & Co", 1970s, Ref. 1016, 12.5 x 35 mm

EXPLORER I / black dial with white indices, 1970s, Ref. 1016, 12.5 x 35.5 mm

EXPLORER I / first model with second stop, original box, 1972, Ref. 1016, Cal. 1570, 12.5 x 34.5 mm

Ref. 1038

EXPLORER I / very rare model for Canadian market, gold lunette, two-tone dial, 1967, Ref. 1038, 12 x 33.5 mm

Ref. 1560

EXPLORER I / arched plastic crystal, stainless steel case, 1959, Cal. 1560, Ref. 1016, 13 x 35 mm

Ref. 5500

EXPLORER / medium size, automatic, stainless steel case, 1960s, Ref. 5500, 11.4 x 34 mm

EXPLORER / medium size, automatic, stainless steel case, 1960s, Ref. 5500, 11.9 x 34 mm

EXPLORER I / medium size, small dial, typically not chronometer, Ref. 5500, 11 x 33 mm

EXPLORER / for Canadian market, white dial with wedge indices, 1960s, Ref. 5500, 12 x 35.5 mm

EXPLORER I for Canadian market, freshened-up dial, medium size, years unknown, Ref. 5500, 12 x 33 mm

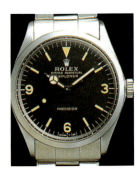

EXPLORER I / made for the English market, originally medium size, 1950s and 1970s, Ref. 5500, 12 x 33 mm

EXPLORER I

Ref. 5501

EXPLORER / medium size, automatic, 18 karat yellow gold and stainless steel bicolor case, 1950s, Ref. 5501, 12.5 x 34 mm

EXPLORER / developed for the Canadian market, 14 karat yellow gold lunette, Ref. 5501, Cal. 1530, 12 x 32.5 mm

EXPLORER / for Canadian market, 14 karat gold lunette, leaf hands, 1950s, Ref. 5501, 12.5 x 32.5 mm

EXPLORER II / rare gold lunette, Ref. 5501, 12 x 32.5 mm

Ref. 5504

EXPLORER I / freshened-up dial, Ref. 5504, 12.5 x 34.5 mm

Ref. 5506

Ref. 6298

Ref. 6305

EXPLORER I / prototype of this model in chronometer form, Ref. 5504, 12.5 x 34.5 mm

EXPLORER I / Jubilee band, 1950s, Ref. 5504, 12 x 34.5 mm

EXPLORER / automatic, gilded case, 1960s, Ref. 5506, 12 x 33 mm

EXPLORER / for Canadian market, guilloched dial, 1960s, Ref. 6298, 13.5 x 34.5 mm

EXPLORER I / faded guilloched dial, red Explorer signature, for the Canadian market, 1956, Ref. 6305, 13 x 34 mm

Ref. 6350

Ref. 6610

EXPLORER I / first Ref. 6350 model, very rare piece with arched plastic crystal, 1950s, 13 x 34.5 mm

EXPLORER / automatic, stainless steel case, 1959, Ref. 6610, 35 mm

EXPLORER / automatic, stainless steel case, 1950s, Ref. 6610, 11 x 35 mm

EXPLORER I / black dial, gold indices, Oyster band, Ref. 6610, 12 x 35 mm

EXPLORER I / added red signature "50 m, 165 ft", 1960s, Ref. 6610, 13 x 34.5 mm

EXPLORER I / faded luminous indices, 1970s, Ref. 6610, 12 x 35 mm

EXPLORER I / back dial, golden indices, Mercedes hands, 1950s, Cal. 1030, Ref. 6610, 13 x 35 mm

EXPLORER I / faded luminous indices, 1960s, Ref. 6610, 13 x 34.5 mm

EXPLORER I / winding rotor works in both directions from this model on, back of case bottom is flat, 1950s, Cal. 1030, Ref. 6610, 13 x 34.5 mm

EXPLORER I / very rare model with Arabic 12, other wedge indices, freshened-up dial, 1950s, Ref. 6610, 12.5 x 34.5 mm

EXPLORER I

Ref. 14270

EXPLORER I / dial in very good condition, 1960s, Ref. 6610, 13 x 35 mm

EXPLORER / original with lengthening band, 1958, Ref. 6610, 13 x 35 mm

EXPLORER / automatic, stainless steel case, 1999, Ref. 14270, 11.7 x 34.9 mm

EXPLORER / automatic, stainless steel case, 1994, Ref. 14270, 11.7 x 34.9 mm

EXPLORER / automatic, stainless steel case, 2000s, Ref. 14270, 11.6 x 35 mm

EXPLORER / automatic, stainless steel case, 2000, Ref. 14270, 10 x 35 mm

EXPLORER / automatic, stainless steel case, 2001, Ref. 14270, 12 x 36 mm

EXPLORER / automatic, stainless steel case, 1998, Ref. 14270, 12 x 35 mm

EXPLORER / automatic, stainless steel case, 1994, Ref. 14270, 12 x 35 mm

EXPLORER / automatic, stainless steel case, 1999, Ref. 14270, 12 x 35 mm

EXPLORER / automatic, stainless steel case, 2001, Ref. 14270, 12 x 35 mm

EXPLORER / automatic, stainless steel case, 1999, Ref. 14270, 12 x 35 mm

EXPLORER / automatic, stainless steel case, 1991, Ref. 14270, 11 x 35 mm

EXPLORER / automatic, stainless steel case, 2999, Ref. 14270, 12 x 35 mm

EXPLORER / automatic, stainless steel case, 1991, Ref. 14270, 11 x 35 mm

EXPLORER / automatic, stainless steel case, 1999, Ref. 14270, 12 x 35 mm

EXPLORER / automatic, stainless steel case, 1999, Ref. 14270, 12 x 35 mm

EXPLORER / automatic, stainless steel case, 2000, Ref. 14270, 12 x 35 mm

EXPLORER / automatic, stainless steel case, 2001, Ref. 14270, 11 x 35 mm

EXPLORER / automatic, stainless steel case, 1998, Ref. 14270, 11 x 35 mm

EXPLORER I

Ref. 114270

EXPLORER / automatic, stainless steel case, 1998, Ref. 14270, 11 x 35 mm

EXPLORER / so-called "Chrome Hearts Edition" model, automatic, silver case, 2000, Ref. 14270, 22 x 41 mm

EXPLORER / automatic, stainless steel case, 2002, Ref. 114270, 11.5 x 35.3 mm

EXPLORER / automatic, stainless steel case, 2001, Ref. 114270, 10 x 35 mm

EXPLORER / good condition, automatic, stainless steel case, 2003, Ref. 114270, 11 x 35 mm

OTHER EXPLORER I

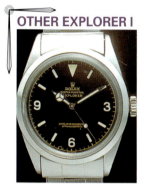

EXPLORER I / early model, dial with gold indices, 1953, 12 x 35 mm

EXPLORER I / developed for the Canadian marked, 1960s, 11.5 x 33 mm

EXPLORER I / early model, faded dial, leather band, 1950s, 12 x 35 mm

EXPLORER I / early type, 1960s, 12 x 35 mm

EXPLORER II

Advertisement: On May 29, 1953 Sir John Hunt and his British expedition conquered Mount Everest. He wore an Oyster Perpetual on his arm.

EXPLORER II

Ref. 1655

EXPLORER II / 1982, Ref. 1655, automatic, stainless steel case, 13 x 38 mm

EXPLORER II / automatic, stainless steel case, 1979, Ref. 1655, 14 x 37.8 mm

EXPLORER II / automatic, stainless steel case, 1970, Ref. 1655, 13 x 38 mm

EXPLORER II / automatic, stainless steel case, 1978, Ref. 1655, 13 x 38 mm

EXPLORER II / automatic, stainless steel case, 1980S, Ref. 1655, 13 X 38 MM

EXPLORER II / automatic, stainless steel case, 1971, Ref. 1655, 13 x 33 mm

EXPLORER II / automatic, stainless steel case, 1980, Ref. 1655, 13 x 34 mm

EXPLORER II / automatic, stainless steel case, 1984, Ref. 1655, 13.5 x 38 mm

EXPLORER II / automatic, stainless steel case, 1971, Ref. 1655, 13 x 37.5 mm

EXPLORER II / improved successor to Explorer I, 1970s, Ref. 1655, 13.5 x 38 mm

EXPLORER II / same movement as GMT-Master, 24-hour hand, 1971, Ref. 1655, 13 x 37.5 mm

EXPLORER II / very good condition, 1970s, Ref. 1655, 13.5 x 38 mm

EXPLORER II / typical orange GMT hand, with box and certificate, 1970s, Ref. 1655, 14 x 38 mm

EXPLORER II / stainless steel case, 1970s, Ref. 1655, 13.5 x 38 mm

EXPLORER II / certificate and box, 1978, Ref. 1655, 13 x 37 mm

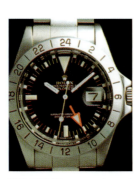

EXPLORER II / rare piece in faultless condition, 1970s, Ref. 1655, 13 x 38 mm

EXPLORER II / movement in good condition, original dial, 1980s, Ref. 1655, 13.5 x 37.5 mm

EXPLORER II / first Explorer II model from the 1980s, dealer's signature "Tiffany & Co", Ref. 1655, 13.5 x 37.5 mm

EXPLORER II / early model with orange 24-hour hand, Ref. 1655, 13.5 x 37.5 mm

EXPLORER II /very good condition, original certificate, 1970s, Ref. 1655, 13.5 x 38 mm

EXPLORER II

EXPLORER II / slim lunette, Ref. 1655, 13 x 37.5 mm

EXPLORER II / early model with orange 24-hour hand, Ref. 1655, 14 x 37.5 mm

EXPLORER II / wide numerals on lunette, Ref. 1655, 14 x 38 mm

EXPLORER II / case in good condition, original dial, 1970s, Ref. 1655, 13.5 x 38 mm

EXPLORER II / 1979, Ref. 1655, 14 x 37 mm

EXPLORER II / 24-hour lunette, 1970s, Ref. 1655, 13 x 37.5 mm

EXPLORER II / case, dial and band in faultless condition, 1980s, Ref. 1655, 13.5 x 38 mm

EXPLORER II / very good condition, 1979, Ref. 1655, 13 x 37.5 mm

EXPLORER II / original dial, 24-hour hand faded, Ref. 1655, 13.5 x 37 mm

EXPLORER II / paint on 24-hour hand well preserved, Ref. 1655, 13.5 x 37.5 mm

EXPLORER II / same movement as GMT-Master, 24-hour hand, second stop, 1970s, Ref. 1655, 11.5 x 37.5 mm

EXPLORER II / Ref. 1655, 13.5 x 37.5 mm

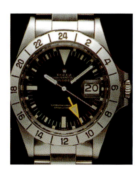
EXPLORER II / early model with wide numerals on lunette, 1970s, Ref. 1655, 13 x 37 mm

EXPLORER II / very fine piece, original box, 1982, Ref. 1655, 13.5 x 37.5 mm

EXPLORER II / unworn original piece with label, box and certificate, Ref. 1655, 13.5 x 37.5 mm

Ref. 16550

EXPLORER II / automatic, stainless steel case, 1984, Ref. 16550, beige dial, 13 x 39 mm

EXPLORER II / automatic, stainless steel case, 1968, Ref. 16550, beige dial, 13 x 39 mm

EXPLORER II / automatic, stainless steel case, 1984, Ref. 16550, beige dial, 12 x 36 mm

EXPLORER II / automatic, stainless steel case, 1984, Ref. 16550, 13 x 39 mm

EXPLORER II / 1990s, Ref. 16550, 13 x 39 mm

EXPLORER II

Ref. 16570

EXPLORER II / ivory dial, very rare model made only two years, 1980s, Ref. 16550, 13 x 39 mm

EXPLORER II / Ref. 16550, 12.5 x 39 mm

EXPLORER II / ivory dial, made only briefly, Ref. 16550, 12 x 39 mm

EXPLORER II / 1991, Ref. 15670, automatic, stainless steel case, 12 x 39 mm

EXPLORER II / automatic, stainless steel case, 1998, Ref. 16570, 12.6 x 39 mm

EXPLORER II / automatic, stainless steel case, 1990, Ref. 16570, 13 x 39 mm

EXPLORER II / automatic, stainless steel case, 1990s, Ref. 16570, 12 x 39 mm

EXPLORER II / automatic, stainless steel case, 1996, Ref. 16570, 10 x 38 mm

EXPLORER II / automatic, stainless steel case, 1996, Ref. 16570, 11 x 38 mm

EXPLORER II / automatic, stainless steel case, 2001, Ref. 16570, 13 x 40 mm

EXPLORER II / automatic, stainless steel case, 1994, Ref. 16570, 12 x 39 mm

EXPLORER II / automatic, stainless steel case, 1996, Ref. 16570, 12 x 39 mm

EXPLORER II / automatic, stainless steel case, 1999, Ref. 16570, 12 x 39 mm

EXPLORER II / automatic, stainless steel case, 1998, Ref. 16570, 12 x 39 mm

EXPLORER II / automatic, stainless steel case, 1999, Ref. 16570, 13 x 39 mm

EXPLORER II / automatic, stainless steel case, 1999, Ref. 16570, 12 x 39 mm

EXPLORER II / automatic, stainless steel case, 1991, Ref. 16570, 12 x 39 mm

EXPLORER II / automatic, stainless steel case, 1993, Ref. 16570, 12 x 39 mm

EXPLORER II / automatic, stainless steel case, 2003, Ref. 16570, 12 x 39 mm

EXPLORER II / automatic, stainless steel case, 1990, Ref. 16570, 12 x 39 mm

EXPLORER II

OTHER EXPLORER II

EXPLORER II / automatic, stainless steel case, 1993, Ref. 16570, 13 x 38 mm

EXPLORER II / automatic, stainless steel case, 1999, Ref. 16570, 13 x 39 mm

EXPLORER II / automatic, stainless steel case, 1998, Ref. 16570, 13 x 39 mm

EXPLORER II / / dealer's signature "Tiffany & Co", box and certificate, 1988, Ref. 16570, 12.5 x 39 mm

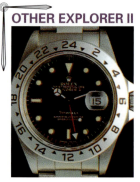
EXPLORER II / dealer's signature "Tiffany & Co", 24-hour hand as in GMT-Master, 12.5 x 39 mm

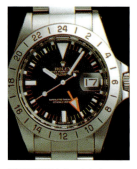
EXPLORER II / all parts but movement replaced, perfectly watertight, 13.5 x 38 mm

EXPLORER II / orange 24-hour hand, 13/5 x 37/5 mm

EXPLORER II / early model, 13 x 38 mm

EXPLORER II / early model, color of 24-hour hand faded, 13.5 x 37.5 mm

EXPLORER II / 24-hour hand, 12.5 x 37,5 mm

EXPLORER II / orange 24-hour hand, 1970s, 14 x 37.5 mm

EXPLORER II / orange 24-hour hand, 13.5 x 37.5 mm

EXPLORER II, yellow 24-hour hand, 13.5 x 37.5 mm

EXPLORER II / orange 24-hour hand, 13.5 x 37.5 mm

EXPLORER II / good condition, 1975, 13.5 x 38.5 mm

EXPLORER II / case, lunette and dial in good condition, stainless steel case and band, 14 x 37 mm

EXPLORER II / 1970s, 13 x 37.5 mm

EXPLORER II / early model, 1970s, back after short pause in 1988 with slight modifications, 13.5 x 37.5 mm

EXPLORER II / early model with orange 24-hour hand, 1971, 13 x 37.5 mm

EXPLORER II / early model, original dial, replaced lunette and band, 13 x 38.5 mm

GMT-MASTER

When the GMT-MASTER came on the market in the 1950s, it was soon accepted officially by Pan Am Airways in 1958. GMT means "Greenwich Mean Time". A significant feature of the GMT-MASTER model is the 24-hour marking in two colors, blue (night) and red (day), on the lunette. With this turning lunette one can instantly read the times of two different places. In 1983 the improved GMT-MASTER II was introduced; it enabled its owner to set three different time zones. The central hour hand of the GMT-MASTER II can be set independently.

Old Advertisement

1966 advertisement

GMT-MASTER I

Ref. 1657   Ref. 1675

GMT-MASTER / with box and certificate, stainless steel case, Cal. 1560, Ref. 1657, 12.5 x 39.5 mm, 5.5 mm crown

GMT-MASTER / automatic, stainless steel case, 1978, Ref. 1675, 12.6 x 39.4 mm

GMT-MASTER / automatic, stainless steel case, 1970, Ref. 1675, 13 x 39 mm

GMT-MASTER / automatic, stainless steel case, 1970, Ref. 1675, 13 x 39 mm

GMT-MASTER / automatic, stainless steel case, 1970, Ref. 1675, 13 x 39 mm

GMT-MASTER / automatic, stainless steel case, 1970s, Ref. 1675, 12 x 39 mm

GMT-MASTER / stainless steel case, 1977, hand-wound, 14 x 39 mm

GMT-MASTER / automatic, 18 karat yellow gold and stainless steel bicolor case, 1972, Ref. 1675, 12 x 39 mm

GMT-MASTER / automatic, 18 karat yellow gold and stainless steel case, 1965, Ref. 1675, 12 x 39 mm

GMT-MASTER / automatic, stainless steel case, 1967, Ref. 1675, 12 x 39 mm

GMT-MASTER / automatic, stainless steel case, 1964, Ref. 1675, 12 x 39 mm

GMT-MASTER / automatic, 19-karat yellow gold and stainless steel bicolor case, Ref. 1675, 13 x 39 mm

GMT-MASTER / stainless steel case, Jubilee band, 1969, Ref. 1675, 13 x 39 mm

GMT-MASTER / automatic, stainless steel case, 1976, Ref. 1675, 13 x 39 mm

GMT-MASTER / automatic, 18 karat yellow gold case, 1972, Ref. 1675, 12 x 40 mm

GMT-MASTER / automatic, stainless steel case, 1970s, Ref. 1675, 12 x 37 mm

GMT-MASTER / automatic, stainless steel case, 1979, Ref. 1675, 12.5 x 39 mm

GMT-MASTER / automatic, stainless steel case, 1978, Ref. 1675, 13 x 39 mm

GMT-MASTER / automatic, stainless steel case, 1965, Ref. 1675, 13 x 39 mm

GMT-MASTER / automatic, stainless steel case, 1960s, Ref. 1675, 13 x 39 mm

GMT-MASTER I

GMT-MASTER / automatic, stainless steel case, 1969, Ref. 1675, 13 x 38 mm

GMT-MASTER / automatic, stainless steel case, 1978, Ref. 1675, for Arabian air force, 12 x 40 mm

GMT-MASTER / automatic, stainless steel case, 1970, Ref. 1675, 13 x 39 mm

GMT-MASTER / automatic, stainless steel case, 1965, Ref. 1675, 13 x 39 mm

GMT-MASTER / 1971, Ref. 1675, 13 x 39.5 mm

GMT-MASTER / blue-red 24-hour lunette, Ref. 1675, 12.5 x 39.5 mm

GMT-MASTER / black 24-hour lunette with yellow numerals, 18 karat gold crown and Jubilee band, Ref. 1675, 13 x 39.5 mm

GMT-MASTER / older type without silver rim for indices, original dial, stainless steel case, Ref. 1675, 12 x 39.5 mm

GMT-MASTER / red-blue 24-hour lunette, Ref. 1675, 12.5 x 39.5 mm

GMT-MASTER / small 24-hour hand, chronometer certificate, 1960s, Ref. 1675, 13 x 39.5 mm

GMT-MASTER / large 24-hour hand, crown guards, 1966, Ref. 1675, 13 x 39.5 mm

GMT-MASTER / very desirable model with black lunette, Cal. 1570, Ref. 1675, 13 x 39.5 mm

GMT-MASTER / very rare, dealer's signature "TIFFANY". Stainless steel case, 1970s, Ref. 1675, 13 x 40 mm

GMT-MASTER / Cal. 1570, luminous indices, 1960s, Ref. 1675, 13 x 40 mm

GMT-MASTER / luminous indices without rims, red/blue lunette, Ref. 1675, 12.5 x 39.5 mm

GMT-MASTER / dealer's signature for "Tiffany" on original dial, expansion band, 1970s, Ref. 1675, 13 x 39.5 mm

GMT-MASTER / chronometer sign on dial, Jubilee band. Ref. 1675, 13 x 39.5 mm

GMT-MASTER / early model, 1970s, Ref. 1675, 13 x 40 mm

GMT-MASTER / red-blue lunette, 1982, Ref. 1675, 12.5 x 39.5 mm

GMT-MASTER / small arrow on 24-hour hand, 1960s, Ref. 1675, 13.5 x 39.5 mm

GMT-MASTER I

GMT-MASTER / dial with unframed luminous indices, Ref. 1675, 12.5 x 39.5 mm

GMT-MASTER / 1970s, Cal. 1575, Ref. 1675, 12.5 x 39.5 mm

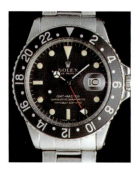
GMT-MASTER / black lunette, no fast date change, 1969, Ref. 1675, 12.5 x 39.5 mm, crown 5.5 mm

GMT-MASTER / dealer's signature "Tiffany" on original dial, Cal. 1570 movement, Ref. 1675, 13 x 39.5 mm

GMT-MASTER / dial with gold ring, early 1960s, Ref. 1675, 5.5 mm crown, 13 x 39.5 mm

GMT-MASTER / red-blue lunette, Ref. 1675, 12.5 x 39.5 mm

GMT-MASTER / black lunette, Ref. 1675, 13 x 39.5 mm, 5.5 mm crown

GMT-MASTER / black lunette, 1966, Cal. 1570, Ref. 1675, 13 x 39 mm

GMT-MASTER / dial enclosed by gold ring, Ref. 1675, 13 x 39.5 mm, 5.5 mm crown

GMT-MASTER / indices without metal rims, 1970s, Cal. 1570, Ref. 1675, 13 x 39.5 mm

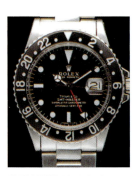
GMT-MASTER / dealer's signature "Tiffany", 1970s, Cal. 1570, Ref. 1675, 13 x e9,5 mm

GMT-MASTER / original dial, Jubilee band, 1970s, Cal. 1565, Ref. 1675, 13 x 40 mm

GMT-MASTER / original dial, late 1960s, Ref. 1675, 12.5 x 39 mm

GMT-MASTER / stainless steel case and band, 5.5 mm crown, 1970s, Cal. 1575, Ref. 1675, 12.5 x 39.5 mm

GMT-MASTER / rare model with black lunette, 5.5 mm crown, 1960s, Ref. 1675, 13 x 39 mm

Ref. 6542

GMT-MASTER / small point on 24-hour hand, Jubilee band, 1960s, Ref. 1675, 13 x 39.5 mm, 5 mm crown

GMT-MASTER / black lunette, 5.5 mm crown, Ref. 1675, 12.5 x 39.5 mm

GMT-MASTER / automatic, 18 karat yellow gold and stainless steel bicolor case, 1950, Ref. 6542, 13 x 39 mm

GMT-MASTER / automatic, stainless steel case, 1950, Ref. 6542, 13 x 38 mm

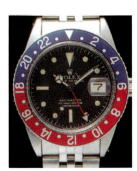
GMT-MASTER / early model without crown guards, 6 mm crown, 1950s, Ref. 6542, 13.5 x 39 mm

GMT-MASTER I

Ref. 16570

Ref. 16700

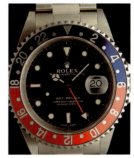

GMT-MASTER / automatic, stainless steel case, 1995, Ref. 16570, 12 x 40 mm

GMT-MASTER / automatic, stainless steel case, 1993, Ref. 16700, 11.9 x 39.5 mm

GMT-MASTER / automatic, stainless steel case, 1997, Ref. 16700, 11.8 x 39.5 mm

GMT-MASTER / automatic, stainless steel case, 1999, Ref. 16700, 11 x 40 mm

GMT-MASTER / automatic, stainless steel case, 1997, Ref. 16700, 10 x 40 mm

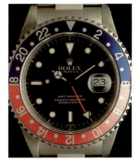

GMT-MASTER / automatic, stainless steel case, 1994, Ref. 16700, 12 x 40 mm

GMT-MASTER / automatic, stainless steel case, 1996, Ref. 16700, 12 x 40 mm

GMT-MASTER / automatic, stainless steel case, 1998, Ref. 16700, 12 x 40 mm

GMT-MASTER / automatic, stainless steel case, 1996, Ref. 16700, 12 x 40 mm

GMT-MASTER / automatic, stainless steel case, 1993, Ref. 16700, 12 x 40 mm

GMT-MASTER / automatic, stainless steel case, 1997, Ref. 16700, 12 x 40 mm

GMT-MASTER / automatic, stainless steel case, 1997, Ref. 16700, 12 x 40 mm

GMT-MASTER / automatic, stainless steel case, 1996, Ref. 16700, 12 x 40 mm

GMT-MASTER / automatic, stainless steel case, 1998, Ref. 16700, 9 x 40 mm

GMT-MASTER / dealer's signature "Tiffany" with box and certificate, Ref. 16700, 12 x 40 mm

Ref. 16713

Ref. 16750

GMT-MASTER / rare brown and yellow bicolor lunette, stainless steel and 18 karat yellow gold bicolor case and band, Ref. 16713, 12.5 x 39.5 mm

GMT-MASTER / automatic, stainless steel case, 1984, Ref. 16750, 13.5 x 39.4 mm

GMT-MASTER / automatic, stainless steel case, 1984, Ref. 16750, 12.5 x 39.3 mm

GMT-MASTER / automatic, stainless steel; case, 1980, Ref. 16750, 13 x 39 mm

GMT-MASTER / automatic, stainless steel case, 1980, Ref. 16750, 12 x 39 mm

GMT-MASTER I

GMT/MASTER / automatic, stainless steel case, 1988, Ref. 16750, 13 x 39 mm

GMT-MASTER / automatic, stainless steel case, 1982, Ref. 16750, 13 x 39 mm

GMT-MASTER / automatic, stainless steel case, 1983, Ref. 16750, 13 x 39 mm

GMT-MASTER / automatic, stainless steel case, 1980s, Ref. 16750, 14 x 39 mm

GMT-MASTER / automatic, stainless steel case, 1985, Ref. 16750, 13 x 39 mm

GMT-MASTER / automatic stainless steel case, 1985, Ref. 16750, 12 x 39 mm

GMT-MASTER / automatic, stainless steel case, 1984, Ref. 16750, 12 x 39 mm

GMT-MASTER automatic, stainless steel case, 1982, Ref. 16750, 13 x 39 mm

GMT-MASTER / automatic, stainless steel case, 1981, Ref. 16750, 13 x 39 mm

GMT-MASTER / automatic, stainless steel case, 1983, Ref. 16750, 13 x 39 mm

GMT-MASTER / automatic, stainless steel case, 1988, Ref. 16750, 12 x 39 mm

GMT-MASTER / automatic, stainless steel case, 1984, Ref. 16750, 12 x 39 mm

GMT-MASTER / automatic, stainless steel case, 1995, 1995, Ref. 16750, 13 x 39 mm

GMT-MASTER automatic, stainless steel case, 1987, Ref. 16750, 13 x 39 mm

GMT-MASTER / desirable sport model with black lunette, 1980s, Ref. 16750, 13 x 39.5 mm

GMT-MASTER / red-blue 24-hour lunette, framed indices, 1980s, Cal. 3075, Ref. 16750, 13 x 39.5 mm

GMT-MASTER / fast date change, 1980s, Ref. 16750, 13 x 39.5 mm

GMT-MASTER / dial with unframed luminous indices, fast date change, 1980s, Ref. 16750, 13.5 x 39.5 mm

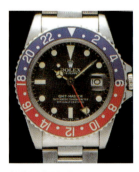
GMT-MASTER / fast date switch, 1980s, Cal. 3075, Ref. 16750, 13 x 40 mm

GMT-MASTER / luminous rimmed indices, original condition, 1985, Ref. 16750, 13 x 40 mm

GMT-MASTER I

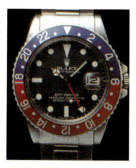
GMT-MASTER / Plexiglas, original dial, 1980s, Ref. 16750, 13 x 39.5 mm

GMT-MASTER fast date switch, original dial, Cal. 3075, Ref. 16750, 12.5 x 39.5 mm

GMT-MASTER / red-blue lunette, jubilee band, 1980s, Ref. 16750, 13 x 39.5 mm

Ref. 16753

GMT-MASTER / automatic, 18 karat yellow gold and stainless steel bicolor case, 1987, Ref. 16753, 12 x 39 mm

GMT-MASTER / 18 karat yellow gold and stainless steel bicolor case, 1980, Ref. 16753, 12 x 39 mm

GMT-MASTER / automatic, 18 karat yellow gold and stainless steel bicolor case, 1980s, Ref. 16753, 13 x 39 mm

GMT-MASTER / automatic, yellow gold and stainless steel bicolor case, 1986, Ref. 16753, 13 x 39 mm

GMT-MASTER / fast date switch, wide rims on indices, 1980s, Cal. 3075, Ref. 16753, 13 x 39.5 mm

Ref. 16758

GMT-MASTER / automatic, yellow gold case, 1983, Ref. 16758, 12 x 39 mm

GMT-MASTER / 18 karat yellow gold and stainless steel bicolor case, 1986, Ref. 16758, 12 x 40 mm

OTHER GMT I

GMT-MASTER / automatic, 18 karat yellow gold case, 1985, Ref. 16758, 12 x 40 mm

GMT-MASTER / very popular model with black lunette, gold and stainless steel bicolor case and band, gold lunette rim, 13 x 39 mm

GMT-MASTER / discolored hands, no fast date change possible, presumably 1970s, 13 x 39.5 mm

GMT-MASTER / early model, no crown guards, plastic lunette, 1950s, 13 x 38 mm

GMT-MASTER / early model without crown guards, freshened-up dial, 13 x 38 mm

GMT-MASTER / rare model with small 24-hour hand, dial in good condition, 1960s, 12.5 x 39.5 mm

GMT-MASTER / small 24-hour hand, crown guards, 1966, 13 x 39.5 mm

GMT-MASTER / early model without crown guards, dial framed with gold ring, small 24-hour hand, 1950s, 13 x 38 mm

GMT-MASTER / rare model without crown guards, 1970s, 13 x 39.5 mm

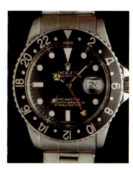
GMT-MASTER / black lunette, latter half of 1970s, 13 x 39.5 mm

GMT-MASTER I

GMT-MASTER / red-blue lunette, 1970s, 14 x 40 mm

GMT-MASTER / brown-gold lunette, brown dial with gold-rimmed indices, steel and gold band, 13 x 34.5 mm

GMT-MASTER / indices with rims, faded lunette, 1980s, 13.5 x 40 mm

GMT-MASTER / early model, no crown guard, small 24-hour hand, lunette replaced, dial with gold ring, 1950s, 13 x 37 mm

2GMT-MASTER / indices heavily rimmed, 24-hour hand not red, bi-color case and band with 14-karat yellow gold, 12 x 39.5 mm

GMT-MASTER II

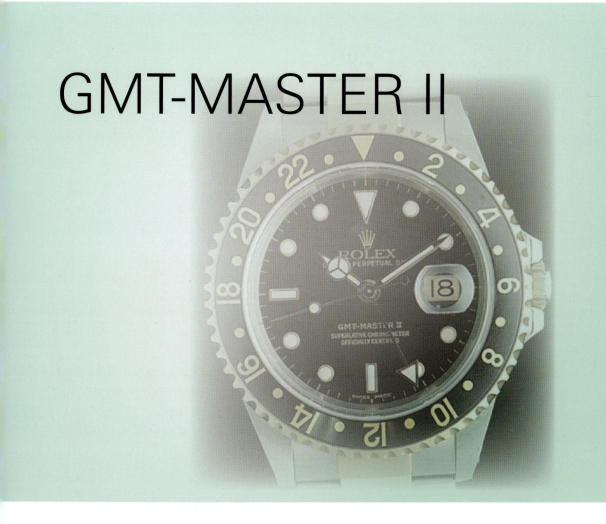

GMT-MASTER II

Ref. 16213

Ref. 16710

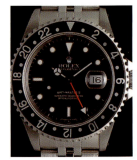

GMT-MASTER II / automatic, yellow gold and stainless steel bicolor case, 1990s, Ref. 16213, 13 x 40 mm

GMT-MASTER II / automatic, stainless steel case, 2003, Ref. 16710, 13 x 40 mm

GMT-MASTER II / automatic, stainless steel case, 1998, Ref. 16710, 13 x 40 mm

GMT-MASTER II / automatic, stainless steel case, 1999, Ref. 16710, 12 x 40 mm

GMT-MASTER II / automatic, stainless steel case, 1994, Ref. 16710, 12 x 40 mm

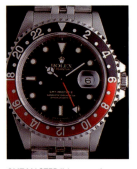

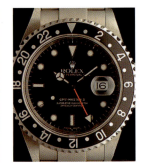

GMT-MASTER II / automatic, stainless steel case, 1990s, Ref. 16710, 12 x 40 mm

GMT-MASTER II / automatic, stainless steel case, 1990s, Ref. 16710, 13 x 40 mm

GMT-MASTER II / automatic, stainless steel case, 1990s, Ref. 16710, 12 x 40 mm

GMT-MASTER II / automatic, yellow gold and stainless steel bicolor case, 1997, Ref. 16710, 13 x 40 mm

GMT-MASTER II / automatic, stainless steel case, 2000, Ref. 16710, 11 x 41 mm

Ref. 16713

GMT-MASTER II / automatic, stainless steel case, 1997, Ref. 16710, 13 x 40 mm

GMT-MASTER II / automatic, yellow gold and stainless steel bicolor case, 1991, Ref. 16713, 12 x 40 mm

2GMT-MASTER II / 18 karat yellow gold and stainless steel case, 1991, Ref. 16713, 12.3 x 40 mm

GMT-MASTER II / automatic, yellow gold and stainless steel bicolor case, 1990s, Ref. 16713, 11 x 39 mm

GMT-MASTER II / automatic, 18 karat yellow gold and stainless steel bicolor case, 1991, Ref. 16713, 12 x 40 mm

GMT-MASTER II / automatic, 18 karat yellow gold and stainless steel bicolor case, 1991, Ref. 16713, 12 x 40 mm

GMT-MASTER II / automatic, 18 karat yellow gold and stainless steel bicolor case, 1993, Ref. 16713, 12 x 40 mm

GMT-MASTER II / automatic, 18 karat yellow gold and stainless steel bicolor case, 1991, Ref. 16713, 13 x 40 mm

GMT-MASTER II / automatic, 18 karat yellow gold and stainless steel bicolor case, 1991, Ref. 16713, 13 x 40 mm

GMT-MASTER II / automatic, yellow gold and stainless steel bicolor case, 1991, Ref. 16713 RGA, 12 x 40 mm

GMT-MASTER II

Ref. 16718

Ref. 16760

GMT-MASTER II / automatic, 18 karat yellow gold case, 1988, Ref. 16718, 12 x 40 mm

GMT-MASTER II / automatic, 18 karat yellow gold case, 1990, Ref. 16718, 11 x 34 mm

GMT-MASTER / automatic, stainless steel case, 1985, Ref. 16760, 13 x 40 mm

GMT-MASTER II / automatic, stainless steel case, 1985, Ref. 16760, 13 x 40 mm

GMT-MASTER II / automatic, stainless steel case, 1987, Ref. 16760, 13 x 40 mm

Ref. 167818

GMT-MASTER II / automatic, stainless steel case, 1988, Ref. 16760, 13 x 40 mm

GMT-MASTER II / automatic, stainless steel case, 1991, Ref. 16760, 13 x 40 mm

2GMT-MASTER II / automatic, 18 karat yellow gold case, 1990, Ref. 16718, 12 x 40 mm

LADIES' WATCHES

From the Art-deco "CHAMELEON" cocktail watch through the white-gold lady's watch with diamonds and gemstones to the "DATEJUST"—today even tennis players were automatic Rolex watches. At the beginning of the 20th century, ladies' watches were mainly pieces of jewelry. Despite their usually small movements, they show the time precisely.

LADIES' WATCHES

LADY ROLEX

NON-OYSTER / enamel dial, silver case, hand-wound, 1920s, 9.9 x 29.1 mm

NON-OYSTER / 18 karat yellow and white gold case, hand-wound, 1940s, 9.1 x 23.5 mm

PRINCESS / 9 karat white gold case, hand-wound, 1930s, 7.4 x 37.8 x 11 mm

NON-OYSTER / 18 karat yellow gold case, 9 karat yellow gold band, hand-wound, 1930, 8.9 x 23.3 mm

NON-OYSTER / 18 karat yellow gold case, hand-wound, 1940s, dial with Arabic numerals, 9.3 x 22.8 mm

PRINCESS / 9 karat yellow gold, hand-wound, 1930s, 7.7 x 31.4 x 15.2 mm

LADY'S WATCH / 9 karat red gold case, hand-wound, 1940s, 7 x 19 mm

LADY'S WATCH / 9 karat red gold case, hand-wound, 1930s, 9 x 25 mm

LADY'S WATCH / 9 karat red gold case, hand-wound, 1920s, 11 x 28 mm

LADY'S WATCH / 9 karat red gold case, hand-wound, 1930s, 10 x 25 mm

LADY'S WATCH / stainless steel case, hand-wound, 1930s, 8 x 27 x 13 mm

LADY'S WATCH / 9 karat red gold case, hand-wound, 1930s, 10 x 26 mm

LADY'S WATCH / 18 karat white gold case, hand-wound, 1930s, 7 x 31 x 14 mm

LADY'S WATCH / 9 karat red gold case, hand-wound, 1930s, 8 x 25 mm

LADY'S WATCH / enamel dial, 9 karat gold case, hand-wound, 1930s, 9 x 27 mm

LADY'S WATCH / enamel dial, 9 karat red gold case, hand-wound, 1940s, 10 x 28 mm

BRACELET / 18 karat gold case, hand-wound, 1950, Ref. 8118, 9 x 16 x 13 mm

LADY CODE / 18 karat gold case, hand-wound, 1940, Ref. 6263, 7 x 22 x 14 mm

OYSTER / stainless steel case, hand-wound, 1934, Ref. 48166, 10 x 23 mm

LADY'S WATCH / 9 karat yellow gold case, hand-wound, 1930s, 9 x 25 mm

LADIES' WATCHES

LADY'S WATCH / 9 karat yellow gold case, hand-wound, 1940s, 8 x 24 mm

LADY'S WATCH / 14 karat yellow gold case, hand-wound, 1940s, cut crystal, 7 x 15 mm

LADY'S WATCH / 14 karat yellow gold case, hand-wound, 1940s, 7 x 15 mm

LADY'S WATCH / 18 karat yellow gold case, hand-wound, 1940s, 9 x 36 x 17 mm

LADY'S WATCH / 14 karat yellow gold case, hand-wound, 1940s, 7 x 16 mm

LADY'S WATCH / 9 karat yellow gold case, hand-wound, 1926, 7 x 23 mm

LADY'S WATCH / enamel dial, 9 karat yellow gold case, hand-wound, 1930, 9 x 29 mm

LADY'S WATCH / 9 karat yellow gold case, hand-wound, 1930, 8 x 21 mm

OCTAGON / 9 karat red gold case, hand-wound, 1930, 9 x 25 mm

LADY'S WATCH / 9 karat yellow gold case, hand-wound, 1935, 9 x 26 mm

LADY'S WATCH / slim band attachments, stainless steel case and band, 12 x 17 mm

LADY'S WATCH / perfect enamel dial with typical red 12, 1920s, hinged 9 karat crystal frame, 9.5 x 22.5 mm

SQUARE / 1950s, 9 karat gold, 7.5 x 26.5 mm

LADY'S WATCH / matte gold band, 7 x 16 x 13 mm

LADY'S WATCH / printed Arabic numerals, 9 karat gold, band is not original, 8 x 29 mm

LADY'S WATCH / 14 karat white gold, band attachments decorated with diamonds, 7 x 15.5 mm

LADY'S WATCH / good as new, 14 karat white gold, 1960s, 7 x 17 mm

LADY'S WATCH / 7 x 34.5 mm

LADY'S WATCH / flower-shaped lunette, 14 karat gold, 7.5 x 15 mm

SQUARE / 9 karat gold, 7.5 x 16.5 mm

LADIES' WATCHES

LADY'S WATCH / guilloched dial, raised indices, 18 karat gold, 8.5 x 16 mm

LADY'S WATCH / enamel dial, 1930s, 9 karat gold, 10 x 26 mm

LADY'S WATCH / red-white lunette, 9 karat gold, 8.5 x 26 mm

ROLCO / early Rolex model, rippled case, silver, 8.5 x 21.5 mm

LADY'S WATCH / matte dial, elegant band, 7 x 17 x 21 mm

LADY'S WATCH / 1930s, crossed lines on dial, 7.5 x 21 mm

PRINCESS / Arabic numerals, 6.5 x 11.5 mm

LADY'S WATCH / enamel dial, 9 karat gold, 10.5 x 29 mm

LADY'S WATCH / engraved on the case side for a 7th anniversary, 8 x 28 mm

LADY'S WATCH / "tonneau" case, 1930s, 6.5 x 25 mm

LADY'S WATCH / elegant dial, overhauled, 7 x 17 mm

LADY'S WATCH / flower-shaped lunette, 14 karat white gold, 7.5 x 20.5 mm

LADY'S WATCH / diamonds on band attachments, 7.5 x 18 x 20 mm

LADY'S WATCH / richly decorated band and case, 9 karat gold, 1950s, 7 x 15 mm

LADY'S WATCH / dial guilloched in ray pattern, octagonal case, 8 x 25.5 mm

LADY'S WATCH / band of braided stylized letter C, 14 karat gold, 7 x 15 mm

LADY'S WATCH / band attachments set with diamonds, 14 karat white gold, 7 x 15 mm

LADY'S WATCH / 9 karat gold, 1920s, 9 x 25 mm

LADY'S WATCH / interesting dial, 7.5 x 19.5 mm

LADY'S WATCH / 7.5 x 21 mm

LADIES' WATCHES

LADY'S WATCH / 1950s, 8 x 16.5 x 13 mm

LADY'S WATCH / rare model, 7 x 24.5 x 15 mm

LADY'S WATCH / slim flexible band of 9 karat gold, 1920s, 8 x 21.5 mm

LADY'S WATCH / raised bar indices, 6 x 15 mm

LADY'S WATCH / dealer's signature "Bucherer", 8 x 27.5 x 17 mm

LADY'S WATCH / slim flexible band, hinged lid with crystal, enamel dial, 8.5 x 26 mm

LADY'S WATCH / early model, 9 karat gold, 9 x 27 mm

LADY'S WATCH / 1930s, blue numerals and red 12 on enamel dial, gold case, 9.5 x 29 mm

LADY'S WATCH / button for hand setting, 9 x 23 mm

LADY'S WATCH / band and attachments set with diamonds, 6.5 x 14.5 mm

LADY'S WATCH / nice design, braided band, 14 karat gold, 9 x 17.5 x 14 mm

PRECISION / like-new condition, elegant 18 karat white gold model, Ref. 2647, 6.5 x 20 x 22 mm

LADY'S WATCH / signed "Mappin", 8.5 x 16 mm

LADY'S WATCH / enamel dial with then-popular blue numerals, hinged case, 9 x 27.5 mm

LADY'S WATCH / gold case, large band attachments, 7.5 x 19.5 mm

LADY'S WATCH / 1940s, 9 karat gold, 9.5 x 20 mm

LADY'S WATCH / case and band of massive 14 karat white gold, 7.5 x 15 mm

LADY'S WATCH / 1960s, 14 karat white gold case, Cal. 1401, 7 x 15 mm

LADY'S WATCH / dealer's signature "London", 9 karat gold case, 9 x 25 mm

LADY'S WATCH / rare octagonal case, good condition, 8 x 17 mm

LADIES' WATCHES

LADY'S WATCH / 8 x 28 x 17 mm

LADY'S WATCH / octagonal case and band of 9 karat gold, 8 x 21.5 mm

LADY'S WATCH / pyramidal case, black dial, 9 x 17 mm

LADY'S WATCH / arched crystal, heart-shaped band, 8 x 14 mm

LADY'S WATCH / gold band set with diamonds, 14 karat gold case, 7.x 15 mm

LADY'S WATCH / stepped case, gold band and raised numerals, 7.5 x 14 x 23 mm

LADY'S WATCH / rare model with Denison case, hand-wound, 9 karat gold, 8 x 21 mm

LADY'S WATCH / 1940s, "Rolex" signature underlined, 8 x 22 mm

LADY'S WATCH / red 12, original band, 1920s, 8 x 22 mm

LADY'S WATCH / interesting hand shape, 9 karat gold, 7 x 21 mm

LADY'S WATCH / 9 karat gold, 1930s, 6.5 x 38 x 11.5 mm

LADY'S WATCH / stainless steel case, 7.5 x 24 mm

LADY'S WATCH / 14 karat gold, 7 x 14.5 mm

LADY'S WATCH / dealer's signature "Bucherer", 10 x 16.5 mm

LADY'S WATCH / hinged case, 9 karat gold, 1930s, 9 x 29.5 mm

LADY'S WATCH / elaborate case, raised indices, 7 x 16 mm

LADY'S WATCH / 9 karat gold, Roman numerals, 10 x 28 mm

LADY'S WATCH / 9 karat gold, enamel dial, movement in good condition, 1920s, 11 x 27.5 mm

LADY'S WATCH / silver case and band, enamel lunette, 9 x 26 mm

LADY'S WATCH / enamel dial, 9.5 x 27.5 mm

LADIES' WATCHES

LADY'S WATCH / straight band attachments, 14 karat gold, 8 x 18 mm

LADY'S WATCH / 14 karat gold, raised indices, 6.5 x 17 mm

LADY'S WATCH / typical cocktail watch design, 9 x 15 mm

LADY'S WATCH / square case, engraved lunette, 7 x 16.5 mm

LADY'S WATCH / enamel dial with red 12, hinged case, 9 x 27 mm

LADY'S WATCH / fine model, dial guilloched in rays, engraved case, 7.5 x 21 mm

LADY'S WATCH / simple model, arched crystal, white gold, 7.5 x 23 x 14 mm

LADY'S WATCH / 9 karat gold case, freshened-up dial, 7.5 x 21 mm

LADY'S WATCH / engraved case, simple dial, 6.5 x 24.5 mm

LADY'S WATCH / 9 karat gold case, dial guilloched in rays, 8.5 x 22.5 mm

LADY'S WATCH / beautiful design, silver case and band, 1919, 9 x 25.5 mm

LADY'S WATCH / rare model, octagonal case, 8 x 21.5 mm

LADY'S WATCH / nice model, stainless steel case, blue steel hands, 9 x 16 mm

LADY'S WATCH / 14 karat gold bicolor case, interesting flexible band attachments, 7.5 x 29 mm

LADY'S WATCH / steel and gold bicolor case, interesting band attachments, 8 x 20.5 mm

LADY'S WATCH / original dial, 7.5 x 22.5 mm

LADY'S WATCH / 9 karat gold case and band, engraved band link, 8.5 x 21.5 mm

LADY'S WATCH / early model, 9 karat gold case and band, 1920s, 9.5 x 28.5 mm

LADY'S WATCH / luxurious case, elaborate band, 8 x 22 mm

LADY'S WATCH / 7.5 x 23 mm

LADIES' WATCHES

LADY'S WATCH / interesting design, 1930s, 7 x 30 mm

LADY'S WATCH / 18 karat gold stepped case, 9 karat gold band, 1940s, 7 x 22.5 mm

LADY'S WATCH / 14 karat gold, crystal faceted inside, 1960s, 6.5 x 14.5 mm

LADY'S WATCH / 1920s, enamel dial with red 12, 9 karat gold case, 8.5 x 28 mm

LADY'S WATCH / 9 karat gold case and original band, 7.5 x 16.5 mm

LADY'S WATCH / very luxurious model, 14 karat gold, lunette set with diamonds, 1960s, 7 x 18 mm

LADY'S WATCH / gold bracelet with watch inset, 14 karat gold, 7 x 15 mm

LADY'S WATCH / 1920s, 9.5 x 27.5 mm

LADY'S WATCH / stainless steel case, covered band attachments, 18 karat gold lunette, braided band, 8 x 17 mm

LADY'S WATCH / enamel dial, flexible silver band, 9.5 x 28.5 mm

LADY'S WATCH / enamel dial with red 12, hinged silver case, 1920s, 9.5 x 28 mm

LADY'S WATCH / 9 karat gold case and band, 8 x 27.5 x 16.5 mm

LADY'S WATCH / 9 karat white gold case, raised gold numerals, 1940s, Ref. 2886

LADY'S WATCH / rare rectangular 14 karat (PG) gold case, 9 x 22 x 13.5 mm

LADY'S WATCH / early 1920s, gold dial, engraved case, 9 x 26.5 mm

LADY'S WATCH / case and band set with diamonds, 18 karat white gold, 7.5 x 15.5 mm

PRINCESS / lightly bowed 9 karat gold case, 6.7 x 26 x 11 mm

LADY'S WATCH / pillow-shaped 18 karat gold case, 1963, 7.5 x 22.5 mm

LADY'S WATCH / arched crystal / 11 x 31.5 mm

ROLCO / square case, rare, 8 x 15.5 mm

LADIES' WATCHES

ROLCO / flat case bottom, 1920s, 7 x 21 mm

ROLCO OYSTER / stainless steel case, hand-wound, 1920, 11.7 x 25.2 mm

NON-OYSTER PRECISION / 18 karat yellow gold case, hand-wound, 1950s, 8.8 x 22.5 mm

NON-OYSTER PRECISION / 18 karat yellow gold case, hand-wound, 1950s, 8.9 x 20.2 mm

NON-OYSTER PRECISION / 18 karat yellow gold case, hand-wound, 1950s, 7.5 x 16.4 mm

PRECISION / 14 karat yellow gold case, hand-wound, 1940s, 8 x 21 mm

PRECISION / 18 karat gold case, hand-wound, 1960s, 7 x 16 mm

PRECISION / 18 karat yellow gold case, hand-wound, 1960s, 6 x 15 mm

PRECISION / 9 karat gold case, hand-wound, 8 x 20 mm

PRECISION / 9 karat gold case, hand-wound, 8 x 20 mm

PRECISION / 9 karat yellow gold case, hand-wound, 1950s, Ref. 130, 7 x 16 mm

PRECISION / 9 karat yellow gold case, hand-wound, 1960s, Cal. 1300, 17 jewels, 8 x 13 mm

PRECISION / 9 karat case, hand-wound, 1950s, Cal. 500, 9 x 23 x 20 mm

PRECISION / 9 karat yellow gold case, hand-wound, 1940s, 9 x 35 x 17 mm

PRECISION / 18 karat yellow gold case, hand-wound, 1967, 7 x 13 x 17 mm

PRECISION / 18 karat yellow gold case, hand-wound, 1969, 7 x 15 mm

PRECISION / 18 karat yellow gold case, hand-wound, 1968, 7 x 15 mm

PRECISION / 18 karat yellow gold case, hand-wound, 1930, 7 x 16 mm

PRECISION / 18 karat white gold case, hand-wound, 1947, 7 x 15 mm

PRECISION / 18 karat gold case and band, 6.5 x 15.5 mm

LADIES' WATCHES

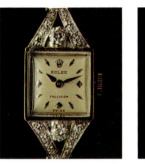
PRECISION / 18 karat white gold with diamonds, simple band, 7.5 x 17 mm

PRECISION / original band, 7 x 15 mm

PRECISION / wide enamel lunette, "Britannia HMS" on dial, 18 karat gold case, 7 x 15,5 mm

PRECISION / 1960s, 14 karat gold, Ref. 300, 7.5 x 17 mm

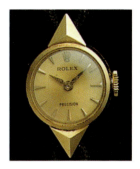
PRECISION / 18 karat gold case, cord band, Ref. 9444, 1.5 x 14.5

PRECISION / dial with raised star indices, rare, 18 karat white gold, 7 x 10 mm

PRECISION / interesting case design, 7.8 x 23 mm (incl. attachments)

PRECISION / 9 x 22.5 mm

PRECISION / 9 karat gold band, simple dial, 8 x 20 mm

PRECISION / 1950s, interesting design, 8.5 x 17.5 x 14 mm

PRECISION / freshened-up dial, 10 x 17.5 mm

PRECISION / simple model, all silver, 1960s, 8.5 x 19.5 mm

PRECISION / American design, 18 karat gold case, braided band, 7 x 14 x 13 mm

PRECISION / bow-shaped band attachments, 9 x 16.5 x 15 mm

PRECISION / nice model, small raised indices, 7.5 x 20 mm

PRECISION / decorative bracelet with hidden watch, 8 x 12.5 mm

PRECISION / 9.5 x 32 x 16.5 mm

PRECISION / simple and elegant model, gold band, 8 x 18 x 14

PRECISION / "Zephyr" model, original box with spare band, like-new condition, 7 x 22 mm

PRECISION / 18 karat white gold case and band, set with diamonds, 7.5 x 14.5 mm

LADIES' WATCHES

PRECISION / 9 karat gold, 7 x 15 mm

PRECISION / lunette with raised indices, 18 karat gold case, raised numerals and indices, 8 x 22 mm

PRECISION / flexible band, 14 karat white gold, 1960s, 7 x 14.5 mm

PRECISION / nice round band attachments, 18 karat gold, 7.5 x 19 mm

PRECISION / American design, 1950s, 9.5 x 17.5 mm

PRECISION / silver dial and indices, 8 x 18 mm

PRECISION / early model, slim band, 9 karat gold, 8 x 19.5 mm

PRECISION / 1950s, 18 karat gold, 9 x 17 mm

PRECISION / crossed band attachments, 1950s, 8 x 20 mm

PRECISION / flower-shaped case, 6.5 x 12 mm

PRECISION / irregularly rippled lunette, 7.5 x 15 mm

PRECISION / asymmetrical band attachments, 7 x 15 mm

PRECISION / like-new condition, 6.5 x 20 x 23 mm

LADY'S WATCH / raised wedge and rectangular indices, 8 x 20 mm

PRECISION / raised indices, 7 x 13 mm

PRECISION / raised indices and Arabic 12, 1920s, 7 x 16.5 x 13 mm

PRECISION / raised numerals and indices, 8.5 x 20 mm

PRECISION / original band, 9 karat gold, 8 x 20 mm

PRECISION / diamonds on hinged lid, 10.5 x 16.5 mm

PRECISION / simple dial, 8 x 21.5 mm

LADIES' WATCHES

LADY'S WATCH / arched crystal, 1950s, 9 x 16.5 mm

PRECISION/ gilded, band attachments, 8 x 16 mm

LADY'S WATCH / rare band design, 9 karat gold, 1944, 7 x 17 mm

PRECISION / interesting band attachments, 8 x 29 mm

PRECISION / simple model, 8 x 16.5 mm

PRECISION / cocktail model, original white gold case with diamonds, original crown, 6.5 x 12 mm

LADY'S WATCH / simple 14 karat gold case, crystal faceted from inside, 18 karat gold band, 6.5 x 15 mm

LADY'S WATCH / typical gold bracelet watch, 18 karat gold, 1960s, 8 x 7 x 16.5 mm

PRECISION / interesting trapezoidal case shape, 1960s, 8.5 x 16.5 mm (top), 12.5 mm (bottom)

PRECISION / original band of hexagonal links, 9 karat gold, 7.5 x 10.5 mm

LADY ROLEX CHAMELEON

PRECISION / lightly bowed trapezoidal case, off-center crown, 6 x 20.5 mm

PRECISION / faded dial, 8.5 x 20.5 mm

CHAMELEON / 18 karat gold case, hand-wound, 1950, Ref. 8789, 9 x 17 mm

CHAMELEON / simple model, 14 karat gold, 9 x 15 mm

CHAMELEON / 14 karat white gold case and rippled lunette, 9.5 x 12 mm

CHAMELEON / round case with engraved lunette, 6.5 x 15 mm

CHAMELEON / 1960s, 10 x 16 mm

CHAMELEON / rare white model, 10 x 24.5 x 17 mm

CHAMELEON / luxurious model, 9.5 x 15.5 mm

CHAMELEON / rare model, 18 karat white gold lunette with raised indices, 9 x 16.5 mm

LADIES' WATCHES

CHAMELEON / 18 karat white gold case and band, good condition, 9 x 24 mm

CHAMELEON / 18 karat gold case and band, 1960s, 10 x 24.5 mm

CHAMELEON / hand-wound, 1960s, 9 x 23.9 x 17.4 mm

CHAMELEON / raised indices, 18 karat gold, 9 x 15.5 mm

CHAMELEON / rare square case, 17 x 15 mm

LADY ROLEX ORCHID

ORCHID / 18 karat white gold case, hand-wound, 1950s, Ref. 2457, 6.8 x 16 mm

ORCHID / raised indices, attachments for cord band, 7 x 15 mm

ORCHID / luxury model, 19 karat white gold, 8 x 16 mm

ORCHID / striking shape of band attachments, 14 karat gold, 7 x 15 mm

ORCHID / braided leather band, 6.5 x 15 mm

L.R. MARCONI   L.R. CELLINI   L.R. PERPETUAL

ORCHID / luxurious design, 18 karat massive white gold case, 8 x 16 mm

ORCHID / 18 karat white gold case and band, 9.5 x 16 mm

MARCONI EXTRA PRIMA / platinum case, hand-wound, 1930s, Ref. 141, 8 x 22 mm

CELLINI / 18 karat white gold case, hand-wound, 1970s, Ref. 3810, 5 x 24 mm

PERPETUAL / 18 karat gold, original box, automatic movement, non-Oyster, 11 x 23 mm

LADY ROLEX OYSTER

OYSTER / stainless steel case, hand-wound, 1960s, Ref. 6022, 11 x 29 mm

OYSTER / small second, stainless steel case, hand-wound, 1940s, 10 x 22 mm

LADY'S WATCH / 9 karat yellow gold case, hand-wound, 1927, 10 x 28 mm

LADY'S WATCH / dealer's signature "Prouds Sidney". Steel Oyster case, 11 x 23.5 mm

OYSTER / dealer's signature "Kalkutta", 1940s, Ref. 3486, 9.5 x 21 mm

LADIES' WATCHES

PRECISION / original dial, Ref. 5004, 10 x 23 mm

PRECISION / hand-wound, 1960s, Ref. 6410, 9.5 x 23.5 mm

OYSTER / white dial, printed Roman numerals, 9.5 x 24 mm

OYSTER / covered band attachments, 14 karat gold bicolor model, stepped lunette, 10 x 24 mm

OYSTER / original dial with luminous Arabic numerals, Ref. 4271, 10 x 27.5 mm

OYSTER / rare cylindrical model, steel and gold bicolor case, 10.5 x 21 mm

OYSTER / signed "Lady Dudley", 9 x 22 mm

OYSTER / nice elegant model, covered band attachments, Ref. 3626, 9.5 x 21 mm

OYSTER / bicolor case with covered band attachments, 10.5 x 27 mm

OYSTER / stepped case, 9.5 x 18 mm

OYSTER / 9 karat gold case, original dial, 10.5 x 23 mm

OYSTER / orange dial, blue steel hands, hand-wound, 11 x 24 mm

OYSTER / stepped case and band attachments, 9.5 x 21 mm

OYSTER / nicely freshened-up white dial, blue steel hands, 9.5 x 24 mm

OYSTER / rare model, cylindrical case, original dial, 11 x 24 mm

LADY ROLEX OYSTER PRECISION

OYSTER / early model, octagonal 18 karat gold case, 1920s, 10 x 30 mm

OYSTER / simple round case, 1940s, 10 x 23,5 mm

OYSTER PRECISION / 18 karat yellow gold case, hand-wound, 1950s, Ref. 6525, 10 x 21 mm

PRECISION / "tonneau" case, 1960s, good as new, 18 karat white gold, Ref. 2645, 6.5 x 18 x 24 mm

PRECISION / non-Oyster stainless steel case, 1960s, Ref. 9631, 8 x 15 mm

LADIES' WATCHES

PRECISION / hand-wound, white gold lunette, small second, Ref. 6525, 9 x 21.5 mm

PRECISION / timeless design, popular dial, 9 x 21 mm

PRECISION / 1940s, 10 x 23 mm

PRECISION / very rare, original Jubilee band, 1948, 10 x 22 mm

PRECISION / lunette with raised indices, 1949, 8.5 x 20.5 mm

LADY ROLEX OYSTER PERPETUAL BUBBLE BACK

PRECISION/ raised indices on lunette and dial, 1950s, 9 x 23.5 mm

PRECISION / good design, Ref. 4360, 10.5 x 20.5 mm

BUBBLE BACK / small second, 18 karat yellow gold case, hand-wound, 1940s, Ref. 4686, 12.5 x 24.4

BUBBLE BACK /automatic, 18 karat yellow gold case, 1940, 12 x 22 mm

BUBBLE BACK / automatic, 14 karat yellow gold case, 1953, Ref. 5002, 11 x 22 mm

BUBBLE BACK / automatic, 18 karat yellow gold case, 1952, 13 x 23 mm

BUBBLE BACK / automatic, 14 karat yellow gold case, 1948, 12 x 22 mm

BUBBLE BACK / automatic, 14 karat yellow gold case, 1940, Ref. 5002, 12 x 22 mm

BUBBLE BACK / automatic, 18 karat yellow gold case, 1951, 11 x 23 mm

BUBBLE BACK / 1940s, automatic, 11.5 x 22 mm

BUBBLE BACK / very rare early model, black dial with luminous hands, 11 x 22 mm

BUBBLE BACK / rare model, lunette with raised indices and gold case, 12.5 x 22.5 mm

BUBBLE BACK rare bamboo band, 1940s, 11 x 24.5 mm

BUBBLE BACK / rare model, 18 karat gold, original dial and band, 11.5 x 22 mm

BUBBLE BACK / rare model, original Jubilee band, Ref. 3869, 12 x 22 mm

LADIES' WATCHES

BUBBLE BACK case and movement in good condition, freshened-up dial, 1940s, 11.5 x 22 mm

BUBBLE BACK late model, original band, 14 karat gold , 11 x 22 mm

BUBBLE BACK / rare original Jubilee band, 1940s, 12 x 22 mm

BUBBLE BACK / 14 karat gold case, discolored dial, 12.5 x 23 mm

BUBBLE BACK / gold lunette, sides of band also gilded, 12.5 x 23 mm

BUBBLE BACK / 18 karat gold case, interesting raised indices, 11.5 x 23 mm

BUBBLE BACK / 14 karat gold case, raised indices, 10.5 x 22.5 mm

BUBBLE BACK / original dial, raised gold numerals and indices, 11 x 22 mm

BUBBLE BACK / arched crystal, freshened up, 1963, 12 x 23 mm

BUBBLE BACK / raised numerals, 1950s, 12 x 22 mm

BUBBLE BACK / gold case, original matte rose dial, 1950s, 12.5 x 24 mm

BUBBLE BACK / 9 karat gold case, raised indices, small second, 11.5 x 22 mm

BUBBLE BACK / dial and 14 karat gold case like new, 1930s, 13 x 22 mm

BUBBLE BACK / black dial and skeletal hands, 12.5 x 22.5 mm

BUBBLE BACK / triangular indices, 11.5 x 23 mm

BUBBLE BACK / rectangular and wedge indices, turning lunette, 11 x 22 mm

BUBBLE BACK / typical of its kind, turning lunette, 18 karat gold case, 12 x 22 mm

BUBBLE BACK / 1950s, 12.5 x 22 mm

BUBBLE BACK / 11.5 x 22 mm

BUBBLE BACK / 18 karat gold case, 1950s, 12.5 x 22 mm

LADIES' WATCHES
LADY ROLEX OYSTER PERPETUAL

OYSTER PERPETUAL / "Zephyr", bicolor, hand-wound, 1970s, Ref. 6724, 10.8 x 27 mm

OYSTER PERPETUAL / 18 karat case, 1996, Ref. 167198G, 11 indices set with diamonds, 9.7 x 25 mm

OYSTER PERPETUAL / automatic, stainless steel case, 1990s, Ref. 67480, 10 x 29 mm

OYSTER PERPETUAL / automatic, stainless steel case, 1970s, Ref. 6618, 10 x 24 mm

OYSTER PERPETUAL / automatic, stainless steel case, 1982, Ref. 6723, 10 x 23 mm

OYSTER PERPETUAL / automatic, stainless steel case, 1982, Ref. 6505, 10 x 23 mm

OYSTER PERPETUAL / automatic, stainless steel case, 1948, Ref. 4436, 11 x 22 mm

OYSTER PERPETUAL /automatic, stainless steel case, 2003, Ref. 76080, 10 x 24 mm

OYSTER PERPETUAL / good condition, automatic, white gold and stainless steel bicolor case, 2003, Ref. 76094, 11 x 25 mm

OYSTER PERPETUAL / good condition, automatic, stainless steel case, 2003, Ref. 76080, 10 x 24 mm

OYSTER PERPETUAL / good condition, automatic, stainless steel case, 2003, Ref. 76080, 10 x 24 mm

OYSTER PERPETUAL / good condition, stainless steel case, 2003, Ref. 76080, 10 x 24 mm

OYSTER PERPETUAL / good condition, automatic, stainless steel case, 2001, Ref. 76080, 10 x 24 mm

OYSTER PERPETUAL "Zephyr" model, automatic, bicolor case, 1970, Ref. 6814, 10 x 23 mm

OYSTER PERPETUAL / automatic, stainless steel case, 1971, Ref. 6718, 10 x 23 mm

OYSTER PERPETUAL / covered band attachments, gold lunette and dial, 10.5 x 23.5 mm

OYSTER PERPETUAL / 1960s, 10.5 x 23.5 mm

OYSTER PERPETUAL / flexible band, Ref. 6618, 11 x 23.5 mm

OYSTER PERPETUAL / freshened-up dial, 10.5 x 23.5 mm

OYSTER PERPETUAL / black dial, 10.5 x 23.5 mm

LADIES' WATCHES

OYSTER PERPETUAL / gold lunette, stainless steel case, 11 x 23.5 mm

OYSTER PERPETUAL / dial with small second, 11 x 23.5 mm

OYSTER PERPETUAL / simple design, 18 karat gold, 10.5 x 23.5 mm

OYSTER PERPETUAL / rare band of 18 karat gold, 1970s, 11.5 x 24 mm

OYSTER PERPETUAL / bicolor band of 14 karat gold and steel, 10 x 23.5 mm

OYSTER PERPETUAL / rare model, small second, Ref. 6504, 10.5 x 23.5 mm

OYSTER PERPETUAL / well-kept piece, small second 1950s, Ref. 6505, 11 x 23.5 mm

BUBBLE BACK / heavy 14 karat gold case, good condition, Ref. 6504, 11 x 23.5 mm

PRECISION / very nice raised numerals, 11.5 x 21.5 mm

OYSTER PERPETUAL / stainless steel case, black dial, Ref. 6623, 10 x 23.5 mm

OYSTER PERPETUAL / wedge indices, bicolor case with 18 karat gold, 10 x 23.5 mm

OYSTER PERPETUAL / bicolor case, Ref. 6619, 10.5 x 23.5 mm

OYSTER PERPETUAL / "Zephyr" model, 11.5 x 24 mm

OYSTER PERPETUAL / 10.5 x 24 mm

OYSTER PERPETUAL / nice blue dial, 11 x 24 mm

OYSTER PERPETUAL / dealer's signature "Tiffany & Co", bicolor case, 11 x 24 mm

OYSTER PERPETUAL / 9 karat gold, 1946, 10.5 x 23.5 mm

OYSTER PERPETUAL / flexible 18 karat gold band, 10.5 x 24 mm

OYSTER PERPETUAL / expiring model, 14 karat gold case, 1970s, 10.5 x 23.5 mm

OYSTER PERPETUAL / Jubilee band of 18 karat gold, 1960s, 10 x 23.5 mm

LADIES' WATCHES

OYSTER PERPETUAL / 18 karat gold, original dial, 10 x 23.5 mm

OYSTER PERPETUAL / raised wedge indices, 10.5 x 24 mm

OYSTER PERPETUAL / small case, 10 x 24 mm

OYSTER PERPETUAL / 18 karat gold case and band, 1950s, 11 x 23 mm

OYSTER PERPETUAL / rare Jubilee band, Ref. 6719, 10.5 x 23.5 mm

OYSTER PERPETUAL / 10.5 x 23.5 mm

OYSTER PERPETUAL / "Zephyr" model, bicolor case with 14 karat gold, 1960s, Ref. 6724

OYSTER PERPETUAL / 14 karat gold, 10.5 x 24 mm

OYSTER PERPETUAL / flexible band, 11 x 24 mm

OYSTER PERPETUAL / rare model with turning lunette, 11 x 24 mm

OYSTER PERPETUAL / 14 karat gold and steel bicolor case, Ref. 6623, 11 x 24 mm

OYSTER PERPETUAL / replaced dial, 11 x 23.5 mm

OYSTER PERPETUAL / steel and 14 karat gold bicolor case, Ref. 6719, 11 x 23.5 mm

OYSTER PERPETUAL / guilloched dial, flexible band, 11 x 23.5 mm

OYSTER PERPETUAL / 1950s, 11 x 23.5 mm

OYSTER PERPETUAL striking minutery, 14 karat gold case, 10.5 x 24 mm

OYSTER PERPETUAL / rare black dial, 1958, 11 x 23.5 mm

OYSTER PERPETUAL / guilloched dial, Ref. 6619, 9.5 x 23.5 mm

OYSTER PERPETUAL / silver dial with firm's logo, 10.5 x 23.5 mm

OYSTER PERPETUAL / indices set with gems on gold dial, 10.5 x 23.5 mm

LADIES' WATCHES

LADY ROLEX OYSTER PERPETUAL DATE

OYSTER PERPETUAL / gold lunette, 10 x 23.5 mm

OYSTER PERPETUAL / stainless steel, smooth lunette, late 1960s, 11 x 23.5 mm

OYSTER PERPETUAL / automatic, red gold and stainless steel bi-color case, 1969, Ref. 6517, 10.9 x 24.3 mm

OYSTER PERPETUAL / automatic, red gold and stainless steel bi-color case, 1968, Ref. 6517, 11.1 x 23.9 mm

OYSTER PERPETUAL DATE / stainless steel case, 1970s, Ref. 6519, 10 x 24 mm

OYSTER PERPETUAL DATE / stainless steel case, 1970s, Ref. 6917, 10 indices set with diamonds, 10 x 24 mm

OYSTER PERPETUAL / automatic, stainless steel case, 1960s, 11 x 24 mm

OYSTER PERPETUAL DATE / automatic, stainless steel case, 2000, Ref. 79160, 11 x 25 mm

OYSTER PERPETUAL DATE / automatic, white gold and stainless steel bicolor case, 1970s, Ref. 6917, 11 x 25 mm

OYSTER PERPETUAL DATE / automatic, white gold and stainless steel bicolor case, 1980s, Ref. 6917, 11 x 25 mm

OYSTER PERPETUAL DATE / automatic, white gold and stainless steel bicolor case, 1970s, Ref. 6924, 11 x 25 mm

OYSTER PERPETUAL DATE / automatic, white gold and stainless steel bicolor case, 1960s, Ref. 6517, 11 x 24 mm

OYSTER PERPETUAL DATE / automatic, stainless steel case, 1980s, Ref. 6516, 11 x 24 mm

OYSTER PERPETUAL DATE / automatic, 14 karat yellow gold and stainless steel bicolor case, 1960s, Ref. 6517, 11 x 24 mm

OYSTER PERPETUAL DATE / automatic, stainless steel case, 1990s, Ref. 79190, engine-turned lunette, 11 x 25 mm

OYSTER PERPETUAL DATE / good condition, automatic, stainless steel case, 2003, Ref. 79160, 11 x 25 mm

OYSTER PERPETUAL DATE / automatic, stainless steel, 1998, Ref. 69160, 11 x 25 mm

OYSTER PERPETUAL / good condition, automatic, stainless steel case, 2003, Ref. 79160, 11 x 25 mm

OYSTER PERPETUAL DATE / good condition, automatic, stainless steel case, 2003, Ref. 79160, 11 x 25 mm

OYSTER PERPETUAL DATE / good condition, automatic, stainless steel case, 2003, Ref. 79160, 11 x 25 mm

LADIES' WATCHES

OYSTER PERPETUAL DATE/ automatic, stainless steel case, 1978, Ref. 6917, 12 x 24 mm

OYSTER PERPETUAL DATE / automatic, stainless steel case, 1968, Ref. 6516, 11 x 24 mm

OYSTER PERPETUAL DATE / automatic, stainless steel case, 1951, Ref. 6519, 11 x 24 mm

OYSTER PERPETUAL DATE, automatic, stainless steel case, 1965, Ref. 6519, 11 x 24 mm

OYSTER DATE / original band, Ref. 6516, 12 x 24.5 mm

OYSTER PERPETUAL DATE / dealer's signature "Tiffany & Co" on dark brown dial, 12 x 25 mm

OYSTER PERPETUAL DATE / finely guilloched lunette, 11 x 25 mm

OYSTER PERPETUAL DATE / bicolor case with 14 karat gold, white dial, 11.5 x 24.5 mm

OYSTER PERPETUAL DATE / bicolor case with 14 karat gold, 11.5 x 24.5 mm

OYSTER PERPETUAL DATE / printed Roman numerals, bicolor case, 12.5 x 25 mm

OYSTER PERPETUAL DATE / Ref. 6917, 12 x 25.5 mm

OYSTER PERPETUAL DATE / bicolor case of gold and stainless steel, 1960s, 10 x 24 mm

OYSTER PERPETUAL DATE / stainless steel case, gray dial, 11.5 x 25 mm

OYSTER PERPETUAL DATE / no sapphire crystal, stainless steel, Ref. 5416, 11 x 24 mm

OYSTER PERPETUAL DATE / 1970s, 11.5 x 24 mm

OYSTER PERPETUAL DATE / lunette with raised indices, 12 x 24 mm

OYSTER PERPETUAL DATE / simple model, smooth lunette, Ref. 6517m 12 x 25 mm

OYSTER PERPETUAL DATE / lunette with raised indices, Jubilee band, 11.5 x 25 mm

OYSTER PERPETUAL DATE / 1970s, Ref. 6517, 11 x 24 mm

OYSTER PERPETUAL DATE / blue dial, 1970s, Ref. 6917, 12 x 25 mm

LADIES' WATCHES

OYSTER PERPETUAL DATE / Ref. 6516, 11.5 x 24 mm

OYSTER PERPETUAL DATE / rare matte black dial, Ref. 6917, 11 x 25 mm

OYSTER PERPETUAL DATE / case and band in good condition, 1970s, 11.5 x 25 mm

OYSTER PERPETUAL DATE / simple model, white gold lunette, 1970s, 11.5 x 22 mm

OYSTER PERPETUAL DATE / white dial, Roman numerals, 1970s, 12 x 25 mm

OYSTER PERPETUAL DATE / white gold lunette, 1952, 10.5 x 24 mm

OYSTER PERPETUAL DATE / stainless steel case, lunette with raised indices, 1969, 11 x 24 mm

OYSTER PERPETUAL DATE / modern model with rippled lunette, 1970s, 11.5 x 25 mm

OYSTER PERPETUAL DATE / Dealer's signature "TIFFANY". Stainless steel case, 11.5 x 24 mm

OYSTER PERPETUAL DATE / stainless steel case, 1960s, 11.5 x 25 mm

LADY ROLEX PERPETUAL DATEJUST

OYSTER PERPETUAL DATE / rare model, gray dial, dealer's signature "Tiffany & Co", 11.5 x 25 mm

OYSTER PERPETUAL DATE / dealer's signature "Cartier", 18 karat gold and stainless steel bicolor case, 11 x 25 mm

OYSTER PERPETUAL DATE / Ref. 6619, 11.5 x 24 mm

OYSTER PERPETUAL / automatic, red gold case, 1960s, Ref. 6517, 11.4 x 23.9 mm

OYSTER PERPETUAL / automatic, 18 karat yellow gold and stainless steel bicolor case, 1991, Ref. 69173G, 11.7 x 25 mm

OYSTER PERPETUAL DATEJUST / platinum case, 2000s, Ref. 79166NG, 10 indices set with diamonds, 10.5 x 25.7 mm

OYSTER PERPETUAL DATEJUST / 18 karat white gold, 1980, Ref. 6917, 10 indices set with diamonds, 11.8 x 25.7 mm

OYSTER PERPETUAL DATEJUST / automatic, 18 karat white gold case, 1960s, Ref. 6702, 10.5 x 24 mm

OYSTER PERPETUAL DATEJUST / automatic, stainless steel case, 1970s, Ref. 6917, 11 x 25 mm

OYSTER PERPETUAL DATEJUST / automatic, white gold case, 1970s, Ref. 6517, 10 x 24 mm

LADIES' WATCHES

OYSTER PERPETUAL DATEJUST / automatic, bicolor, 18 karat yellow gold, 1980s, Ref. 69163, 11 x 25 mm

OYSTER PERPETUAL DATEJUST / automatic, 18 karat yellow gold bicolor case, 1970s, Ref. 6917, 11 x 25 mm

OYSTER PERPETUAL DATEJUST / automatic, bicolor case, 1980s, Ref. 69163, 11 x 25 mm

OYSTER PERPETUAL DATEJUST / automatic, stainless steel case, 1970s, Ref. 6917, 11 x 25 mm

OYSTER PERPETUAL DATEJUST / automatic, gold case, 1980s, Ref. 69178G, dial with 10 indices set with diamonds, 11 x 25 mm

OYSTER PERPETUAL DATEJUST / automatic, 18 karat red gold case, 1950, Ref. 6517, 11 x 24 mm

DATEJUST / automatic, 18 karat gold and stainless steel bicolor case, 1993, Ref. 69179BIC, 11 x 25 mm

OYSTER PERPETUAL DATEJUST / automatic, 18 karat yellow gold case, 1995, Ref. 69178, 11 x 25 mm

OYSTER PERPETUAL DATEJUST / 18 karat, 1991, Ref. 69298, 10 indices set with diamonds, 11 x 27 mm

OYSTER PERPETUAL DATEJUST / automatic, white gold and stainless steel bicolor case, 1997, Ref. 69174, 11x 25 mm

OYSTER PERPETUAL DATEJUST / bicolor case, 10 indices set with diamonds, 2001, Ref. 79173, 11 x 25 mm

OYSTER PERPETUAL DATEJUST / bicolor, Ref. 79174NG, 10 indices set with diamonds, 2003, 11 x 25 mm

OYSTER PERPETUAL DATEJUST / automatic, white gold and stainless steel bicolor case, 1990s, Ref. 69174, 11 x 25 mm

OYSTER PERPETUAL DATEJUST / automatic, 18 karat yellow gold and stainless steel bicolor case, 1990s, Ref. 69163, 11 x 25 mm

OYSTER PERPETUAL DATEJUST / automatic, 18 karat yellow gold case, 1990, Ref. 69178, 10 indices set with diamonds, 11 x 25 mm

OYSTER PERPETUAL DATEJUST / 18 karat yellow gold, 1990s, Ref. 69178G, 10 indices set with diamonds, 11 x 25 mm

OYSTER PERPETUAL DATEJUST / white gold and stainless steel bicolor case, 2003, Ref. 79174, 11 x 25 mm

OYSTER PERPETUAL DATEJUST / automatic, white gold and stainless steel bicolor case, 2003, Ref. 79174, 10 indices set with diamonds, 11 x 25 mm

OYSTER PERPETUAL DATEJUST / automatic, white gold and stainless steel bicolor case, 2003, Ref. 79174, beige dial, 11 x 25 mm

OYSTER PERPETUAL DATEJUST / white gold and stainless steel bicolor case, 2003, Ref. 79174, mother-of-pearl color dial, 11 x 25 mm

LADIES' WATCHES

OYSTER PERPETUAL DATEJUST / automatic, 18 karat yellow gold case, 1960, Ref. 6517, 10 x 24 mm

OYSTER PERPETUAL DATE / red date indication, 18 karat gold case, Ref. 6517

OYSTER PERPETUAL DATE / 14 karat gold case and band, 10 diamond-set indices, Ref. 6917, 11.5 x 25 mm

OYSTER PERPETUAL DATE / not original band, 18 karat gold, 11 x 24 mm

OYSTER PERPETUAL DATE / expiring model, gold case, 11.5 x 24.5 mm

OYSTER PERPETUAL DATE / rippled lunette, 1970s, Ref. 6517, 11 x 24 mm

OYSTER PERPETUAL DATEJUST / blue dial, 10 x 24 mm

OYSTER PERPETUAL DATEJUST / 1962, 12 x 23 mm

OYSTER PERPETUAL DATE / popular rose dial, 11 x 25 mm

OYSTER PERPETUAL DATE / 18 karat gold case and band, 1970s, 10.5 x 25 mm

OYSTER PERPETUAL DATE / 10.5 x 24 mm

OYSTER PERPETUAL DATEJUST / dealer's signature "Tiffany & Co", original black dial, 12 x 25 mm

OYSTER PERPETUAL DATEJUST / dealer's signature "Tiffany & Co", unusual dial with Arabic numerals, 11 x 25 mm

OYSTER PERPETUAL DATEJUST / rare green enamel dial, Ref. 6516, 11 x 24

OYSTER PERPETUAL DATEJUST / rippled lunette and band (Broken) of 18 karat gold, Ref. 6927, 11 x 25 mm

LADY ROLEX YACHT-MASTER

OYSTER PERPETUAL DATEJUST / blue dial, raised indices, 1977, 11.5 x 25 mm

OYSTER PERPETUAL DATEJUST / bicolor case, dealer's signature "Tiffany & Co", 10.5 x 23.5 mm

OYSTER PERPETUAL DATEJUST / replaced dial, 10 indices and points set with gems, Ref. 6517, 11 x 24 mm

YACHT-MASTER / automatic, bicolor case, 1990s, Ref. 169623, 11 x 23 mm

YACHT-MASTER / automatic, yellow gold case, 1996, Ref. 69628, 11 x 29 mm

POCKET WATCHES

POCKET WATCHES

NURSE WATCH / pendant watch for nurses, reversed dial, 1934, 12 x 34 mm

POCKET WATCH / B-watch with wooden box, "broad arrow" symbol and B6239 engraved on case bottom, 14.5 x 52.5 mm

TRAVEL WATCH / very rare model, unique dial with small second, hand-wound, Ref. 272B, 8 x 30 mm

POCKET WATCH / guilloched dial, 9 karat gold-plated case, hand-wound, 1950s, 15 x 44.5 mm

POCKET WATCH / for the British Army, "broad arrow" symbol engraved on case bottom, 15.5 x 50 mm

TRAVEL WATCH / good condition, stainless steel case, hand-wound, 8 x 26 mm

TRAVEL WATCH / 1940s, can be set up, 8 x 26 mm

POCKET WATCH / rare "Prince" model as pocket watch. Interesting design, hand-wound, 14 karat gold, 7.5 x 41 mm

POCKET WATCH / 1930s, dealer's signature "Marconi sunburst" on dial, 9 karat gold case, 9.8 x 46 mm

POCKET WATCH / modern design, "Prince" model, 18 karat gold case, 7.5 x 40.8 mm

POCKET WATCH / dealer's signature "H. Newman", Denison case, 14.5 x 50 mm

POCKET WATCH / for British Army, "broad arrow" symbol and "G.S.MK.II" engraved on case bottom, slightly yellow crystal, 15.5 x 49.5 mm

POCKET WATCH / for British Army, enamel dial, fault by the 11, "broad arrow" design and "B8003" engraved on the case bottom, 14.5 x 52 mm

POCKET WATCH / freshened up, Arabic numerals, elegant color combination, 10 x 45.5 mm

POCKET WATCH / enamel dial, for British Army, "B1008" engraved on case bottom, hand-wound, 15 x 52 mm

PANERAI / unique dial, 1954, 15 x 43 mm

PANERAI / Rolex movement and case, 19 x 45.5 mm, compass and depth gauge by Panerai

POCKET WATCH / "Century Club", 1943, 9 x 41.5 mm

POCKET WATCH / rare model, engraved case and dial, white gold plate, movement in good condition, 10 x 41 mm

POCKET WATCH / signed "Windsor", silver case, hand-wound, 13 x 29 mm